The Collected Sermons of

William H. Willimon

The Collected Sermons of

William H. Willimon

William H. Willimon

WESTMINSTER
JOHN KNOX PRESS
LOUISVILLE • KENTUCKY

To Katherine Grace
Who knows? Maybe you will be a preacher like your
great-great-grandmother; great-great-grandfather;
great-grandfather; and grandfather.

© 2010 William H. Willimon
Foreword © 2010 Westminster John Knox Press

First edition
Published by Westminster John Knox Press
Louisville, Kentucky

10 11 12 13 14 15 16 17 18 19—10 9 8 7 6 5 4 3 2 1

Book design by Sharon Adams
Cover design by Lisa Buckley
Cover photo: Duke Photography, Jim Wallace

Library of Congress Cataloging-in-Publication Data

Willimon, William H.
  The collected sermons of William H. Willimon / William H. Willimon.
    p. cm.
  ISBN 978-0-664-23446-1 (alk. paper)
  1. Sermons, American—20th century. 2. Sermons, American—21st century. 3. United Methodist Church (U.S.)—Sermons. I. Title.
  BV4253.W46 2010
  254'.076—dc22

2010003673

Contents

122778

Episcopal Sermons

Foreword

For nearly four decades, William H. Willimon has been a singular voice in American preaching. His rare blend of wit and wisdom, prophetic jabbing and pastoral nurturing, biblical insight and common sense, poetic soarings and country store musings have made him a welcome and refreshing presence in pulpits across the country and around the world.

Like many others, I first came to know Will through his writing, not his preaching. As a relatively young seminary professor, trying to teach worship as well as homiletics, I picked up a copy of Will's *Worship as Pastoral Care* (Nashville: Abingdon Press, 1979) and was immediately enchanted by his writing style. The words leapt off the page in a graceful manner that was, at one and the same time, academically substantial and conversational. On paper, Will seemed to be this fellow who had traveled widely, read abundantly, and thought deeply about the relationship between worship and life, and now he had put another log on the fire, tipped his chair back, and was just talking with you about what he had observed. This volume of sermons ably demonstrates that Willimon the preacher displays the same rhetorical virtue as Willimon the writer, namely, that he always shows up in the pulpit as the friend leaning on the backyard fence and engaging a neighbor in conversation. He is sometimes the witty friend, sometimes the comfortable friend, sometimes the demanding and challenging friend, sometimes even the irascible friend—but always the friend, bearing news and provocative ideas.

We see in this collection of sermons Willimon's versatility as a preacher. He has preached as a pastor, as a chaplain, as a celebrated guest, and, in the last few years, as a United Methodist bishop. He has preached effectively in tiny rural churches and in the Washington National Cathedral, at Methodist camp meetings and in the pulpits of major universities, including twenty remarkable years as the preacher at Duke University Chapel. He has preached in the ancient halls of King's College, Cambridge, and he has preached on television from California's Crystal Cathedral. In his range of venues, Willimon seems like Paul, willing to stand up and talk about the gospel anywhere and anytime, always in language that can be appreciated by his hearers, regardless of whether they are a gaggle of academics and philosophers on Mars Hill or a tiny group of women meeting in a prayer cell on a Macedonian riverbank.

The sermons in this volume cover the period from 1974 to the present, a tumultuous era in the life of the old mainline churches, and one of the marks of Willimon's preaching is a keen awareness of the travails of the church and the general cultural drift away from religious commitment. In *Resident Aliens: Life in the Christian Colony* (Nashville: Abingdon Press, 1989), Willimon and his friend, theologian and ethicist Stanley Hauerwas, celebrate the demise of Christendom with its cozy relationship to the dominant powers and enthusiastically underscore the cultural oddness and the displaced character of the Christian community. This book has been widely influential and has found an appreciative readership, but its vigorous critics have charged Willimon and Hauerwas with sectarianism, fideism, and other infractions against the spirit of progressive, open-minded theology.

The act of reading these sermons as an ensemble, however, will perhaps prompt any otherwise wary readers to drop the charges of sectarianism. Seeing the variety of approaches Willimon takes to the classic "Christ and Culture" problem certainly gives one a more nuanced portrait of his views of the relationship between the church and the larger society. At times, Will does forcefully embrace Christianity's newfound minority status, and he rejoices in the cultural homelessness that inevitably becomes the lot of those who truly follow Jesus. At other times, however, Will is almost wistful about an America where faith and the larger community life were woven inextricably together, and he is confidently hopeful about a world upheld by a God who desires to be all in all. In some sermons, he is the ardent defender and promoter of the Christian theological tradition, a repository of wisdom that an autonomy-loving, freedom-seeking culture can never seize on its own but must, rather, turn and receive as a gift. On the other hand, Will surely surprised the baccalaureate congregation at an Alabama Methodist college when he quoted as advice to the graduates what the anarchist and erstwhile midwife Emma Goldmann would whisper in the ears of newborn baby girls she had helped to deliver: "Rebel! Rebel!"

The years covered in this sermon collection, so rife with changes in church and society, were also a time of profound shifts in sermon fashion and preaching style. When Willimon graduated from Yale Divinity School in 1971, what has lately come to be called the "new homiletic," a move toward more poetic, listener-oriented, and narrative-shaped sermons, was barely visible on the landscape. There were early signs that preaching was changing. As early as 1969, homiletician David J. Randolph sensed a new preaching pulse gathering and had trumpeted it in *The Renewal of Preaching* (Philadelphia: Fortress, 1969). While Willimon was in seminary, another homiletician, Charles Rice, had published *Interpretation and Imagination* (Philadelphia: Fortress, 1970), an appeal to employ plays, movies, and short stories as preaching "texts." In

1971, theologian Thor Hall, in *The Future Shape of Preaching* (Philadelphia: Fortress, 1971), called for sermons to be arranged as instruments of dynamic communication and not just as vessels for content, and in that same year biblical scholar and homiletician Fred Craddock published his monograph *As One without Authority* (Enid, OK: Phillips University Press, 1971), which was, with its discussion of inductive preaching, to become the most significant book of the new wave in homiletics. Clearly something was afoot in the world of homiletics, but none of these books had yet made much of an impact on the actual practice of preaching in America, which remained largely allegiant to the more didactic strategies of the 1950s.

But in the 1970s and 1980s all of that changed, and Willimon, as a young pastor and then as the minister to the university at Duke, was not only a participant in this new trend in preaching, he also became a major influence in it. His natural gifts as a storyteller and his engaging conversational approach both fit and shaped a way of American preaching that was rapidly becoming more narrative and more attentive to the rich possibilities of metaphorical language. In this volume he teasingly refers to this as his "narrative phase," but in most ways this was no mere passing phase for Will as a preacher. He has a strong and enduring sense of the gospel and of the Bible as structurally narrative-shaped and an intuitive grasp of the power of contemporary story to connect Scripture and life.

This by no means implies, however, that Will has been blind to the excesses of the new homiletic, or uncritical even of his own preaching. A Wesleyan with a long attraction to the Word-of-God theology of Karl Barth, Willimon has a healthy suspicion of all homiletical techniques and strategies, even his own, and sees them as potentially prideful intrusions upon the wild freedom of God to speak in unexpected ways and beyond human capacities. A strong dose of Barth can produce an embarrassed pulpit paralysis ("Who are *you*, little man, to take the Word of God on your lips?"), but in Willimon's case his understanding of the freedom of God and the fragility of the preacher has encouraged a lively sense of experimentation. Some preachers are always holding their finger to the wind, trying to say only what is pleasing to an ever fickle culture. Willimon, on the other hand, tries to sense the blowing of another wind, the breath of the Spirit, and he has been quite willing to adjust his preaching accordingly. Thus, he will sometimes thunder for a month of Sundays like an Old Testament prophet, sometimes dip down for a season into the deep pool of sanctification, and sometimes will exude as much joy and praise as Bach's *Magnificat*.

Will reports that a friend of his playfully claims that Willimon has only three sermon themes, which he repeats over and again: (1) God is big, great, and confusing and I can't explain God to someone like you, (2) the Christian life is demanding and difficult and I can't make it easier for someone like you, and (3) the Bible is big and strange and I can't explain this passage to someone like you (Michael Turner and William F. Malambri, III, eds., *A Peculiar Prophet: William H. Willimon and the Art of Preaching* [Nashville: Abingdon Press, 2004], 120–31). While this tri-fold catalog by no means encompasses the breadth and depth of a lifetime of Will's preaching, there is truth here nonetheless. Willimon is constantly pointing to a God and a Christian faith that have size and majesty, a gospel that is big and difficult and great and confusing and strange and so wonderful and life-changing that one cannot truly hear it without being overwhelmed by awe.

What could appear as contradictions in Willimon's ministry and in his preaching are actually the result of the pull of two powerful forces in his sense of call. Willimon is a prophet and he is also a pastor. In fact, it is sometimes hard to tell whether Will is a Jeremiah with a Methodist appointment or a country preacher who, as Kierkegaard said of Luther, always acts as if lightning is about to strike behind him. Sometimes Willimon testifies to the strange and astonishing good news with homiletical left jabs, prophetic punches, angular and unexpected sermons that unsettle his hearers (who else would preach on "fornication" during the university's parents' weekend?), and on other occasions the very oddness of the gospel evokes surprising tenderness from his mouth. Read, for example, the touching and powerful sermon Willimon preached on Easter in 2007. Willimon did not preach that day as a bishop but as a caring ministerial colleague of the heartbroken pastor of the congregation whose son had committed suicide only a few days before. When he closes that sermon by assuring the shaken congregation that "the Easter story was not just that Jesus came back from the dead but that he came back to a set of sad losers like us. Therein is our hope in life, in death, in life beyond death . . ." he was showing not only why he is viewed as a fine preacher but also why he is experienced as a good man and a treasured friend by so many of us.

Thomas G. Long
Bandy Professor of Preaching
Candler School of Theology
Emory University
Atlanta, GA

Preface

I can't believe that God called me to be a preacher. My own dear mother predicted that I would be a disaster. "Preachers must flatter and ingratiate themselves to church members, all the time telling people what they want to hear. Let's just say that you are not gifted in that." Many of my congregations respond in unison, "You should have listened to your mother."

My life in the pulpit has been either a credit to the mercy and resourcefulness of God or a validation of my mother's good judgment. Read these sermons; you make the call.

I love talking, love being in front of a congregation, thrill to saying something that elicits the old, "You really preached to me today, preacher." I rejoice at being a fellow worker with Matthew, Mark, Luke, and John, using any talents God has given me to bring the gospel out in the open through words. I adore having something more interesting to talk about than myself and my grandchildren. I love that sinking feeling in the pit of my stomach, in the last thirty seconds before I rise to speak, that terror that comes of wondering, "Is there any word from the Lord?" I delight to kill and to make alive, to slay and to give birth, and where else can one do that except in a sermon?

Thinking about these sermons is something like what one thinks about when one collides into a brick wall at sixty miles an hour. Your whole life flashes before you. I've kept most of my sermons in file boxes in the attic but I never had the courage to pore over them. When contemplating my turn one day to stand before the judgment throne, my prayer has always been that of the psalmist, "Remember not the sins of my youth, remember me!" (Ps. 25:7). Now my youthful homiletical indiscretions—misdeeds that continued well into my fifties, sixties even—are here exposed for all to see. It's humbling.

Assembling this collection of sermons was thus both painful and gratifying. It was painful to hear my thoughts from decades ago repeated. I really hope that God is in a forgetful, forgiving mood when the Lord looks over some of my sermons. Did I really compare my first sermon to a Carolina congregation in 1984 to a first date? Why on earth did I take time during Holy Week for a discourse on cockfighting in Louisiana? What was I thinking?

It was also gratifying to see that, in spite of all the odds against it, in a variety of times and places, I kept talking about Jesus. I have a deeply ingratiating personality and I so want to please. (My mother was wrong about that.) The few truly courageous sermons here are a credit to the prodding of the Holy Spirit. Telling the truth does not come naturally to me. Did I really dare to stand up to the university and call *alma mater*, for all her virtues, an enemy of the gospel? What was I thinking?

I hope these sermons reveal what a great God we've got in Father, Son, and Holy Spirit. Thank God our God did not leave us to talk to ourselves. Our God has said more than I'll ever be able to process in a lifetime of sermons. Some of the strangest stories ever told (Scripture) were weekly fuel for my preaching. I can't imagine having to talk about a less interesting God, in nearly fifty years of sermons, than the God who is Trinity. May these sermons display the joy of being called to be a Trinitarian preacher.

No one is more surprised than I that I actually preached over 2,000 sermons and can still muster a fair amount of enthusiasm for preaching this coming Sunday. As I note in one of these sermons, Christians are blessed by having a loquacious God who delights in self-revelation. Thus we preachers, if we're listening, always have something to say.

I selected these sermons as snapshots of a preacher at work over four decades, trying to give a sample sermon from nearly every year of my ministry. These sermons were not selected because they are brilliant or grand examples of the homiletical art but rather because they are fairly typical of me at a given period of time and I thought that others might—even now, years later—enjoy them.

It's rather odd for a preacher to have his sermons reappear in print. It feels almost like I'm dead. It's not preaching if it's not the live human voice thrown out to an unsuspecting congregation. Immortality is not a proper aspiration for a biblical preacher. Preaching is occasional. An oral event, like a sermon, cannot be duplicated in print. If you really want to know how a sermon actually sounded on a summer Sunday in 2008, well, sorry, you had to be there. Preachers practice a fragile, ethereal art. We know from the beginning that our sermons are not meant to live too long after the benediction. Our words bounce off the church's walls, ricochet off the heads of the faithful, by God's grace manage to penetrate a few in the congregation, and then are heard no more. We pour out sweat and blood on a weekly basis, try to turn words about the Word Made Flesh back into flesh and blood in the pulpit, and then the sermon is over. The best we can hope is that the Holy Spirit might condescend to seize upon something we said in a sermon and wallop some soul, but that's up to God and not to us.

Looking over these sermons, I am surprised by how few ideas I've had over the years. I have been working and reworking some of the same exegetical insights for decades. Some of my ideas that I thought were recently developed, as it turns out, have been bumping around in my brain since seminary. I haven't grown or developed as much in my thought as I thought. Perhaps this is a good thing. All my life I've been accused of inconsistency; these sermons suggest that I'm more coherent in my thinking than my critics have charged. I've got a friend who says, "Will only has about three sermon themes that he keeps repeating: (1) God is big, great, and confusing and I can't explain God to someone like you. (2) The Christian life is demanding and difficult and I can't make it easier for someone like you. (3) The Bible is big and strange and I can't explain this passage to someone like you" (Michael Turner and William F. Malambri, III, eds., *A Peculiar Prophet: William H. Willimon and the Art of Preaching* [Nashville: Abingdon Press, 2004], 120–31). Thus, when friend Stanley Hauerwas was asked to write about my preaching, he titled his essay "Why Willimon Never Explains."

You will watch me go through various phases—me trying to sound like Fred Craddock, me appearing as Walter Brueggemann, me attempting to do Karl Barth with a southern accent, me as Stanley Hauerwas, only nice. There was my parables-of-Jesus period and my "Gee-isn't-the-Old Testament-great" era. Thank God that Scripture is so much richer than my imagination. I literally could go on for another fifty years if the United Methodist Church were not putting me out to pasture. One day, not too long from now, the Lord will say to me, "Enough, already" and I shall at last have nothing else to say.

Some time ago I, with a group of preachers, was asked to respond to the question, "What do you think about in the moments just before you deliver a sermon?" What goes on in you during that pause just before you preach? Some of the respondents confessed terror in that moment, feelings of inadequacy or worries about what they ought to have done differently in the coming sermon.

I, of course, have rarely had such feelings when I preach, not because I'm so very competent in what I'm doing, but rather because I have not an ounce of perfectionism in me—my depravity is ever before me. As Paul said, I am what I am, by the grace of God. My sermon is what it is; the rest is up to God.

I, unlike some of my preacher friends, relish that moment just before I preach. I will miss it in retirement. In that moment, just prior to the first words of a sermon, it's as if I am freed from all thought, especially thoughts about me. I find my little life swept up in the life of God, subsumed by whatever work the Holy Spirit intends to do through me that day. In that sacred instant, I have no problems, am beset by no worries, and am gloriously without self-concern—no small achievement in a culture of narcissism. I become the artist who is totally consumed in the act of creation, subsumed in the art itself. I become the sermon. I have no needs, want nothing else. I am what I'm trying to talk about. I can't believe I've been lucky enough to have been called to such a wonderfully self-forgetful vocation.

In the Museum of Fine Arts in Boston there is a small, rather unusual Rembrandt—a self-portrait of the artist in a darkened studio (done around

1638). Near the center of the painting is a large canvas on an easel. But the painting in progress is turned away from us, the viewers, facing the artist. The artist stands in the shadows across the room, holding his palate, staring not at us but intently at the painting that we cannot see.

It's a painting of a painting and an artist preoccupied by his art, neither of which is fully visible to the rest of us. Here is the artist at work, totally absorbed by his art that we outsiders cannot see. The subject of the painting is painting.

I hope that will be the fate of this collection of my sermons. The subject of this book of sermons is the sermon. The greatest value of these sermons is not that they are great sermons by a great preacher. They are glimpses of the life of a preacher who was privileged to be so absorbed in his work that he hardly knew the listeners were there. If these sermons have abiding interest after their moment of delivery, it is similar to that of Rembrandt's 1638 painting of the artist at work—here was the primal Christian event of a preacher attempting to listen to God, then trying to speak for God to God's people. May you be edified by watching this preacher work on the gospel and watching the gospel work on this preacher.

I am honored to have Tom Long give the benediction on the time I've done in the pulpit. These sermons show my indebtedness to friends like Tom who, in the company of preachers, urge us on in the weekly task of bringing the gospel to speech.

As Luther stirringly ended many of his sermons, "That's enough about that for today."

Will Willimon

Trinity United Methodist Church

1

First Sermon

March 3, 1974

I CORINTHIANS 1:26–2:5

Trinity's pastor came out of the closet in a Christmas Eve sermon, and then left the church crippled by debt and in disarray. A crusty old retired Navy chaplain held things together for a few months then, midyear, with no warning and only two weeks to pack, the bishop sent me to Trinity, North Myrtle Beach. My father-in-law, Carl Parker, had given birth to Trinity the year I was born, but the congregation had never thrived. So I went there in fear and trepidation, as witnessed in this first sermon. Trinity turned out to be a wonderful place to begin my ministry, a congregation whose rebirth validated the importance of faithful preaching as the key to congregational renewal.

A first sermon is much like a first date—I want to do well, put my best foot forward, not say anything too dumb that might render impossible a future relationship, impress you, reassure you that the bishop made a wise decision in sending me to Trinity.

To continue the dating analogy, my anxiety is much like that of a "blind date." I don't know you and you don't know me. You have heard about me, but only through the advance information from the district superintendent, and you know that district superintendents are sometimes not to be trusted.

So here I am—wanting to appear wise—but not overly wise, not offensively wise like William Buckley. I want to entertain, to engage you, but not to appear trite or comical. I'm thinking now, "I wonder what they expect of me? What would they like to hear?"

And there you are—wanting to appear likeable, congenial, a nice group of people with whom any preacher would love to live, wanting to impress me that the bishop is really impressed by you and looking out for you when he sent me to you.

And here I am thinking . . . there are lots of empty pews out there; am I equal to the task? I wonder why they pay so little of their fair share of mission giving? Why did Peggy have such a pained look on her face when I mentioned finances to her? How come Joan said to me, after handing me a lemon pie, "Well, you really have got your work cut out for you, preacher"?

The district superintendent told me that this church had lots of "potential," but I don't trust D.S.'s anymore than you do!

And there you are thinking . . . he looks young, too young. Some are thinking . . . he looks old, or if not old, at least short. He can't play softball, I can tell that by looking at his arms. Oh well, maybe we can use him, second string, right field. I wonder why he really left his last appointment? How long will the "honeymoon last"?

Will there be a honeymoon?

I'm sure that George Baker told you that I had a good reputation, even though I've only been a pastor for a couple of years. But then George told me the story of the preacher who left a congregation. It was his last Sunday. End of the service the preacher is standing at the door. One woman was overcome with weeping and emotion. The preacher, touched by her grief attempted to reassure her with, "O Sister, don't weep. Even if I'm leaving I know that the bishop will send you a wonderful preacher."

She replied through tears, "That's what they've been telling this church for twenty years and it ain't happened yet!"

Here I am and there you are and you are wondering—will he take time for me? Will he listen to my story? Will he care that I've got problems? And will his ministry be adequate to meet my needs?

And here I am wondering—will I have time for all of them? Will they take time to know me as a person, or will they only know me as "The Preacher"? Will my talents be adequate to their need?

In other words, here I am—wondering, if I'm honest, "are they good enough, kind enough, enlightened enough for me?" Will they receive my offbeat way with sermons? Will they pay me enough so that next year I can go to Annual Conference and look good enough to all my fellow preachers so I can say, "Look how I turned around things at Trinity?"

And there you are wondering—can he fix my marriage? Can he make my children behave? Can he keep me interested on a Sunday in a sermon? Can he attract more young couples to our church? Will he embarrass us in town?

For you and for me the first sermon is like a first date; we're both putting each other on trial.

Knowing all this, I tossed and turned in preparing my first sermon, wondering what should I say and how I should say it to you.

"Preach that one on redemption that worked so well at Broad Street. You really wowed them with that one."

Too heavy. Don't want them to think they've got an egghead for a preacher.

"Use some football analogy; can't go wrong by mentioning sports. They all love football."

Better stay out of controversial matters—don't know whether they tend to be for Clemson or for Carolina.

And so it continued, rummaging about in my old files, frantically searching for something impressive enough, entertaining enough, yet spiritual and humble enough, inspirational too—and do it all in about twenty minutes in my first sermon!

Then, as so often happens, I managed to get some good advice from an older, wiser friend of mine, a fired old preacher who has served (and even survived!) some of the toughest, meanest, hard-to-please congregations that ever were—Brother Paul.

In reminiscing about his preaching at First Church Corinth—a difficult appointment if ever there were one—Paul said:

> Consider your own call, brothers and sisters, not many of you were wise by human standards, not many were powerful, not many were of noble birth. But God chose what is foolish in the world to shame the wise; God chose what is weak in the world to shame the strong. God chose what is low and despised in the world, things that are not, to reduce to nothing things that are, so that no one might boast in the presence of God. He is the source of your life in Christ Jesus who became for us wisdom from God, and righteousness and sanctification, and redemption in order that, as it is written, "Let the one who boasts, boast in the Lord."
>
> When I came to you, brothers and sisters, I did not come proclaiming the mystery of God to you in lofty words or wisdom. For I decided to know nothing among you except Jesus Christ, and him crucified. And I came to you in weakness and in fear and in much trembling. My speech and my proclamation were not with plausible words of wisdom, but with a demonstration of the Spirit and of power, so that your faith might not rest on human wisdom but on the power of God.

Saint Paul says to his first church: there you are, not wise by the world's standards of wisdom, not the brightest candles in the box, not by a long shot. No PhD's among you. Few of you rich, few prestigious. Not much ground for boasting among you.

And here I am, Paul: no silver-tongued orator here. Just a poor, often inadequate, sometimes disconnected, often boring, poor Bible-quoting preacher. No charismatic, good-looking TV Oral Roberts. Just a plain speaker of the plain, unadorned Good News.

That's all.

Not that wise a congregation, not that wise a preacher, says Paul. Just you, just me, *just the gospel.*

Paul's sermonic strategies are interesting in that they don't try to be interesting. "I decided to know nothing among you—no six steps to salvation, no surefire way to riches and happiness, no smooth, religious-sounding big words—I was determined to know nothing but the gospel. That's the only good reason for you, or for me, to be here. The church isn't about me and it's not about you. It's the wisdom and power of God. It's about the gospel.

That's a tough gospel truth. It's so easy to get confused that we could really have a great church—if we could find just the right pastor who—along with being good with older folks and youth, also visits everybody all the time, prepares profound and moving sermons, and walks on water to boot! Or we could have a really great church if we could weed out all the halfway committed people and get this down to the really, really serious Christians.

But Paul says that's not the way Christ works. Christ works by taking a group of people—not many all that wise, none too powerful and competent, not many rich—and uses them to show what a great, wise, powerful, competent God can do.

In my better moments I know: any good that I'm able to work here is that good that only God can do. God is going to have to work through frail, all-too-human, flawed people like you, like me, or no real good will get done.

I was asking one of you last week (I'm not going to tell you who it was but I bet you can guess), "What do you love most about Trinity Church?" And you responded, "I love that God really is here. When I think of the sorry preaching we have endured over the past years I think it's a miracle that we are still here! With the sorry preachers we've had it's a testimony to the power of God that there is a Trinity Methodist Church!"

Can you guess who said that to me? And you know: he was absolutely right. Maybe not right about preachers but right about God. That there is a church here. That people like us are being saved, being used by God to take over the world for the kingdom of God. It's "a miracle."

So here I am wanting to come up with something brilliant for you and there you are wanting to be brilliant and Paul tells all of us: It's not about brilliant people; it's about a God who loves to create something out of nothing.

I confess I'd rather trust what wisdom I've got than to risk trusting the goodness of God to create a world out of chaos (Genesis 1), to raise the dead back to life (Luke 24), and to make the people of God out of those who were once nobodies and strangers (Trinity United Methodist Church).

There I am and there you are. Despite our weaknesses and inadequacies, a loving, resourceful God is stupefying the world, using what the world regards as low, foolish, and dumb to make something wonderful. We've only been in town a week now and yet already we have been amazed at what God is doing through you at Trinity Church. A Baptist mechanic was testifying to what a good church I was getting just this past Wednesday.

I'm not the greatest preacher in the world and you're not the greatest church in the world but that's OK because the greatest God in the world is surprising the world with God's ability to create something out of nothing, right here in this congregation. So on this our first Sunday together pray for me that I would, week-after-week, keep real clear about why we're here, that I would look to Jesus and not to myself to make this a faithful church. Pray that on my last day here, when I'm preaching my very last sermon to you, I'll be able to say, "When I came to Trinity Church, I didn't come preaching lofty words of wisdom, fancy spiritual stuff, and highfalutin theology. I preached Jesus Christ and him crucified. I preached the simple, unadorned good news that God is saving the world through us. My only boast is the wisdom and power of God."

There you are and here I am with nothing to bring us together, and no hope in life or in death, no chance of ever being the body of Christ—nothing except Christ, the wisdom and power of God.

Frankly, I can't wait to discover just how great and wise a God we've got. Let's go!

2

On the Jericho Road

September 15, 1974

"But a Samaritan, as he journeyed, came to where he was; and when he saw him, he had compassion."

Luke 10:33 RSV

I show my increasing fascination with the literary form of Scripture in the shape of this sermon from 1974. Egged on by Augustine's sermon on the Good Samaritan, I attempted to reframe the overly familiar story. I think I also show an increasing confidence in my own peculiar voice in the sermon.

I love to travel—the lure of faraway places, new adventures, and unusual experiences. Name a place to go, and my bags are packed. But there are hazards of travel, chief among them: travel puts you at the mercy of other people, strangers—innkeepers, mechanics, hotel doctors, cooks—strangers who don't know you and you don't know them.

Being far away from home is usually fine—as long as you don't have trouble. But if you do run into difficulty—your car breaks down, your wallet is stolen, or the hotel loses your reservation—you are totally dependent on the beneficence of strangers.

Misfortune brings odd people together, out on the road.

A few years ago, traveling home one night after a speaking engagement in a remote part of South Carolina my car began to sputter, to falter, and finally rolled to a stop. It was 10 or 10:30 on a summer evening. The stars were out but otherwise no light could be seen anywhere. I had no idea where I was.

8

I got out and stood beside the car in the darkness. Five, ten minutes passed. At last, I could hear a car in the distance. I could see its lights, now and yes, here it came. I looked into its lights, smiled hopefully, as it—passed on by, barely slowing for me.

"Well, at least someone is on this road tonight," I thought. But it was another fifteen minutes, a virtual eternity, before another car came. And it, too, passed by.

I got in the car, put my tie back on, straightened my hair, and resumed my post beside my stricken auto. It was late now. Who in their right mind would stop for me at midnight on a country road? Would I be stranded here all night?

Again, I saw lights coming toward me. As they came closer, I could hear music, loud music, emanating from this car. It was coming at a high rate of speed. I could tell that this car was really flying. No chance of *them* stopping. But as its lights shined in my eyes, the driver of the car put on brakes and skidded, finally coming to a stop a hundred or so feet beyond me, sliding all the way around on the pavement. Then throwing the car into reverse, backing up nearly as fast as he had come, he screeched to a stop when he was even with my car.

I gulped. It was a multicolored old Lincoln with fender skirts, some part of some sort of animal waving from the radio antenna, and two little red, blinkup lights on the back of the rearview mirror.

"Oh, no," I thought. "What now? Here I am in the middle of nowhere, I'm gonna die."

I could see two large men in the car. The one on the driver's side was wearing a T-shirt, the man on the passenger side was bare-chested. He held a large can of beer and looked at me through a pair of dark glasses.

"Hey, man," he shouted at me from his window. "You got trouble?"

I thought, "*Now* I've got trouble." I'm just resting, counting stars, letting my engine cool. Before I could say anything else these strangers were out of their car, had my hood up, offered me refreshments, and were tinkering with my motor. Nearly an hour later, long after a dozen other cars had passed by on the other side, with the moon well on its way down the western sky, the two shook my hand, bid me farewell with, "Take it easy, neighbor," and squealed off into the darkness of a low country summer night. I headed home.

Misfortunate on the road brings together the most unlikely of neighbors.

One day, on the long road to Jerusalem, a lawyer stopped Jesus and asked, "Teacher, what must I do to inherit eternal life?"

"Hey, Teacher," he says to Jesus. "I've got a question for you. . . ." Bill Mallard notes that just about every time Jesus is addressed as "Teacher" in Luke, it's a term of contempt, a sign of derision. "Hey! Teach! Mr. Scholar! *Didas-kalu*"—you can hear the hiss in the Greek.

Here is a learned lawyer making fun of this yokel, this layman, this carpenter's son named Jesus. "You think you're smart; here's a question for you, Mr. Teacher."

Remember, Jesus' encounters with critics occurred before a crowd. Here the lawyer is grandstanding in a public debate. Who will win the crowd's approval—the professional theologian, or this unlearned "teacher"?

"What does the law say?" Jesus asks. And the lawyer, quoting Scripture known by everyone, a verse learned in Sabbath school, "You shall love the Lord thy God, with everything that you have . . . and your neighbor as yourself."

"But who is my neighbor?" the lawyer asks.

Isn't it interesting that the lawyer doesn't ask, "Who is this God that I am supposed to love with all my heart, mind, and soul?" Rather he asks, "Who is this neighbor whom I am supposed to love as myself?" He knows, or thinks he knows, who God is. He just wants to know who his neighbor is.

That's us on Sunday morning. I ask people, "What's the point of Sunday worship? They reply: I come to church to learn where I've gone wrong in life and to find out how I can do better." We come with our little notepads to get our assignments for the week. In the sermon the minister says, "What do we have to do to be good?" Then, in the rest of the sermon, the preacher answers his questions: You must do the following three things this week in order to be good.

1. Love your neighbor.
2. Be nice to people at the supermarket.
3. Tithe.

We are practical, utilitarian, down-to-earth folk. Our religion is reduced to the level of petty moralisms: Do this, don't do that. "Don't bother us with God; we want things kept safely tied down here. Tell us what we are supposed to do this week to be good. After all, why else would we be here at church?"

The lawyer doesn't want to know about God. He wants to know more about himself, "Tell me, what must I do to have eternal life?" He wants to save himself, be God to himself. Tell me, Jesus, who is my neighbor so that I can go out and love him? What do I have to do so that I might win my salvation? Who has the Gallup Poll declared to be the latest trend in neighbors?

Jesus answers, as he so often does, by a story. Jesus' story is a little travelogue. A man was on the road from Jerusalem to Jericho. He gets beaten up, left "half dead" in the ditch by a bunch of robbers. There he lies, dying, hurting, forsaken. Down the road comes a priest. (Crowd perks up.) But the priest, rather than helping the man, passes by on the other side. (The crowd loves it. "Go get 'em, Jesus. We are sick and tired of these money-grabbing, self-righteous, TV preachers from Tulsa. Sock it to 'em." The people always tend to be anticlerical.) Then, down the road comes a Levite, a lay leader of First Church Jerusalem. (Yes, a Levite, with his little fish license plate and his black leather Bible on the dashboard.) He—passes by on the other side of the road. ("Great!" says the crowd. "Those Levites who sit on the front pew every Sunday and act so holy, so damn pious. They think they own the church just because they are the top ten tithers. Go get 'em, Jesus! This is wonderful!")

There lies the man in the ditch . . . you hear more footsteps coming down the road toward you. The sun beats down. You know you've lost a lot of blood. This may be your last hope. You open your eyes, one last time, blurred by loss of blood, and you see, you see coming toward you—a humble, sincere, religious, but not showy, ordinary Methodist person like you and me? No. You see, you see, a *Samaritan!*

"Oh no!" A Samaritan! We Israelites hate those Samaritan half-breeds, racial mixers, heretics—hate them so much we would wade through the Jordan just to avoid having to meet them on the same road. (In Luke 9:54, James and John want to call down fire on the Samaritans.) "A Samaritan! I'd rather die than to be saved by the likes of you!"

And you know the story. The Samaritan stops. But the thing that impresses us about this Samaritan is not only that he stops and helps. We would have done that. The thing that the story drives home is the sheer extravagance of his helpfulness. He not only stops, risks his own life (after all, the bandits who got the man in the ditch could still be lurking in the shadows), unties his headband and dresses your bloody wounds. Then he puts you in his Lincoln. He not only stops from his busy work, he goes to the Inn, pays for everything and more. He tells the innkeeper to look after you and when the Samaritan returns, he will pay whatever it costs.

You see (this is important) it's not that the priest and the Levite were bad men. They were important, busy men. For all we know, good men. They had serious responsibilities. Their religion was their work. And all you good, hardworking, busy good people know how it is when you're on the road and you are due at the temple by 11:00. It's not that you don't want to help, it's that you can't help right now.

The priest and the Levite's work was religious, all consuming good work like ours. You can't help everyone who needs help. You can't give everyone as much help as they need. There must be limits. "Maybe a highway patrolman will help if you put your hood up. I can't help, not just now. I have other responsibility beyond your misfortune." It's just too dangerous to stop on an interstate these days. Isn't it illegal to pick up or discharge hitchhikers on these highways?

See? These are not bad people. They are just busy people, this priest and Levite, people like us. It's not that they are bad and the Samaritan is good. It is that the Samaritan is excessive, extravagant in his goodness, in taking time, risk, sacrifice. Most of the verses in this story are expended in describing in great detail the extravagant, risky nature of what the Samaritan did. It wasn't just that he stopped to help the man in the ditch. It was the way he stopped, the extravagant way he helped.

We like to think of the Samaritan as a decent sort of fellow—like us. We picture him as the one who writes a check to the United Fund, or gives a pint of blood to the Red Cross, or spends an hour a week as a volunteer at the public school. But these are all things we can afford, things that really don't call for any risk, any extravagance on our part. We are simply giving others from our oversupply, giving something we don't need anyway—an hour a week, $25 a year, a pint of blood. This giving is merely another form of self-love, a shrewd and cautious way of justifying ourselves, making ourselves look good, saving ourselves by our little acts of charity. No wonder the priest and the Levite look evil when they won't even stop and toss the man a quarter to call the highway patrol. We would do that.

But that's just the point. Jesus carefully emphasizes the excessiveness of the Samaritan. "All you spend," he tells the innkeeper, "I will repay you when I return." I'll pay it all. Jesus asks, "Now, think clearly, Mr. Theologian, who of the three was the neighbor?" "Wait," says the lawyer. "I asked you who is my neighbor? That is, whom should I love as my neighbor? Who is neighbor enough to me so that I should love him as I love myself?"

But the fascinating thing is that Jesus reverses the lawyer's question. Not, How can I be a neighbor to others, but *who is neighbor to me?* Which of these three—the priest, the Levite, the Samaritan—was a neighbor to that wounded man in the ditch? Which of these three should the wounded man love as much as he loves himself? Not, "Who is my neighbor?" but, "Who is the neighbor to the wounded man?"

And the lawyer begrudgingly replies, "I guess, I suppose it was the one who had compassion. The Samaritan."

You have to put yourself in the right place. You see, the story is not about the man in the ditch whom we are supposed to be charitable toward; it's a story about three people who came down a road one day and only one was a neighbor—the neighbor is a despised Samaritan. We'd rather die than to have a neighbor like that.

The lawyer who wanted to justify himself is confronted not by the poor wounded man in a ditch but by the anything-but-poor Samaritan—the despised, rejected, disgusting Samaritan. This is the neighbor whom the lawyer only saw as an enemy. It's a story about a Samaritan.

Three people passed by—a preacher and the head for the Full Gospel Business Men's Association. The only one who stopped was—a member of the P.L.O., or a Communist, or a Sandinista rebel—you fill in whatever person you most despise, some Samaritan.

And we all responded: *We'd rather die than be saved by the likes of you.*

I've seen it in the church. I once knew a woman who was assaulted in broad daylight in her backyard. It was horrible. We got her a great counselor who specializes in such violent tragedies. One day she said, "My counselor wants me to tell my story to someone who is not a member of my family, as a therapeutic help."

"Have you thought of someone?" I asked. "Yes. I'd like to tell Harry Jones," she said. Harry Jones was a sometimes recovering, often not, unemployed alcoholic.

"Why Harry?" I asked. "I thought you might want to tell another woman."

"Why Harry? Because he knows what it's like to go to hell," she replied.

And I thought: only in the church would someone whom the world despises and regards as a failure be your savior.

So once again we are surprised that, as in Jesus' other parables, this is not a story about us and what we are to do. It's a story about God; what God does. It's not a story about how we are to save ourselves by doing this or that, but a story of the strange, peculiar way Jesus saves us.

We, like the lawyer, want to know the limits of our responsibilities. Who are *we* supposed to love? The deserving poor? How much are *we* supposed to give? Would you settle for 10 percent? Let's send 50 million in aid to El Salvador so we can spend 50 billion to blow the Russians to high heaven? Who is our neighbor?

But the story is not about to whom are *we* to be neighbors? It's about who is a neighbor to *us*?

Remember, this whole argument with the lawyer is preceded by the observation that, "this one (this teacher) receives sinners and eats with them." This one welcomes back Prodigal Sons. This one forgives adulterous women. This one admits thieves into heaven. This one claims that God's sun shines on the good and the bad. "Father, forgive them," he says. This one's love is so—extravagant—that it makes our charity look miserly.

And we despise him for it. The despised, offensive Samaritan savior is *Christ.*

Like his other parables, this Jesus story is not about how we can go about loving poor people. It tells us about a God whose love is so extravagant that it makes us all look poor. And we, like the lawyer, don't like to look poor and helpless. We want to be liberated, self-sufficient, big, rich, justified. Why do we give a few bucks a year to the poor—to make ourselves look big as we cast a crumb their way. So we hate the extravagantly self-giving Samaritan who reminds us of our spiritual poverty.

As Augustine noted, it was Jesus' critics who sneered, "Thou art a Samaritan, and hast a devil" (John 8:48 KJV).

We are the one dying in the ditch. Our neighbor is the one whose love is so—extravagant—that it saves us. Here is a story, not about the difficulty we good ones face in being neighbors to the needy, but the difficulty we all have in seeing this despised stranger, Jesus, is our neighbor to those of us who are in more need than we admit.

The lawyer's question—who is my neighbor that I ought to love him as much as myself?—is answered. It is this despised Samaritan-like savior who, though he was God, emptied himself, risked all, stooped down, washed feet, healed, died. Our problem is not just that we don't know who are our neighbors; we don't know who is our God. *Our* God is powerful, omnipotent, the God of the rich and successful, a powerful being who sends a little charitable power to his lowly creatures. So we are shocked out on the Jericho road to meet *this* extravagant God who gives away *everything*.

The teacher leaves the lawyer and travels up the road toward Jerusalem. There, at the end of the road, they betray him, mock him, deride him, strip, beat, and crucify this—Samaritan. He came to the wounded, the naked, and the dying. We looked upon him and said with one voice, "We'd rather die than be saved by the likes of *you*."

3

On the Perils of *NOT* Passing By on the Other Side

October 12, 1975

Just then a lawyer stood up to test Jesus. "Teacher," he said, "what must I do to inherit eternal life?" He said to him, "What is written in the law? What do you read there?" He answered, "You shall love the Lord your God with all your heart, and with all your soul, and with all your strength, and with all your mind; and your neighbor as yourself." And he said to him, "You have given the right answer; do this, and you will live."

But wanting to justify himself, he asked Jesus, "And who is my neighbor?" Jesus replied, "A man was going down from Jerusalem to Jericho, and fell into the hands of robbers. . . ."

Luke 10:25–30a

Even after a decade of preaching, I was blessed by a weekly fascination with the way that the Gospels present the truth who is Jesus Christ. I felt a kinship with the Gospel writers in their originating presentation of Jesus. Scripture tended to be mostly narrative, whereas I realized that many of my sermons were propositional. Thus began my narrative phase, attempting to interpret story with story, determined to keep close to the literary form of the originating text.

We were coming out of the diner, my friend and I, he a preacher and I one too. Heading down the street toward our respective churches, we came across a poor old man, sprawled out on the edge of the sidewalk, head swirling around in a drunken stupor. I'm sure we thought of passing by on the other side; the old man was a pitiful mess. But then I thought, "Wait. I'm a Christian, a Christian pastor, for God's sake." I'm sure that my friend thought the same.

So we did the only thing Jesus permitted us to do. We stopped and showed compassion on the man in need.

> A man was going down from Jerusalem to Jericho, and fell into the hands of robbers. . . . Now by chance a priest was going down that road; and when he saw him, he passed by on the other side. . . .

"Poor old fool," said my friend.

"You know, we really ought to do something," said I. "He could get hurt out here in his condition. Someone might take advantage of him."

"After all, we're in the business, right?" said my friend.

"Yea, right," said I. That's how it started.

> But a Samaritan while traveling came near him; and when he saw him, he was moved with pity. He went to him and bandaged his wounds, having poured oil and wine on them.

My friend took one of the man's arms and I took the other. With some difficulty, we got him to his feet. He was dressed in a rumpled, terribly dirty, old suit, with a crumpled hat. As he attempted to steady himself, he swerved and staggered back and forth on the sidewalk, my friend and I staggering with him, trying to get him upright.

"Easy does it," the man mumbled, "look out for those slippery places in the river."

"Hey, old man, you really ought to get some help," said my friend. The three of us staggered, tottered down the sidewalk, the man with my friend and I on either side, people scurrying out of our way.

"Where do we take someone in this condition," I wondered aloud.

"There's got to be somewhere for people like him," said my friend.

"Would you mind what you're doing," said the old man in an aggravated tone of voice, "you're going to run aground and kill everybody on the boat!"

We staggered and tottered, the three of us, to a phone booth on the next corner.

My friend left me outside to wrestle with the recipient of our compassion while he began thumbing madly through the phone book.

"Well, are we going to just stand here, or are we going to go inside and eat lunch?" asked the man, gesturing toward the phone booth.

"Aha! Here we are, the Greenville Alcohol Information Center," said my friend, relieved. "It's not too far from here. We can drive it in five minutes."

We staggered, the three of us, on down the street, with the man mumbling, "What was wrong with that restaurant, it looked good to me?"

> Then he put him on his own animal, brought him to an inn, and took care of him.

Once in my friend's car, he in the front driving, and our ward and I in the back, we headed toward the Greenville Alcohol Information Center. By the time we reached Main Street, the old man had passed out again and was snoring quietly on my shoulder, a sort of beatific smile on his dirty face.

Then, just after we turned on to busy Main Street, without warning, the old man began to shout, curse, and kick.

"Hold him!" said my friend, looking over into the back seat where I was wrestling for all that I was worth. "I just bought this car last month."

He was kicking, screaming something about "Snakes, everywhere, snakes!"

With that he somehow managed to kick the back door open and fell forward out of the car and into the street.

All I had to hold him back was the seat of his pants, pants which, with his struggling to get away, and my struggling to hold him, were now being pulled down his hips.

"Help me!" he began shouting to the people on the sidewalk. "Help me! I don't even know these people and they are trying to take me someplace! Help!"

There I was, traffic stopped in the middle of Main Street, attempting to wrestle this old man back into the car while also speaking to the now gathering crowd on the street, "I am a Methodist minister. My friend is a Baptist. We are clergy. We are professionals. We are helping this old man here."

"I don't want no help from nobody, specially no damn preachers!" he was shouting to the crowd. "I'm Church of God. Baptists is the ones that put me in this fix in the first place. For the love of God, help!" he screamed to the onlookers.

I finally succeeded in forcing him back into the backseat and the car sped away. After a few more moments of struggle, the old man passed out once again and slept peacefully until we arrived at the big office building which housed the Greenville Alcohol Information Center.

It wasn't easy getting a totally unconscious man out of the car, dragging him across the street, into the lobby, on to the elevator, and up to the ninth floor. I had him propped up in one corner of the elevator where he kept sliding down into a hovel on the floor.

"I am a Methodist minister," I kept saying to people who got on the elevator. "We are helping this man. My friend is a Baptist. This is part of our work."

The Alcohol Information Center consisted of a young woman seated behind a desk. On the desk were stacks of leaflets about substance abuse. That was it. It was obvious, when the three of us staggered into her office, that she had never actually seen an inebriated person in her life, probably never seen two clergy, either.

"You can't bring him in here," she said to us.

"But he needs help," protested my friend.

"Not here," she said. "We provide information, phone numbers. We are not a certified treatment facility."

When he persisted, she agreed to go upstairs and ask her boss what we might do with the man (who now slept in one of the metal chairs, his head resting peacefully on her desk between the stacks of pamphlets).

> The next day he took out two denarii, gave them to the innkeeper, and said, "Take care of him; and when I come back, I will repay you whatever more you spend."

As soon as she left the office my friend and I looked at one another and, without a word of deliberation, quietly but quickly tiptoed out of the office and dashed for the elevator, leaving the intended recipient of our good will sleeping between stacks of pamphlets.

Once downstairs and on the street, we sped away, my friend to work on next Sunday's sermon, me to the tennis court.

> "Which of these three, do you think, was a neighbor to the man who fell into the hands of the robbers?" He said, "The one who showed him mercy." Jesus said to him, "Go and do likewise."

Luke 10:29–37. Easier to preach than to practice. Hey, people! Be careful with the, "Go and do likewise."

Northside United Methodist Church

4

The Peril of Forgiveness

September 6, 1981

MATTHEW 18:12–22

"'Lord, how often shall my brother [or sister] sin against me, and I forgive . . . ? As many as seven times?' Jesus said to him, 'I do not say to you seven times, but seventy times seven.'"

Matthew 18:21–22 RSV

My sermons at Northside have a distinctly pastoral cast to them. Life in a congregation definitely affects a pastor's reading of Scripture. I remember being impressed, in my pastoral conversations with my people, that forgiveness is an ever-present reality of congregational life. Can it be that Jesus' command to forgive sins against us is not some heroic act but rather a basic requirement for any people who would live in community in the name of Jesus? I hoped, in this sermon, to remind the people at Northside of the adventure of being saved by a savior like Jesus.

You see, my problem is that I just hate to see anybody get away with something. A Texas tycoon milks a savings and loan for millions, I think the rat ought to pay. A North Carolina wife feeds her husband arsenic, throw her in the slammer—particularly when her poisonee was a preacher, for heaven's sake. "Throw the book at 'em," today Texas, tomorrow my neighborhood. Next they'll be running for president and then where will we be?

I am all in favor of forgiveness, as long as it is appropriate. Mercy is fine, as long as it is not an excuse for indifference to wrong. Let us have no weak-kneed, syrupy moral ooze masquerading as Christian mercy. Forgiveness is fine, as long as it is not a means for somebody getting off scot-free. Debts must be paid. There are penalties for broken rules. Such is the mathematics of justice. You let someone off the moral hook, he'll think that his behavior is OK and just go do wrong again. Then where would we be, morally speaking? They'd be running naked in the streets.

And don't try to cover up sloppy moral thinking with sentimental little stories about lost sheep (Matt. 18:12–14).

"A shepherd has a hundred sheep," says Jesus. "One goes astray. The shepherd leaves the ninety-nine and goes out to look for the one lost sheep and, when he finds it, rejoices more over that recovered sheep than over the ninety-nine that never went astray. It is not the will of my Father that one of these little ones should perish."

The Father, the Shepherd, has this thing for lost sheep, just loves to go looking for the lost, doesn't want any sheep to stray from the fold. Sweet thought.

But say we're not talking about little lost lambs but a goat like Manuel Noriega. Say the one little bleating lamb who can't find his way home is named Jim Bakker, or Pol Pot. Do you still think it's sweet that the Shepherd is out beating the bushes for the lost?

I want you to think of the worst thing anyone has ever done to you. The lie that was told about you, the time you were falsely punished, the deal on which you were cheated, the person who gave you the shaft. Focus on that act and the person behind it. Now, picture yourself extending the hand, forgiving that person who has so terribly wronged you.

Will you agree with me that there is just about nothing so tough as forgiving someone?

Now, few would accuse Matthew of ethical permissiveness. Matthew's Gospel is full of rules and regulations, standards for and stress upon righteousness, higher righteousness for Jesus' people than even the righteousness of the scribes and Pharisees. Which makes all the more perplexing the sloppy way in which Matthew records this story of the Lost Sheep. When Luke tells this same story (remember, Jesus told the story in Luke when his critics attacked him saying, "This man receives sinners and eats with them," Luke 15:2), Luke has the Shepherd say, "Rejoice with me, for I have found my sheep which was lost . . . I tell you, there will be more joy in heaven over one sinner who *repents* (get that, who *repents*) than over ninety-nine righteous persons (like all you good church people here) who have no need of repentance."

Now wouldn't the story of the Good Shepherd make more sense in Matthew if he were Luke's Good Shepherd out looking for repentant sheep? Forgiveness is fine—wrapped in sackcloth and ashes. There have got to be limits. Unfortunately, Matthew's Shepherd is out looking for strays, whether they be repentant or not.

A woman of my acquaintance has a husband who has broken marriage vows, committed adultery, humiliated her, and broken her heart. She asks me, as someone tight with Jesus, what she should do.

"Why, don't you know the story about the little lost lamb? Take him back. Go out, search for the poor lost philanderer. Bring the little wandering lamb back. Throw a party as soon as he returns from Vegas! It is not the will of our Father that any of these little ones should perish."

She's a Christian. She forgives him, takes him back. Next spring, the sap is rising, he's on his way to Vegas again, different blonde sitting beside him in the Pinto, but it's him, the unrepentant old goat.

"Pastor, what should I do?"

"Don't you know the story about the little lost lamb? Take him back . . ."

"Wait a minute, pastor. That was the sappy story you told me this time last year. This is the same stupid sheep that got lost last time. Don't you know any other stories?"

The sweet sheep story sort of disintegrates, doesn't it, when the one sheep the Shepherd shows up with is named Al Capone?

So maybe that's why Jesus catches himself, after that sweet little story about the Shepherd taking back the lost sheep, and follows it with more realistic, sensible advice.

"If your brother or sister sins against you, go tell him about it. If he listens, great. If he doesn't listen, squeal on him to the whole church and, if he won't even listen to the church and do right, let him be to you as a Gentile and a tax collector" (18:15–17).

You, you Gentile! You IRS-tax-collecting stoolie you!

"So much for these losers," Jesus now seems to say. "Sure, go out and seek them like the Shepherd. But no need to overdo it. Go out and beat the rough for the lost ball, wave the next foursome through, then to heck with it. Drop another ball in the fairway and play on."

And I take some comfort that Jesus threw this qualification in here. Otherwise, if he had left it with just that story of the Shepherd and the sheep, someone might have justly accused Jesus of irresponsibility, moral permissiveness, ethical sentimentality. When you've been wronged, try to settle it on your own. If that doesn't work, go public with your gripe. And if that fails, treat him as a Gentile and a tax collector.

Gentiles? We're talking Roman Army Officers here, the first-century equivalent of the Nazi S.S. tax collectors? Those conniving quislings who collaborated with the Romans to fleece their own people. When forgiveness is rejected and repentance is refused, the stakes appear to be high indeed—treat them as no better than a Gentile or a tax collector.

When I taught in seminary, I told my students in classes on pastoral care, "Make it a rule to go anywhere, anytime with your people once. But twice, three times to bail them out at midnight? Forget it. Even pastors, especially pastors as the moral guardians of the community must have their limits."

So it was at this point that Peter's hand went up, Peter, who is there for all of us. "Lord, did you say limits? What are the limits? Three strikes, then you're out? One verbal warning, then you get a Technical? No? That's right. We're Christians. The world's doormats. OK, let's say, just to show that we are long-suffering, we forgive seven times. How do you like those numbers, Jesus?"

And Jesus replies, "I'd suggest something more akin to seventy times seven or (in the RSV), seventy-seven."

And even Peter, who was about as lousy at arithmetic as he was at theology, knew that Jesus was talking big money.

"Why, if we forgave people who wronged us that often, we'd go to our grave forgiving, we'd lose count forgiving by the time we were in our thirties."

Right, says the Shepherd. Think about it. You'd go to your grave forgiving.

So what about that earlier business of telling them to their face, then to the church, then treating them as a Gentile and a tax collector? I think that business is the key to this whole passage. If it isn't, then these verses are a hopeless muddle; Jesus saying one thing in his parable about the Shepherd and the lost sheep, taking it back with his hard line on the limits of forgiveness, then linking it with a complete non sequitur about forgiving seventy times seven—which means, for all intents and purposes, forgiving without limits. If Jesus was playing this thing straight, about calling our brother or sister a Gentile and a tax collector, then the whole thing is a muddle.

You have to watch Jesus. There are times when Jesus will say something, even in a Gospel as straightforward as that of Matthew, when you think he means one thing, only to find out later that he meant something quite different. I think it's Jesus' sly way of showing us that the good news he brings isn't self-evident. Sometimes it doesn't make sense, as we are accustomed to make sense, isn't reasonable, the way we define reason.

You have to watch Jesus also because *you have to interpret what he says by what he does.*

Many times in our congregation we don't confront one another with wrong doing or offense. We overlook it. Refuse to mention it. We say we do it for "love" but to be honest we do it because it's just too risky and troublesome to get into such "private" matters. Jesus here insists that wrongdoing be made public, that we take lots of time and trouble with one another in the church. Jesus gives explicit instruction on how to handle wrongdoing. But even with this detailed instruction on forgiveness, there seem to be limits. "Tell him to his face," he says, "then, if he still doesn't say he's sorry, tell it to the church.

And if even that doesn't work, treat him like you would a Gentile or a tax collector, that'll fix him."

And we think we know what that means. We know what *we* would mean. Gentile? Tax collector? In other words, treat him as an outcast, excommunicate, incarcerate (or in South Carolina and a few other states), incinerate. That'll fix him. But when Jesus follows up with his advice to Peter on the limits of forgiving someone seventy times seven—that is, no limits at all—we know that what we would mean is *not* what Jesus means by treating someone as a Gentile and a tax collector. It's a setup.

The one who speaks is the one of whom it was said, "Now the tax collectors and sinners were all drawing near to hear him. And the Pharisees and the scribes murmured, saying, 'This man receives sinners and eats with them'" (Luke 15:1–2 RSV).

At his birth, the way Mr. Higher Righteousness Matthew tells the story, the first people to show up in Bethlehem were three astrologers bearing perfume (Matt. 2). Three *Gentile* magi, they were.

It was said, at the opening of his work, "The land . . . across the Jordan, Galilee of the *Gentiles*—the people who sat in darkness have seen a great light" (Matt. 4:15–16 RSV). One of his first healings was of the servant of a Roman centurion (Matt. 8:5–13). He was a light, not just to the Chosen, but also to *Gentiles*.

And one day, when he was fooling around with a bunch of sinners, he called as a disciple one whose name would be given to this Gospel, Matthew. Do you remember what Matthew was doing for a living when Jesus called him? He was not a Gentile. He was a tax collector.

Get my drift? He told us to treat the unrepentant offender as a "Gentile and a tax collector" and he ought to know; he had enough firsthand experiences with that sort of folk.

And when they criticized him for the way he broke the law and stepped over the tradition, he answered, "If any of you have a sheep who falls into a pit on the Sabbath, will you not lay hold of it and pull it out? Now, if you'd break a rule or two to save a lost sheep, but how much more valuable is a person!" (Matt. 12:11–12, paraphr.).

He criticized the religious leaders of his day for the burdens they heaped on people's backs. Is that why he said, "Truly, I say to you, whatever you bind or loose on earth will be bound and loosed in heaven. Where two or three are gathered in my name, there am I in the midst of them" (Matt. 18:18–20, paraphr.)? Why should we be busy binding sins on other people's backs, acting as if it's three strikes and they're out, when this Shepherd of a God is forever out beating the bushes looking for some stray sheep, some Gentile or tax collector to bring back in?

Is that why Jesus says, "Where two or three are so gathered (eating and drinking with sinners and tax collectors?) in my name (the way I gathered unto myself the folk whom you exclude) I am there in the middle of 'em"? If we are going to be close to Jesus, we must act toward the world as he acted. And so he put the words in our mouth (in Matthew's version of the Lord's Prayer), "Forgive us our sins, as we have (already!) forgiven those who sin against us" (Matt. 6:12, paraphr.).

Especially because sometimes, the sins we are so busy binding on those Gentiles and tax collectors are our own. Sometimes the forgiveness we pronounce on another is forgiveness for ourselves. We saw on the news, a couple of years ago, the fire-breathing TV prophet, denouncing those evil pornographers and dirty movie makers while all the while was secretly making a few dirty movies of his own. The pious preacher, so quick to denounce the greed of the capitalist church members, is the one the board fears most in annual salary negotiations. There is some kind of link between our self-righteous condemnation of others and dishonesty about ourselves. The worst kind of lostness of all is not knowing how lost we are. The worst sort of sin is to believe we are without sin. The worst sort of unforgiveness is to presume that we don't need forgiveness. So sometimes the Gentile and tax collector that we are busy excluding from the fellowship and binding up with condemnation is *us*. For in the searching moral gaze of God's eyes, *we're all Gentiles and tax collectors*. The stray sheep that the Shepherd is out seeking is us, whether we have strayed from the path of moral rectitude through whom we slept with last night, or we have strayed from the meaning of true discipleship through whom we condemned in church this morning.

To our surprise, we have met the Gentiles and tax collectors, and they are us. And today's good news is, that's just the sort of lost sheep Jesus loves to save.

5

Graciousness and Grumbling

September 20, 1981

MATTHEW 20:1–15

In seminary I got the impression that the preacher's job is to explain the gospel, to make it relevant to everyday life, and to make first-century Jesus accessible to people who drive Toyotas. As a pastor of a mostly blue-collar, inner-city congregation, I certainly had parishioners who were grateful for any sermonic attempt to make life more comprehensible. Yet I also discovered that an important role of the preacher is to talk about Jesus in a way that is at least as disturbingly odd as Jesus. Scripture is a model for this sort of preaching. The Bible says, "Let me show you God," then seems to go out of its way to make God obtuse and strange.

Whenever a preacher portrays the gospel in such a way that hearers say, "That's odd. That's not the way that I'm accustomed to looking at things," the preacher is performing an important pastoral work—restoring the excitement of discipleship.

Well, religion has suddenly become the burning concern of politicians. I can't remember when religion has been so important in a presidential campaign. Mr. Reagan wining and dining the Rev. Falwell (or at least dining him). Everybody boasting about how great they are with their families. It wasn't long ago that John Kennedy had to explain why, although he was a Catholic, his religion would not hinder him from being a good president. And a very short time ago, Jimmy Carter stood before the voters and admitted that, although he was a faithful Baptist, he would perform his presidential duties as if he were nothing at all—or something like that.

So I suppose we preachers ought to be pleased that suddenly everyone wants the voters to think that he or she is a good Christian, that our president

wants us all to be praying in schools and reading our Bibles and strengthen-
ing our families. One would expect us preachers to be on the front row of
the cheering section as Democrats and Republicans beat each other into dust
debating who is *really* religious!

But if you listen to the Bible, sometimes it's difficult to decide if we would
be better off if we just got the Bible back in our public schools and homes.
"We need to get back to the Bible," said someone the other day, "it has all the
solutions to our problems." Good thing, the Bible. We ought to take a dose
or two of it every morning before work. It would do us all good.

But every now and then, if you really listen to the Bible, you come across
a story, a story so strange, so against the grain of our cherished suppositions,
that the Bible doesn't seem to be the solution for anything. In fact, it seems to
be the problem. Take this story of the Laborers in the Vineyard, for instance.

Here we are, Sunday morning, a beautiful September day in church, good
music, so much substantial stone, order, and pleasing harmony. Then comes
this parable about people going to work, some for eight hours (and in the heat
of the day, too), some for three, some for only one hour. Then the master
of the vineyard calls them together and pays everybody the same wage. The
workers who have been lounging in the marketplace until 4:00 p.m., get paid
as much as those who punched in at dawn. There is grumbling among those
who have been sweating in the vines all day, and why not? Is this any way to
run a business? they want to know. What kind of justice is this?

And even the most casual reader of the Bible, even the most complacent
mind, even a politician who thinks a little religion is a good thing, realizes
that it has arrived within a strange new world where everything is topsy-turvy.

You don't expect to find a story like this in Matthew. Other Gospels may
be stuck on the love and gracious acceptance of God, but not Matthew. As
far as Matthew is concerned, Jesus Christ brings us salvation, but that doesn't
change one thing about the rules. The rules still apply. Therefore Matthew
is filled with stern demands, and lists of injunctions, and the gavel coming
down in the great court of the Almighty. Other Gospels have stories about
good little bad boys who come back home after a week of carousing in the
family car with Dad's credit cards all gone and a terrible hangover and the old
man—welcomes the prodigal with open arms and orders a banquet thrown in
honor of his homecoming. Not Matthew. He tells stories of foolish virgins
standing in the darkness, clawing at the door, but no, they had their chance,
the door is now shut. Too bad for them. Matthew is fond of little moralistic
lessons about a poor servant who tried to gyp his fellow servants out of a few
dollars and, when the master found out about his scheme, has him beaten
and thrown into jail forever. For Matthew, you get what you deserve; if you
make your bed, you must lie in it; and what you sow, you reap. Actions have

consequences in this Gospel. There is a cause-effect relationship between our ethics and our ultimate destiny. Be careful what you do because, in the end, we shall be judged, the sheep shall be separated from the goats, and we must answer for our actions.

In other words, Matthew is the Gospel that your mother wanted you most to read when you were in high school. In Matthew, the focus is wages, not gifts; just deserts, not surprise parties.

So, you can see why I have enjoyed having Matthew as our Gospel in this year's lectionary. Every week it's morality and accountability and, after all, as a preacher, I'm in the morality business.

"If you do your job," said a policeman to me a few weeks ago, "we don't have to do ours."

That's why we're all here, right? The preacher warns us about getting out of step so we can mend our ways and get right so right will be dealt to us in life. Do what Jesus says, read your Bibles daily, say a little prayer for good luck, keep your nose clean, and you'll do well. That's religion.

But what does Jesus say? Let me tell you a little story. A man hired some workers. Some worked for him all day long. Some managed to get in a few hours after lunch. Others, who got there late, worked only one hour. At quitting time, all of the workers got paid the same. The result: there was grumbling, murmurings of injustice, righteous indignation, and envy. The parable ends with the employer asking, "Do you begrudge my generosity?" or, more literally, "Is your eye evil because I am good?"

You and I should be glad that the Master is generous. Yet the parable ends, not in gladness but in grumbling. Why are we so upset that the Master is so generous?

As I was growing up, teachers and parents were forever telling us, "If you cheat, you hurt no one but yourself." And I believed them. Thus, when he came to me every morning before class and said, "Hey, got your Latin homework? Let me see it. I had a late date last night and didn't get it done. . . ." And sometimes I'd let him see it—but always with the understanding that he was hurting no one but himself. He would get what he deserved. Just you wait.

Well, we waited. Then came Senior Honors Day, the whole school gathered in the auditorium to pay homage to the best in our class. Whose name was called out, and who walked across the stage to claim the prize in Latin?

I wanted to stand up and shout, "Wait, there's been a miscue here! Something's wrong. Remember? If you cheat, you hurt no one but yourself. The world's got an odd way of punishing cheaters. He's hurting?"

Such an insight is particularly threatening to those of us who are here, in this congregation. We are here because we are not shirkers. We didn't sleep in. We got up and we came to church, waving good-bye to our neighbor who was washing his car—the shirker. One day, in his eleventh hour, he'll be sorry! We are here at church because, on the whole, we are conscientious, dependable, hardworking, high achievers who have been laboring in the ecclesiastical vineyard since early morning, or at least since 9:45. We didn't get here by relying on grace.

We all know that if you fool around the whole semester and wait until the night before the exam to open the book, you're going to pay for it, and that's as it should be. No one should grumble about that. "Sure, I flunked the course, but I had a great semester while doing it," says one. "I got an A, but I worked for it," says another. And everything is as it should be, tit for tat. Cause-effect, labor-wages, study-grades.

Yet . . . just enough of those shirkers *do* get by to keep us conscientious ones wondering, What if Jesus was right when he noted that God "makes his rain to fall upon the heads of the good and the bad and his sun to shine on the just and unjust"? What if Paul really means that "God is kind to the ungrateful and the selfish"?

Recently Studs Terkel noted that the typical American attitude is, "I've got it made because I deserve it. And if you don't have it made, you don't deserve it."

Then he says, "When things don't work that way, as has been the case for lots of Americans these days, a kind of meanness sets in" (*CBS Evening News*, Sept. 12, 1981).

Meanness. Grumbling.

Two men went into church to pray, said Jesus, one, a money-grabbing, traitorous, idolatrous swindler of a tax collector; the other a Bible-believing, tithing, deacon. Two men left church; the former was justified, accepted, but not the latter.

A boy demanded his inheritance from his father and then left the father's house and blew it all on booze, loose living, and bad women. When he finally crawled back home in rags, his father—threw a party.

How did you feel when you heard that millionaire John DeLorean was acquitted of charges of drug dealing? How did you feel when you heard that Mr. DeLorean is now a born-again Christian? I've been a Methodist all my life; that ought to count for something! We're not talking about cheap grace, we're talking *free* grace. When a John DeLorean, a Charles Colson, a Velma Barfield gets reborn . . .

Those who assume—whether they be politicians of the right or left, judicial board members, or ordinary, Bible-believing Christians—that a little dose of religion, a little helping of the Bible, would do us all a lot of good, must come to terms with the frequently unexpected nature of biblical religion such as we encounter in this parable. The gospel resists our attempt to appropriate it in our own programs of social justice, our notions of what is fair and good, our expectations for the way the world ought to work. In here, there is some good help for daily living, but there are also a good many stories like this one where the first are last and the last first, where we are shocked into the realization that our ways are not God's ways. Here is what the Reformers called the *verbum externum*—the external word, the alien word which cuts into me from without.

Here sits a ticking bomb in the middle of the straightlaced, ethically earnest Gospel of Matthew, this little parable. It is not a story about how God helps those who help themselves. It is not a call to do good so that good might be done to us. It is not (and I heard Brother Falwell preach it this way not long ago) a story of how employers ought not to be limited by governmental regulations regarding fair treatment of employees!

It's not even a sermonette on how we ought to feel kindly toward those prodigal sons and daughters who somehow manage to slip through our system of ethical cause and effect and get saved. Jesus goes out of his way to avoid any intrusion of some moralistic point in the story. There is no suggestion of laziness or merit on the part of any of the workers—they are just people who got to work early or late. There is no lesson for us to learn or put into practice to make the world a better place to live. God's gracious generosity, when it cuts through my little moral equations, elicits not gratitude, but grumbling. When you receive grace, I grumble. When I receive it, I assume that I have earned it. Either way, grace is utterly beyond my human powers of comprehension. It will always be a shocker.

Any lesson of the story, if you are looking for a lesson, is that *God's ways often make the world a surprising, sometimes confusing place in which to live.* Jesus takes a little story and rams it into our self-satisfied, smug assumption that we have figured it all out. And if we don't like hearing such stories, we best not bother with Jesus. He won't be a plank in my political platform.

Here is a story of how God's grace is so surprising, so beyond our comprehension or appropriation as to be downright—exasperating. It's either a story about a generous God or a grumbling humanity; either way, it isn't easy to take. I don't like to be thrown off balance. I like my world more predictable than that.

We had predicted it. At age fourteen she was on the rear end of a Honda, screaming up and down the street as if it were Daytona. "She will end up bad," we said. At fifteen I could tell, by the empty beer cans in my front yard the next day, what kind of weekend she had enjoyed. "They're just going to have to take her in hand," I said. "She's headed for trouble." More than once, on those Saturday nights, her car radio electrified my sleep, sending me hurtling through space at 3 a.m. "People like that are a menace to society," we declared. Then at sixteen, there was a story in the papers, the trial, and she was sent away for a year at the Youth Correctional Institution. "We told you so," we said. "Only a matter of time," we agreed. While there, she gave birth to the child she was carrying.

The day of reckoning came. I was cutting my hedge at the time. I could see them, though. Cars began gathering about ten or eleven that morning. Loud music coming from the house. People came and went, bringing baskets of food, dishes, stacks of plates. Chairs were put out on the lawn. The music grew louder. Finally, a car pulled up. They came pouring out of the house and huddled around the car. Everybody "oohing" and "aahing." I was hacking at the hedge, cutting it down to the roots by this time. Some kind of little basket, decorated with pink ribbons, was unloaded. They paraded behind it into the house. I watched them from my now sparse hedge. Before going in, he stood at the door and called, "Hey, she's home, and the baby too. Come on over and join us. We're having a party!"

Who? Me? A Bible-believing Christian? Humph!

6

The Best Little Harlot's House in Jericho

October 31, 1982

By faith Rahab the harlot did not perish with those who were disobedient, because she had given friendly welcome to the spies.
Hebrews 11:31 RSV

A highlight of the year at Northside Church was All Saints, when the lay leader would read the names of the honored dead and we would celebrate Communion. Northside had an inferiority complex when compared with other congregations in town. Having set a national record for attrition during a turbulent time in the seventies, Northside had been shrinking rapidly from a congregation of a thousand to only about three hundred by the time I got there in 1980. Looking back over the sermons during my years at Northside, they seem affirmative, benedictory. This declining, inner-city congregation needed a boost. In short, here was a congregation in much the same situation as whatever congregation it was that first heard the Letter to the Hebrews.

This is one reason why the Bible's chief locus of interpretation is the gathered congregation, not a college religion department or even a seminary classroom. The church keeps raising the questions for which Scripture is the right answer. When interpretation is detached from the congregational attempt to embody the faith, bad things happen. When Scripture is preached in the struggling congregation, Scripture is in its native habitat.

It takes a congregation full of Rahabs to know that the Scripture's word is an address to them.

Few of us come to church to be jolted. But with a living God, who knows?

33

It's shocking, in the midst of the epistle for All Saints, to come across the name of one engaged in a most unsaintly profession—Rahab the harlot. How dare the writer of Hebrews? *We've got young people present.*

Noah, Abraham, Sarah, Moses, yes. But *Rahab?* One can imagine "Rahab the Sunday school teacher," or "Rahab the president of the United Methodist Women," among the saints, but Rahab the *harlot?* It takes the honor out of sainthood, doesn't it?

Here's the story: Joshua has led the army of Israel to the threshold of the Promised Land. Two spies were sent to reconnoiter Jericho. As soldiers so often do, they end up at Rahab's Place in a seedy section of town.

The king got word that spies were about and sent messengers to seize them. When they inquired at Rahab's, she lied. Batting her heavily mascaraed, false eyelashes, she said, "True, a couple of Jewish boys were here earlier, but when the gate was closed, at dark, they paid their bill in cash and left. Go quickly, maybe you'll overtake them."

The king's men rushed on, not knowing that Madame Rahab had hidden the Israelites on her roof. Rahab told the spies that she had heard of the mighty works of their God. All she asks is that the Israelites show her family mercy when the walls of Jericho come tumbling down.

Then, while it was still night, Rahab let them down by a rope, trying a scarlet thread in her window to identify her place for the invading Israelites. When Joshua and his army finally entered the city, the folk of the red thread house in the red light district were the only ones spared when Jericho was leveled.

A harlot, a liar, what a seedy sort of saint! And yet, Rahab was not alone in her seediness. Drunken, naked Noah; Abraham with his squabbling family; old conniving Sarah; murderer Moses; lustful David; bigoted Paul—a rogues' gallery. Men and women of ill repute. If people like them can be saints, anybody can. Anybody.

Who is a "saint"? Israel is called a nation of saints:

> You are a people holy to the LORD your God; the LORD your God has chosen you to be a people for his own possession, out of all the peoples that are on the face of the earth.

Why choose Israel? Perhaps because Israel was more religious than other nations, more pious? Have you never read Scripture? The Bible is clear:

> It was not because you were more in number than any other people that the LORD set his love upon you and chose you, for you were the fewest of all peoples; but it is because the LORD loves you. (Deut. 7:6–8a RSV)

It was out of love that God chose Israel. Biblical writers bend over backwards to say that divine choice was not due to any achievement on Israel's part. Israel played the harlot many times. Waywardness, infidelity, idolatry, pride, were among the sins charged to Israel's account. Whatever is meant by "a people holy to the Lord," it means something other than a person pure and spotless.

A biblical saint is not a person who lives such a virtuous life that a committee nominates her for the honor of Chief Moral Virtuoso. No, biblical saintliness is a matter of what God does with people. A person is called "saint" in the Bible because God wants that person to do something holy, not because that person is holy. Saints are people who are called by God to do God's work.

As Karl Barth says, a person is sanctified in the Bible when that person is "dedicated to the service of God" by God's "separation, claiming, commandeering," of him or her for service. That's what happened to Rahab. On a typical day, going about her typical business, in the world's oldest profession, the old girl got "commandeered" for God.

The New Testament shares this definition of saints. "You are a chosen race, a royal priesthood, a holy nation," declares 1 Peter 2:9 to the first Christians because God has work for them to do, "that you may declare the wonderful deeds of him who called you out of darkness into his marvelous light." God wants to make something out of them: "Once you were no people but now you are God's people . . ." (2:10 RSV). It is in this sense that the New Testament refers to the whole church as saints. Like Israel before it, out of a bunch of nobodies come somebodies, made saints by God's gracious choice.

On All Saints' Sunday, we remember the saints. But this *all* saints, let's be sure to remember all of them; Rahab the harlot and all the rest. What looks like seediness to you and me often looks like potential saintliness to God. Maybe God passes over the nice, pure people, the ones we regard as so "saintly," because nice, pure, sweet people can't always get the job done—especially when the jobs which need doing are as tough as the ones God takes on.

Although Rahab lacked a bit in the area of conventional sexual morals— she was a survivor. She wasn't born yesterday. Rahab had been in business long enough to know how to take care of her own and therefore proved quite helpful in looking after God's own.

Whom do you think about when you hear the word "saints"? Perhaps you think of some sweet, pious Sunday school teacher who taught you in the third grade, whose memory challenges the Rahab image of sainthood. But I submit that any person who is capable of running a third-grade Sunday school class without receiving or administering bodily injury and still is able to convert a few eight-year-old pagans along the way has got more to commend her for God's work than sweetness.

This is how saints are made. Saints are made by listening for God and saying, "yes," trusting God to know who ought to be saints.

Do you know the book *Lest Innocent Blood Be Shed* by Philip Hallie? It's an inspiring account of how an ordinary little village in the French Alps—Le Chambon, hid its Jews in World War II. Hallie went there to interview the survivors wondering, What heroism motivated people to risk all? He discovered the source in interviewing an old woman who faked a stroke when the Nazis came to look for the Jews she had hiding beneath her chicken coop. What was the source of her courage?

> "Pastor always said in sermons, 'There is a time in every life when Jesus asks you to do something for him.'"
> "The day the Nazis came to our village, they entered the church during the service and stood around the room. And, in his sermon that day, Pastor Trocme said, 'Children, I have often said, "Jesus comes into every life and asks you to do something good for him."'"
> "And we knew what we had to do."

Rahab was minding her own business, looking after things in her place in Jericho when the Lord, through two frightened spies, asked her to mind his business. She said yes, and thereby is justly listed among the heroes of faith. The Epistle of James says that Rahab got to be a saint by her good work (Jas. 2:15). That's part of the story. But I think the author of Hebrews is more correct in saying that it is by faith more than good work, that she entered sainthood—faith that God could use even a harlot.

Despite your misgivings concerning her morals, you have to grant Rahab: she got the job done. Perhaps she had misgivings. Perhaps she wondered if the Lord might have chosen a more eminent person, a more holy one for such work. Whatever the misgivings of Madame Rahab, she put them aside and went on about God's business. As one of her kin said to his own unlikely, ordinary, disciples years later, "You did not choose me, but I chose you and appointed you that you should go and bear fruit . . ." (John 15:16 RSV).

He was complaining that he hadn't been able to sleep, that something was tugging at him, deep inside. He just couldn't get those pictures of people in South Africa out of his mind. It was as if he had to do something, say something.

"Could the voices, the ones you hear late at night, could they be God?" I wondered.

"Ridiculous," he said. "Me? I'm no Joan of Arc. You don't know me. Look, you'd be shocked to know the stuff I've done."

"Look, kid, God has used worse people before," I said, in love.

This All Saints, let us remember the saints—*all* of them, including the odd ones, the good little bad boys among them, the unlikely, unsuspecting ones, the Rahabs, the Abrahams, the Sarahs and all the rest, who listened and said *yes*, and thereby point the way for the rest of us. If they can be saints, anybody can!

7

Being Good

February 7, 1982

Think not that I have come to abolish the law ... unless your righteousness exceeds that of the scribes and Pharisees, you will never enter the kingdom of heaven.

Matthew 5:17, 20 RSV

During this year I rediscovered Wesley about the same time Stanley Hauerwas discovered me. I became a sanctificationist as if for the first time. I'm not sure what my little congregation at Northside made of my theological transformation. This sermon was one of my attempts to share my discovery with them. Yet they were a big part of my discovery. Wesley believed that it was possible for ordinary people (Northside Church) to be saints—if they got good preaching!

I got help on this sermon from W. D. Davies' commentary on the Sermon on the Mount in which he notes that in Matthew 5:17–20 Jesus clearly puts himself on the side of the "law and the prophets." I also felt that Calvin's interpretation of the three uses of the law (Geneva Catechism, 1541) had continuing usefulness. The law must be taken with great seriousness by Christians and, when it is taken seriously, we find out how unable we are to be faithful and are thus driven back into the arms of a gracious God.

Most of my really good theological discoveries and rediscoveries occurred in the parish, in the tug and pull of pastoral life, stretched between Scripture and the church.

Let's say that we're all here today because we want to be better people. We are here to be good, to become more righteous. After all, surely this is one of the main functions of religion, the Christian or any other, to make us better than we would have been if we had not gotten up on a cold February morning and come to church. And let's agree that, even if we have not arrived, we are at least on our way toward goodness because we did get up and come to church, which in no way is meant to detract from those of you who are listening to this service on the radio. You are on your way too, even though you are traveling in the prone position on your sofa.

Yet the trouble with knowing the story of Jesus is that you know that it was good people, "scribes and Pharisees," people who never cheated on their taxes or their spouses, people who knew Scripture backwards and forwards, people who lived by the book and kept themselves clean were those who eventually cried, "Crucify him!"

Why? Well, one reason was the way Jesus lived. Shortly after saying, in his Sermon on the Mount, that he did not want to "abolish the law," he did just that.

"Why does your teacher eat with tax collectors and sinners?" the scribes and Pharisees asked Jesus' disciples (9:9–13). A clear violation of Torah.

"I haven't come for you good people," replied Jesus, with a smirk, "I've come to seek and to save the bad."

"Doesn't the wedding party begin when the bridegroom arrives?" asked Jesus (9:15–17). "Forget your rules about fasting, let's party!"

"Look!" they said. "Your disciples are doing what is not lawful on the Sabbath!" (12:1–14).

"The Sabbath was made for humanity, not humanity for the Sabbath," said Jesus.

"Master, heal my daughter," pleaded the Canaanite woman. "Well, I'm really supposed to only go to the House of Israel," said Jesus, "but what the heck?" (15:21ff.). He heals her.

"Rabbi, Moses said a man could get out of marriage by giving his wife a certificate of divorce."

"It was a dumb law made for dummies like you," said Jesus (10:3–9). "Sometimes you've got to break a rule to do what's right. Stay married."

"You have heard it said of old. . . . But I say to you" (5:21–48). That's our Jesus. It is possible to be so good, so right, that you are wrong. You can be so religious that you miss the point of religion. As Paul says, "The law kills!" Dry, dead, jot-and-tittle legalism can just suck the life out of religion until it is a cold, calculating, posturing, ugly thing.

Mark Twain once described someone as "a good man—in the very worst sense of the word."

John tells a story (Matthew doesn't, but let's say that he would approve) of a woman who was caught in adultery (John 8:1–11). They had gathered to fulfill the law, namely, to stone her to death. That's how Torah, the law, handled adultery.

"What do you think about our version of People's Court, Jesus? A law is a law, right?"

"Wrong. Let he who is without sin throw the first stone," said Jesus. And one by one, they dropped their stones and slipped away.

Scholars don't think that story appeared in John's original. It was added later. But let's imagine that there was good reason to add it later. If Jesus didn't actually do this, it was certainly true to form for Jesus. And by the time they added it to John's Gospel, the church had been around long enough to have thoroughly confused Jesus' earlier religion of grace and acceptance with the older rules-and-regulations righteousness. So here's Jesus against sneering self-righteousness, Jesus versus the cruelty of misguidedly "good" people.

Yet I don't think any of this is our problem with today's gospel. The message that rules and regulations can't save, if once interesting material for a sermon, has become conventional wisdom. For us, the law holds not much of a threat. Most of us are in greater danger of antinomianism than legalism. Can you say antinomianism? We have moved from thinking that just obeying a few rules makes you right to the conviction that *no* rules are right. Learning that sometimes a rule must be broken, we now assume that anything goes. In a fight between legalistic scribes and Pharisees on the one hand and rule-breaking tax collectors and harlots on the other, you know on whose side we stand. We are all drawn toward the whore with a heart of gold.

Big deal that Jesus abrogates religious laws about how we keep the Sabbath holy, how we prepare ourselves for worship, the sort of company we keep, the sanctity of the marriage bond—we stopped keeping all those rules long ago.

They gathered to stone a person to death for adultery. Jesus says to them, "Let the one who is without sin throw the first stone."

As they silently drop their stones and slip away, Jesus says to the woman, "I do not condemn you, go and sin no more."

And she says, "What do you mean by 'sin'?" And Jesus says, "Well, I mean like adultery. That's wrong."

And she says, "So what gives you the right to judge me? How do you know it was wrong when you know nothing about the relationship?"

So Jesus says, "But you weren't married to this man."

"So?" she says. "It was a loving and fulfilling relationship."

"But . . ." says Jesus.

"And before that, there was Sam. That loving relationship was fulfilling for about three months. Then there was Joe. So what's with this sin bit, Mr. High and Mighty Morality?"

The next verse is not in Scripture but it ought to be: Jesus looked around at his feet, searching for a large stone. . . .

> Think not that I have come to abolish the law and the prophets . . . till heaven and earth pass away, not an iota, not a dot, will pass from the law until all is accomplished. Whoever then relaxes one of the least of these commandments and teaches [others to do] so, shall be called least in the kingdom . . . unless your righteousness exceeds that of the scribes and Pharisees, you will never enter the kingdom of heaven. (Matt. 5:17–20 RSV)

Go through the rest of the Sermon. Jesus takes an older command, difficult enough to keep even for a scribe or a Pharisee, and he intensifies the command, raises the bar, becomes even more demanding than the Torah.

You know you are forbidden to kill your brother. I forbid you even to be angry with your brother. Call him a fool, you'll go to hell (5:21–22).

You know that adultery is a no-no. I say, look at another person lustfully, it's adultery of the heart (5:27–28). All of us lustful lookers wince.

If your right hand causes you to sin, cut if off (5:29–30).

Remarry after divorce? I don't care what the law calls it, I call it adultery (5:31–32).

Somebody hits you on the right cheek, offer them your left as well (5:38–42).

Love your neighbor, invade your enemy? I say, love your enemy, pray for those who persecute you. Do not lay up treasure for yourself on earth. Judge not, least you be judged. Enter by the narrow gate.

No wonder Matthew reports that, when Jesus got finished with this Sermon, "the crowds were astonished at his teaching" (7:28 RSV)!

You want to be good? Don't just keep the law like the scribes and Pharisees, go beyond the law. W. D. Davies, in his classic commentary on the Sermon, says that this text, opening the Sermon on the Mount, "stands as a guardian against every immoral or antinomian misunderstanding of the gospel." And what a guardian it is. Here we encounter the bracing unsentimentality of Matthew's moral Gospel. It challenges us to be good, really good, if we would be God's. To enter a narrow gate.

Yet we are accustomed to coming to church and, if we should stumble over a difficult passage like this one, it usually takes no more than twenty minutes for a skillful preacher, using the skills of historical criticism and pop psychology, to explain it away, reassuring you that a nice person like Jesus would have never said something tough like this to a good person like you.

I know of no way to do that with this text. In fact, the tougher the text, the greater the chance that it came straight from the lips of Jesus. If we the church could have dumped Matthew 5 and gotten away with it, we would have.

"You think I've come to help you weasel out of the law? Forget it," says Jesus. "I've come to intensify, exceed, deepen the frontal assault of the law."

And all of our sweet Jesus sentimentality and gushy grace just crumbles before these searing commands. We are, as Matthew says of Jesus' first congregation, astonished.

You want to be good? "Do *all* that I have commanded you" (28:20), says Jesus.

There is the arrogance of the rule-stressing, self-righteous, puritanical legalist, yes. But there is the arrogance of the rule-ignoring antinomian. Paul showed us the delusion of thinking that fallible, limited human beings like us had the resources for attaining so high a righteousness. Goodness comes as a gift of God's grace, not through our determined human efforts. Grace assaults the legalist.

But I'm saying that the peculiar brand of contemporary arrogance is that of the antinomian. I am the only one who knows what's right for me. My opinion is the measure of all things. The rules are made up as we go along to suit the situation. Don't bother me with your judgments, I'm doing the best I can. What right has Jesus or anyone else to tell me what I should do? There's no way that the grace of God is grand enough to enable a slouch like me to rise that high.

Such antinomianism arises not out of an appreciation for the limits of the Law but rather out of a lack of appreciation for any limits upon my own ego. At least the scribes and the Pharisees studied God's law, pondering its implications for their lives. We have no object for study other than our own feelings.

Against such modern parochialism, Jesus slams these demands for a higher righteousness. He refuses to back off in deference to our human frailty. He will not pander to our ethical sentimentality, patting us on the head, saying, "There, there, I know that you're doing the best you can which is certainly good enough for me." No, he refuses to withdraw one iota, one dot. How can Jesus, knowing our frailty, our arrogant moralism and our arrogant antinomianism, intensify, exceed the law, knowing our inability to keep the law?

About fifteen chapters later, Matthew tells the story of Jesus' encounter with the rich young ruler (19:16–22). You know it. A rich, successful young man comes to Jesus, saying, "Good teacher, what must I do to get 'eternal life'?" The successful *yuppie* has been so successful at getting everything he wanted in life, he now wants to get what Jesus is selling.

First Jesus says, "What's with this 'good' business? Nobody's good but God." But then Jesus tells him, "You know what the Good Book says. Obey the commands of God, all of them, then you will have eternal life."

Now, in telling the young man this, Jesus probably hopes that the smart young man will say something like, "Gosh, Jesus! I guess I haven't been such a success after all, when you put it like that. Why should I be going around looking for even more rules to break when I haven't kept the rules that God has given already!"

But this young man was a hard-core success. That isn't what he said. What he said was, "No problem! I've kept all those commands since I was a kid. Never have I cursed, stolen, fornicated, coveted, blasphemed, killed, lied, talked back to Mom. How 'bout giving me some real commands, something a morally successful person like me can really sink his teeth into."

And then Jesus, in one of the greatest understatements in all of the gospel says, "OK. You want to be good? All you must do is one teeny, weeny little thing. Go. Sell all that you have and give it to the poor."

Matthew says that, with that, the young man slumped down and got real depressed and went away. Isn't that typical of Jesus in Matthew? Here you've got these commands which are already burdensome enough and he lays an even tougher command on you!

So the disciples spoke for us all when they then asked, "God, who can be saved?"

And Jesus responds with the good news: with you, it's impossible, but with God, all things, even the salvation of people like you, is possible. With God, it's possible.

The law, the excessive righteousness which Jesus demands of you and me, is a means of making us good, but it is not as though goodness were the result of our own earnest efforts. Goodness arises out of our being driven into the arms of a merciful and just God. The commands are the means of taking us there.

John Calvin spoke of three uses of the law: First, we must obey God's laws, all of them, because thereby we are given something that doesn't come naturally—humility. Go out tomorrow and try to live truthfully, nonviolently; you'll be humbled. Secondly, because God always requires more of us through the law than we'll ever be able to do, the law teaches us to pray to the Lord for more strength than we have on our own, teaching us that we are more guilty of sin than we like to admit. Thirdly, the law is like a bridle on a horse, keeping us under the rein of God. If God demanded only easy, little things of us, then we could be good through our own effort. We wouldn't need a just, loving, and forgiving God to save us. Fortunately, God demands excessive things of us, responding to our failures through excessive forgiveness.

Luther says that's why Jesus begins his Sermon with, "Blessed are the poor in spirit" (5:3), because even if you felt rather rich in spirit when we began this sermon, by the time Jesus gets done with demonstrating your lust, violence, covetousness, and sin, everybody looks poor . . . thus rendering you into exactly the sort of person Jesus loves to love.

The foundation for goodness that would be Christian is this: It is not the mere mastery of God's rules or their merely skillful reinterpretation but relationship with Christ, who both commands us to keep God's holy law and gives us the resources to do so, namely, his presence among us.

At the end of Matthew's Gospel, after the Sermon has been preached to astonished disciples, after the Rich Young Man has gone away and the disciples have wondered who could possibly be saved, Jesus tells us to baptize and teach the whole world "all that I have commanded you." All? Yea, all, even the bit about turning the other cheek, giving away all that you have, not remarrying after divorce, all.

Then comes the punch line that makes the fulfillment of the commands possible and the burden of the law bearable: "Lo, I am with you always."

Duke University Chapel

8

First Things First

June 17, 1984

GENESIS 1:1–2:3
2 CORINTHIANS 13:5–14
MATTHEW 28:16–20

In the beginning . . . God

It was not only Father's Day and Trinity Sunday but also my very first Sunday at Duke Chapel. I stuck with the lectionary for the day, "In the beginning . . . God." A preacher can't go wrong always beginning with God, and ending there too. The only good reason to stand up and say anything to a congregation is God. As Barth believed, the First Commandment is the "axiom for all theology."

Nearly twenty years later, the Sunday after the 9/11 tragedy, when I thrashed about, desperate for a hopeful word to say to the congregation amid all the dust and ash, I went back to this same text. In life, in death, in life beyond death, here is the first and last word: In the beginning, God.

The lection for the first Sunday after Pentecost is the first verse of the first chapter of the first book of the Bible, "In the beginning when God created the heavens and the earth . . ."

How fitting a text for my first Sunday as minister to this university.

How fitting a text for Father's Day—a reflection upon the work of God the Father. For whether you take this as a description of God as Father or God as Mother (all this creating and begatting seem a good deal more maternal than paternal to me), it is a delightful, childlike, moving symphony of creativity. God is the busy masterworker, making light and dark, moon and stars, fish and fowl, begatting, birthing, shaping, muttering to him/herself, "good," "yes, very good," finally knocking off at the end of the week for a well-deserved rest.

47

How primitive the story is to our ears. How childlike and innocent. Imagine the first people who heard this tale of creativity. Israel was no longer a wandering tribe of nomads squatting around a campfire. This, scholars tell us, is a sophisticated literary creation from the hand of the priestly writer, probably the last part of the Book of Genesis to be written.

But still, at round 500 B.C., there was enough chaos, enough darkness to make one appreciative of a little divine order. A century or so before, the nation had been obliterated, sent into exile. We who sometimes put down conservative calls for "law and order" ought to remember that there was a time, say 500 B.C., when any shred of political order and stability seemed so miraculous as to be of divine origin.

Even without the political mess, there was still enough sickness, natural disaster, and famine about to make one wonder just who is in charge of our earthhome.

The first tellers of this tale, at 500 B.C., achieved a good deal of what we call civilization. But just beyond the city limits, only a stone's throw or a season of bad weather away, there was the desert, the encroaching, chaotic wilderness ready to take over.

A few years ago I came upon a little South Carolina town—not a town anymore, a ghost town of boarded up stores and houses that time had forgotten. When I asked what happened I was told, "This used to be the center of the country, then came the 1917 epidemic, wiped out all but one male in the town, boys and men. The place died; went back to being cotton fields and woods."

An eerie, threatening thought, a reminder of how fragile is the toehold of civilization, anywhere, when you think about it.

The Genesis affirmation that God is on the side of order, that God is the great, cosmic artist who combats chaos and nothingness, fights disorder in favor of design and somethingness, is a great act of faith. Here was the first article of the creed upon which Israel was built—God creates, begats, pushes back the nothingness, makes form out of void, order out of chaos.

People of 500 B.C. knew that chaos surrounded the little islands of civilization. Just when you thought that you had it together, there came this flood roaring through the canyon, your beloved child began coughing and died, the skies grew clear and hot and stayed that way for months. Ancient people knew, firsthand—life is suspended by a thin thread above a formless void, an abyss, the (in Hebrew) *tohu wa-bohu* by waters of chaos. "But for the grace of the Creator God . . . we wouldn't be here," they said to one another.

Of course, the world is different. For us children of the Enlightenment. Since Darwin, we look upon the earth, not so much with wonder, but rather with curiosity. Our world is a thing to be poked at, examined like a cadaver, mined, developed, bulldozed. The earth was without form and void until the advent of the biologist, who explained it, the engineer, who fixed it, the real estate developer who subdivided it, put up a sign reading, "PARADISE ESTATES—RESTRICTED LOTS."

The closest God comes to this world is the Deist clockmaker who set the whole, whirring machine to working a billion or so years ago and retired. Seasons change, the planets turn, apples fall in obedience to gravity's law. Our world is not creation but rather a giant, mechanical toy. Just another machine. No need for God, once the thing gets going, so we have none in this great, clockwork, reproducing, clicking, cosmos.

The machine usually works quite well and, when it doesn't, someone has a government grant to find out why, and when they do, we'll fix that too!

And yet . . . more than we moderns may admit, there is still the threat of chaos, nothingness, the void. Maybe even more so. We have our world, but it is not so firmly fixed in place as we like to think. Science has shown us, not only the order and rhythm of the universe, but also its fragility. The wrong virus gets loose, a certain insect appears for which there is no DDT, the big bang, or the black hole, genetic engineering goes—we live only a step or two from disaster at the push of a button, then the flash, the roar, the great mushroom cloud, and we are no better off, perhaps a good deal worse, than our ancestors who first told this tale of chaos and creation in 500 B.C.

Need we be so dramatic? My own life is but a heartbeat away, a bad report on this year's physical, from the void. And one reason I find it hard to sleep at night sometimes, is that, as a pastor, being with people in all of life, I know firsthand, how fragile life can be, how close the chaos. I have my happy family now, my home, a new job, health . . . but all of it floats, just barely sometimes, over the abyss. . . .

"Cancer," I read in *Time*, "is basically the normal reproductive processes of the body gone crazy for some strange reason. Normal cells go crazy, normal cellular checks and balances malfunction and the destruction begins."

Isn't this a layperson's explanation for simple, everyday, horrible, primordial, disfiguring—chaos?

It's frightening, the fragility of it all. Sure, it's a warm, beautiful, summer Sunday today, but what happens when the chaos bubbles up and the mountains shake and the sea roars? The midlife crisis, the screech of brakes and the crash, the note from the boss . . . into every life, a little chaos must come. And what then? Our allegedly orderly, whirling, efficient, natural-law-abiding machine isn't much comfort to us in times like that.

In such times when we are reduced to the level of children, frightened by the dark, fearful of the void, crouched in helplessness, what can we do? We can then turn, like little children, and remember the story. "In the beginning God created the heavens and the earth. The earth was without form and void, and darkness was upon the face of the deep; and the Spirit of God was moving over the face of the waters. And God said, let there be light" . . . let there be Heaven . . . let there be land, let there be plants, stars, sun, moon, swarms of living creatures, sea monsters, winged birds, cattle, creeping things, and let us make humanity, male and female, in our image, and give them dominion. And God said, 'It is good.'"

So the first article of Luther's catechism taught the little child to say, "I believe, that God created me and all creatures." If you don't get any further than that in your faith, it's as good a place as any to begin, and end.

In times of chaos in your life, when your somethingness is in danger of being overswept by the nothingness, imagine this father/mother of a God, bending over your world, like (in the image of Langston Hughes) "a Mammy bending over her baby," birthing, forming, caressing you with the joy of a great, cosmic artist. "He's got the whole world in his hands."

So on this beautiful June day, but most of all for the dark, chaotic, abysmal stormy days, know this: In the beginning God created. In the end, God creates. Without God's love and creativity, chaos would prevail, this earth would return to a watery abyss. We float today by a slender thread of creative love.

In the words of the psalmist:

> God is our refuge and strength,
> a very present help in trouble.
> Therefore we will not fear though the earth should change,
> though the mountains shake in the heart of the sea;
> though its waters roar and foam,
> though the mountains tremble.
> . . . .
> The LORD of hosts is with us;
> the God of Jacob is our refuge.
>
> (Ps. 46:1–3, 7 RSV)

As it was in the beginning, is now and ever shall be, world without end, Amen.

9

Pharisees and Publicans All

October 26, 1986

LUKE 18:9–14

I am now deep in my parables of Jesus phase, fascinated by the twists and turns and the surprises in Jesus' most distinctive literary device, the parable. This sermon is remarkable for how little development or explication occurs. It's mostly a walk through the text, laying Jesus' story alongside one of my own. I seem reluctant to give much commentary on Jesus' story of the Pharisee and the Publican, content to let the narrative stay narrative.

It was Saturday night. There was a knock at my door. I opened the door to find a policeman standing on my doorstep.

"Preacher," he said, "could you come with me? Some of your church members have gotten into a big brawl and the Chief thinks you might be able to help us settle them down."

I was aghast. Some of my *church* members. How could this be?

"Now cut out that shooting, Joe, and you two settle down and come on out. You're going to hurt somebody if you ain't careful," blared the Chief's voice across the debris-strewn yard. I could see broken glass and overturned furniture, some inside, some outside of the house. It was an apocalyptic vision of chaos and battle. Another shot rang out from the house and the Chief ducked back down behind his car.

This is no place for a man of the cloth, I thought, as I inched my way over to the Chief's car.

"How are you doing, Reverend?" the Chief asked amicably as I joined him in his improvised bunker.

"Not all that well, at the moment," I replied.

"Joe and his wife are having a little argument, it seems. It has gotten a bit rough and we thought that maybe you could help us settle them down," said the Chief.

"A little argument?" I asked in amazement.

"Yes, they usually have one of these every spring."

"You mean to tell me this has happened before?"

"Oh sure, it's not all that big a deal. They just seem to let things build up during the winter and then every spring they let it all out, so to speak."

I was appalled. And to think, one of my "best" church members.

No shots or curses came from the house for five or ten minutes and, after repeated attempts by the Chief to elicit some response from Joe or his wife, the Chief pronounced that "They have probably passed out now. It's safe to go on in and get them."

I accompanied the police into the scene of the heart of battle (at a safe distance) where we found Joe and his wife, just as the Chief had predicted, passed out on their living room sofa, a bit bruised, scratched up here and there, but apparently in surprisingly good condition for two battle-weary veterans. By that time, neighbors had arrived and were clearing away the debris and helping the two groggy combatants into bed. The Chief led his men back to their cars saying something about, "Well, that ought to hold them until this time next year."

As for me, I was shocked, disappointed, angry, but mainly I was embarrassed. I returned home determined to relieve Joe of his church duties as soon as possible. Was this any way for one of my members to act?

The next morning, in the quietness and beauty of church, the disorder of the evening seemed far away. As I moved through the worship service, I had hardly given the episode a thought until we came to the Offering. I dutifully got the offering plates and turned to hand them to the head usher. And who should be the head usher on this Sunday? Joe. I nearly passed out when I turned around and saw him standing there, smiling sheepishly, bandages on his bruised hands and a cut under one eye, more or less reverently waiting for the plates; Joe, standing there before me, God, and everybody else. This was more than I could take. The nerve of the man. Had he no pride? Had he no self-respect? Can you imagine someone having the nerve to stand up before the altar on Sunday morning after a Saturday night like that?

He had no pride?

> He also told this parable to some who trusted in themselves that they were righteous and despised others: "Two men went up into the temple to pray, one a Pharisee and the other a tax collector. The Pharisee stood and prayed thus with himself, 'God, I thank thee that I am not

like other men, extortioners, unjust, adulterers, or even like this tax collector. I fast twice a week, I give tithes of all that I get.'"

"But the tax collector, standing far off, would not even lift up his eyes to heaven, but beat his breast, saying, 'God, be merciful to me a sinner!'"

"I tell you, this man went down to his house justified rather than the other." (Luke 18:9–14 RSV)

Jesus told this parable of the Pharisee and the publican to those who "trusted in their own righteousness and despised everybody else." Who is that?

"Two men went up to the temple to pray . . . ," they go up for the 3:00 p.m. sacrifice, a regular service of worship. It's a story about worship, about people who pray.

Two people go up to pray, to worship. Their posture is the first thing you notice. The Pharisee "stood with himself." He stood by himself, one assumes in some prominent position, yet alone, detached, not too close to "sinners," the other worshipers. As was the custom, he was standing praying aloud, under his breath. Listen to his prayer:

First he lists the sins from which he has refrained, then his good deeds. He not only avoids sin, he does good. Among his good deeds were those he was in no way expected to perform: voluntary fasting twice a week, no doubt interceding for others' sins while he fasts. He tithes everything he buys so as to be sure he uses nothing which has not been previously tithed. He goes beyond the "second mile" in his giving. Nowhere is the Pharisee's piety or goodness condemned. Here we have a good man, a very good man.

Some have rapped the Pharisee for his prayer, but as a professor of liturgics, I find nothing amiss in his prayer. His prayer begins "I thank thee." The man is thankful. He knows his virtues come as gifts from God. The tax collector over there is materially better off than the Pharisee, but the Pharisee wouldn't change places with him. Unlike a lot of *our* prayers, the Pharisee doesn't bother God with a string of petitions. He asks for nothing for himself. He only wants to give thanks. He feels gratitude because he is so well off.

The stance and prayer of the publican, the tax collector, are equally revealing. As a tax collector he has had ample opportunity to defraud. In contrast to the Pharisee, he stands "afar off." And why not? He, sinner that he is, lackey for the Roman overlords, no wonder he dares not even to lift his eyes toward God. He can only bow his head, beat his breast. For him, repentance, true repentance which the law demands, requires not only abandonment of his profession but restitution of his evil gains plus an added fifth. How can he know all whom he has cheated? He is hopeless. He doesn't pray, he cries out, raves—"God have mercy."

The cheating tax collector claims nothing, but asks everything. Lacking anything to give God, he asks for a gift.

Then comes the surprising line, "I tell you this publican, this fraudulent tax collector, went back down to his house after worship justified (righteous, blessed with God's pleasure) *not* the Pharisee."

Two men, says Jesus, went up to worship before the altar—one, a good, Bible-believing, faith-practicing, liberally giving Pharisee. The other, a bad, money-grabbing, immoral, tax collector. Two men went back home. One, the publican, was atoned for, forgiven, justified, blessed. The Pharisee was not.

The point?

It can't be, "OK, gang, let's get out there and get humble." Such self-conscious, posturing "humility" infects too much of our worship already. Besides, have you ever *tried* to be humble? In regard to being humble, you either are or you aren't.

Pride takes many forms, doesn't it? "God, I thank thee that I don't make a big deal of my religion and pray showy prayers, not like all those religious fanatics on TV." "God, I thank thee that I know my weaknesses and I admit them, not like that Pharisee." "God, I thank thee that my social attitudes are correct, not like those South Africans."

Like the Pharisee, it's so easy for our best intentioned prayers of thanksgiving to slip into self-congratulation, just as even our best acts of charity can become self-aggrandizing, a subtle means of making ourselves look good. "God, I thank thee for *me*."

Like the Pharisee, we don't seek God's mercy in such prayers—so we usually find none. We come with hands clenched and full, so it's understandable why we go back home empty. The hard truth of prayer; you often get what you ask for. Like the Pharisee, we don't also ask for God, so we get none.

The publican is not a good man. He is a sinful man. A man without merit. A man without hope. His breast-beating humility is not a virtue for us to emulate—it is simply his realistic assessment of his own real wretchedness. He *is* humble.

Neither man is the hero of the story. Both sin, though one sins knowingly and the other sins unknowingly, but both sin. Some sin by stealing and others sin by praying. "God, I thank thee that I am not like others," but both sin. Both come to worship that way.

I think this is a parable about prayer, about Sunday morning in the Chapel. Jesus says, before any altar of God, in any service of worship, you mainly find two sorts of folk—Pharisees and publicans. A few of us are one or the other all of the time. But most of us are some of each some of the time. There are times when we enter to worship as good, Bible-believing, righteous Pharisees who ask nothing and get nothing. We are so pleased with ourselves, so competent, so well fixed. We go home to Sunday dinner with a gnawing emptiness because we were so full before we came. But there are also times in life when we enter this place to worship as publicans, needing everything, empty, lost, without hope and (surprise!) return home with more than we dared to ask.

In other words, sometimes we fail at prayer and sometimes we succeed. Sometimes what happens here on Sunday works for us, and sometimes it doesn't. It is not for us to know when we will go back home "made righteous." All we know (according to Luke's preceding parable of the Unrighteous Judge) is that we are to keep at it. The gift of righteousness, atonement, justification is only God's to give. Grace is a gift, grace is not grace if it is expected. Sometimes it is there for us and sometimes it is not.

Why?

Jesus does not answer that one here. The gift is God's to give out of his unfathomable mercy. Christians do not go back home righteous and justified because we have prayed correctly, or done it all in proper fashion, or struck a sufficiently humble stance. If we be justified, if we be blessed in our worship and prayer, it is only as a *gift* of God's love. His mercy is without bounds, extending to sinners of all kinds and their well-said or half-blurted-out prayers. It is only through the mercy that we ever return home from church any different than we came. Only through the mercy for us sinners, only through the mercy.

No, Joe, I would not have been caught dead up there before the altar, before God and all the righteous that Sunday morning after your kind of Saturday night. You see, I am too good for that kind of imprudence in worship. It's bad form. I must keep my distance. I have too much pride to bare my bandaged and still bleeding wounds before the altar, smiling sheepishly, holding out my bruised knuckles as if I had come here expecting to be given some gift. Unlike you, Joe, I have my pride. I have my pride.

Two men went up to the temple to pray one Sunday morning, the first a Methodist preacher, the second a wife-abusing, drunken lout . . . the latter went back down to his house justified, not the former.

10

Jews and Christians: All in the Family

December 7, 1986

ROMANS 15:4–13

May the God of steadfastness and encouragement grant you to live in such harmony with one another, in accord with Christ Jesus, that together you may with one voice glorify the God and Father of our Lord Jesus Christ. Welcome one another, . . . as Christ has welcomed you, for the glory of God.

Romans 15:5–7 RSV

Duke offered me the opportunity to work closely with Jews on a regular basis. I became fascinated by the ways in which Jewish students on campus, at least those who still practiced Judaism, developed rather sophisticated skills of analysis and resistance within a majority Christian culture. I admired their ability to stay Jewish in a campus world that seemed determined to make them less Jewish than when they arrived at Duke. I also saw some fruitful survival practices that we Christians (now losing our grip on the society we once thought we owned) could utilize for our own survival.

In the summer of 1986 I was engaged in research on Christian preaching about Jews, looking through the history of Christian preaching in Germany and elsewhere. It was not a pretty picture. Anti-Jewish preaching has a long, sad history and even continues in subtle but no less detrimental ways.

In this sermon I tried to speak to the relationship of Christians and Jews by working exclusively from Christian Scripture. The local newspaper reprinted the sermon and I began warm relationships with a number of Jewish faculty members.

Any law enforcement officer will tell you that a policeman would rather try to stop a bank robbery than to intervene in a domestic argument. Bank robbers want only to take the money and run. But an estranged husband or wife, two feuding brothers fighting it out in the kitchen or the bedroom—someone is likely to be hurt. More people are murdered by relatives than by strangers. Family feuds are the worst fights.

Luke tells (Luke 15) of a family feud in which an older brother and a younger brother contend with one another for their father's love. You know the story about how the younger one left home and wasted his inheritance in prodigality. When the boy returned, his father welcomed him, but not his older brother who pouted bitterly in the darkness and refused to go to his homecoming celebration. Family fights can be bitter. I have known more than one set of brothers and sisters to honor their dead parent's memory by refusing to speak to one another after a fight over who got the family farm.

In graduate school, when we lacked enough money to go out on a Saturday night, we would sometimes amuse ourselves by listening in on the marital disagreements of the couple who lived in the apartment next to ours. One didn't even need a glass to the wall to hear their altercations. It was harmless, cheap fun for us. Often, when we read the New Testament, we are peeking in listening at the door, with glass put to the wall, on a family feud that has lasted centuries, a feud in which there has been little fun and much bitterness, even bloodshed—a family feud between Christian and Jew.

Today's Scripture from Romans, like much of that epistle, is part of that debate. In some of his letters, Paul pleads to his fellow Jews to accept Gentile Christians into the family of God. Here, Paul works the other side, pleading to new Gentile Christians to get along with their Jewish Christian brothers and sisters. "Welcome one another, . . . as Christ has welcomed you," Paul says. To those Gentiles who put on airs and behaved haughtily towards their (probably poorer) Jewish relations, Paul says, "Look, you know what it's like to be outsiders. You were outsiders, now you are insiders. You ought to welcome others in the same way that Israel has graciously welcomed you."

We, as Gentiles, are the Johnny-and-Susie-Come-Latelies to faith. We Gentiles are the eleventh-hour worker, the younger prodigal son, the foolish virgin beating on God's door, hoping that the promises given to Israel might also be given to us.

"Will the Jews be saved?" That question is sometimes asked in the church and may be of interest to us but it is of little interest to the New Testament. The question of the status of the Jews had already been answered by Scripture beginning with the promises to Abraham and Sarah, reiterated to Jacob, made manifest to Moses and the children of Israel in the exodus, and the birth of Joshua (Jesus) at Bethlehem. God promised always to love Israel and Scripture is the testimony to God's faithfulness. As Paul says here in Romans,

"Christ became a servant to the circumcised to show God's truthfulness, in order to confirm the promises given to the patriarchs" (15:8 RSV).

Will the Jews be saved? No, the New Testament question, the question which occupies today's epistle is: Will the *Gentiles* be saved? When God made the promise to Abraham, it was a promise to make a great nation of his descendents, not the whole world. When God stretched forth a mighty arm in the exodus from Egypt, it was to deliver Israel, not all oppressed peoples everywhere. The promises of God to save, to deliver, to love, to preserve are promises to Israel, the Chosen People, the Light to the Nations, God's family. Will the Jews be saved? is not, according to Paul in Romans 9, 10, and 11, a question which any Bible-believing, promise-trusting Christian may ask. We already know the answer. God is gracious, faithful to his promises.

The New Testament question, the debate which required massive argument and all of the theological and literary skills at Paul's disposal was, "Will the *Gentiles* be saved?" In what way is the good news of the Jew, Jesus, addressed to his fellow Jews, our good news? How do we stand in relation to the people who first taught us to look for a Messiah? What are we doing here today, Gentiles, reading somebody else's mail? For Paul, the ultimate wonder of Christ, the deepest marvel of the coming of Jesus, was not the virgin birth, or angels in the skies, but the gracious inclusion even of Gentiles into the promises of God to Israel. The glory of God, he says in today's Scripture, is that God has welcomed you! The father has welcomed home the younger prodigal. The door has been opened at midnight to the beseeching outsider. Those who have entered the vineyard at the close of the day are given as much as those who have trusted, believed, suffered, and been persecuted for thousands of years. God is amazingly gracious to save *even Gentiles*.

But if you have even a superficial knowledge of the history of the church's relationship to the Jews, a shudder goes down our Gentile spines. The gospel which first enabled Jews to welcome Gentiles became perverted into the separation of Gentile from Jew. By crusader's sword, Hitler's ovens, or even Christian evangelism, the once persecuted church became the persecutor of Jesus' own people. I do not have to recount for this congregation the long, tragic story of the church's complicity and outright persecution of the Chosen People. Our infidelity, our perversion of the gospel, transformed the cross of Christ from a symbol of salvation to the symbol of oppression and death for millions. We Christians are hurt when others say that our cross, the symbol which we honor as our hope, is a feared sign of past and potential persecution for others. It is a bitter irony that the instrument of torture and death for Jesus (not the first, and alas, not the last Jewish martyr) has been perverted into a sword of oppression of Jesus' kinfolk. Advent is a season of penitence, and there is much repenting for the church to do in our relationship with our brothers and sisters, the Jews.

In this sense the presence of the Jews continues to be a kind of scandal to Christians. Where Christians have become a smug, powerful majority, complacent, affluent and secure, the Jew—the millions of victims of pogroms and concentration camps—reminds us of how painful belief in God can be. But more than that, the presence of the Jew poses a stark and threatening question to us Christians: We look back upon the centuries of Christian cruelty to the Jews and wonder why our gospel failed to give more of us the resources rightly to live with, defend, and even to die for the brothers and sisters whom our Lord died to save. Why weren't there more Christian families, like that Polish family we have been hearing about in the news, that welcomed their Jewish kinfolk in their time of trial?

How many Christian doors would open to a poor Jewish carpenter and his pregnant wife who had nowhere to stay during Caesar's taxation? How many of us would risk our families to save some Rachel and her Jewish boy-child from Herod's sword? This is only my theory, but I believe that one reason why there is animosity between Christian and Jew is that we Christians know, in our moments of deep honesty, how miserably our religion failed when it needed to be laid on the line for Jesus' family. We had our chance to show that faith in Jesus enables us to be courageous, peaceful, heroic, and true and we blew it. We turned away Joseph and Mary from our door; we stopped our ears to the wailing of Rachel in Ramah.

Paul's solution to this sadness is a simple one of hospitality: Welcome the Jew as the Jew has welcomed you. The one who is hospitable knows what it's like to be a stranger, for he has been a stranger himself. We Gentiles have stood out in the cold. Once we were nobodies, now we are family. Let us act like it.

This does not deny that we Christians really do have differences with the Jews. The church is not the replacement for Israel. The Jews look at Jesus and do not see what we see. Rather, the Jew still asks us Christians, "If Jesus is the Redeemer, why doesn't the world look more redeemed?" It is a tough question, one which goes to the heart of our faith. But we must not answer it in ways which forsake the religion of Jesus—with hatred, violence, or resentment. We must answer it in the way that Jesus answered: by living lives which do not blatantly contradict the truth of which we speak.

We Gentile latecomers will not get out of our dilemma with the Jews through some sort of liberal, intellectual imperialism which first demands that both Christians and Jews be converted into bland, universalized, American pagans before we can live together. Some of the silliest arguments over the future of the Duke class ring took this point of view: Let's all agree to act less religious, suppress our distinctive beliefs and act like rational, universal human beings and then that will settle the problems of our differences. No. Religion, for Jew or Gentile, is not something we check at the door when we come to the university or walk in the voting booth. It accounts for who we are, what we want, what we are trying to be. If I am to welcome the Jew, I must welcome the Jew as a Jew, in all his or her differences and he or she must welcome me in the same way. We cannot render up our belief in Jesus as the Christ as a sort of guilt payment for our past sins against the Jews. That solves nothing.

Right after I came here, I received a rather irate phone call from a faculty member who complained about something one of the fundamentalist Christian groups on campus had done. I tried to tell him that those fundamentalists would probably listen to me less than they would listen to him. But he was upset about their Christian dogmatism and, to him, offensive tactics. I said that I, as a Christian, was embarrassed too. He continued, saying how inappropriate it was, on the Duke campus, for people to be pushing their religion. I disagreed. "Wait a minute," I said. "You are talking as if you are a minority negotiating with the majority. There are about as many Jews on this campus as Methodists. I'm not the majority anymore. I'm not your problem, nor are those conservative Christians. It's all of us believers against all of those pagans! They are the majority, we believers—Christian and Jew—are the minority."

The way for Christian and Jew to live together, on the Duke campus or anywhere else, is for us both to be more faithful to our beliefs. The more we Christians come to see our Christ as the fulfillment of God's promises to Israel, the more keenly we feel the unmerited quality of our amazing inclusion into those promises, the more quickly will be healed the tragic separation within the Family of God. To the extent that we believers—Christian and Jew—allow our faith in God to be diluted through nationalistic loyalties, pagan philosophies, or other alien truth claims, we forfeit the theological resources whereby we are enabled to live together as family. The only way I can be hospitable to any stranger is constantly to be reminded that I was a stranger, I was out in the cold, I was taken in even when I didn't deserve to be.

Luke told a story about a troubled family in which a younger son, after a lurid sojourn, returned home in rags and smelling of the cheap perfume of harlots. The waiting father received him with joy (Luke 15:1–32). A party began. But the older brother—working for the father—refused to go to the party. The father came out into the darkness and pled with the brother to come in, but to no avail.

In our day, the story has taken a sad and unexpected turn, one which Luke couldn't have imagined. The younger brother soon lost his repentant, contrite spirit. The shock of his father's gracious reception wore off. He came to resent his older brother's failure to party at his homecoming. He began to scheme against his brother, to take on airs, to forget how fortunate he was to be in his Father's house. At last he even resorted to locking the older brother out of the house. He bolted the door and the party which had been a celebration for the reception of a stranger, became the victory bash of the arrogant usurper.

The music and dancing resumed. The smug younger brother had it all to himself now. But outside in the December darkness stood the Father where he had left him, out in the darkness, standing where he had always been, beside the older brother.

The younger brother had succeeded in locking out his brother, he had the whole house to himself but, alas, he had locked out his loving father as well.

11

When Bad Things Happen to Good People

May 17, 1987

LUKE 13:1–5

Some Christians on campus seemed to think that by talking about justice or "peace with justice" we could sidestep all of the difficulties involved in talking about Jesus to people who were more interested in justice than Jesus. As far as I can tell, Jesus has little interest in justice, certainly no interest in theodicy. Therefore this May sermon became an occasion simply to remind my thinking congregation that though we think about many deep matters in some depth, we rarely think like Jesus.

In freshman philosophy, I learned "Philosophy deals with two types of questions—questions to which everyone already knows the answers." That's one reason I enjoy teaching religion. Nobody knows any of the answers to the questions. This is bad if you're a student, but good if you're a professor. So, when the student comes back to complain about a C on the religion exam, I answered the question, "Why did I get a C?"

I can say, "Well, see here, you partly answered the question but you didn't deal with the larger philosophical issues, the existential and phenomenological dimensions."

Then as the student stumbles out of my office, bumping into the furniture, bouncing off the walls, he says, "You know I really did quite well to get a C on this paper."

Religion deals with so many questions like that—but so does life. And when we don't get answers we're apt to get cynicism. We're apt to find a story.

We were standing in the hall. Her child had been struck by a rare, often fatal illness. "Your little boy may not make it." She grabbed me by the lapel, pushed her face loose and said, "All right, preacher, tell me. Why did this happen to my little boy? What have we done to deserve this?"

And I was silent.

Now, I don't know what you think of the rare phenomenon of a speechless preacher. You may think that, if I were really a good preacher, I would have something to say to this question. There are preachers who do. But at least give me credit—I may not be the most comforting pastor, but I wasn't as tough on her as Jesus.

[Read Luke 13:1–5.]

Who can explain Jesus in today's gospel? They come to Jesus with two instances: How about those Galileans whom Pilate put to the sword at the Temple, their throats slit before the very altar of God? Why did they deserve such a fate?

And Jesus, so sensitive to human need, says, "I tell you unless you repent you will all likewise perish."

In their instances, they have covered the waterfront of tragedy. The Galileans were outsiders, the Jerusalemites were insiders. The Galileans were killed by the government, among the millions of victims of cruel and oppressive tyrants. The Jerusalemites were killed by a natural disaster, among the millions who have perished in earthquakes, wind, and fire. That just about covers tragedy, doesn't it—human-initiated and naturally caused disaster? Why did this happen to me?

It's a wonderfully philosophical dilemma.

The best-selling book on campus three years ago was Rabbi Harold Kushner's *When Bad Things Happen to Good People.* Thousands perish by famine in Africa, people are crushed in a Mexican earthquake, and others die in a ball of flame over Cape Kennedy. How can God be good and still allow bad things like these to inflict good people like us? "O Lord, why hast thou forsaken me?" "When I saw the prospect of the wicked . . ."

As interesting as we may find such questions, let us note that Jesus could care less. First, Jesus lumps all violence and suffering together—whether it be caused by natural calamity or by human perversity. Makes no difference to him. Evil is evil. Hurt is hurt.

Worse, Jesus refuses to answer the two-part question. The exam questions were: (a) What did those poor Galileans do to get slaughtered by Pilate? (b) Why were those Jerusalemites in the wrong place at the wrong time when the tower fell?

And to these perfectly good philosophical questions, Jesus responds, "Do you think that these Galileans were worse sinners than all the other Galileans, because they suffered thus? I tell you, No; but unless you repent you will all likewise perish" (Luke 13:2–3 RSV).

Now of course, Jesus, uneducated Jew that he was, wasn't too good at philosophy. When asked, on another occasion, about theodicy, he responded, "Well, God makes his sun to shine on the good and the bad; his rain to fall on the just and the unjust." That's all. The good and the bad get both sun and rain. That's all.

Elsewhere, the disciples asked, "Rabbi, who sinned, this man or his parents, that he was born blind?" (John 9:2 RSV). Surely there must be some reason, some direct correlation between sin and misfortune, between bad people and bad luck. "I have never seen a righteous man's children beg for bread." "Blessed is the one who walks not in the way of sinners, everything he does will prosper." No, Jesus denies a correlation. Still the idea persists: There is a direct relation between the sort of person I am and the bad or good things which come my way in life. I am suffering—what did I do wrong to deserve this? In my church: Teenager goes bad. What did they do?

Thornton Wilder's novel *The Bridge of San Luis Rey* tells of a little village in South America. Each day, the villagers made their way across a bridge to go to the fields. One day, without warning, the bridge snapped. Six persons fell to their deaths. There was a priest in the village who said, "Aha! I will do research into these people's lives and show why those six people were on the bridge when it fell. I will prove beyond a doubt that if you do bad things, bad will happen to you and if you do good things, good will be done to you."

He studied every aspect of their lives and came to a conclusion: Those six people were no worse, nor no better than anyone in the village. God does allow the sun and the rain to fall upon the good and the bad.

All right, I can take it. I can see the fallacy of our neat little distinctions between deserving and undeserving when they are blurred so by God's sunshine and rain. Jesus didn't give an answer when questioned about those Galileans and Jerusalemites because there isn't one. When a Pilate swings a sword, the closest person gets cut. When the earth heaves and a tower falls, anyone underneath, good or bad, perishes. Rabbi Kushner calls it luck. There is good luck or bad—neither of which is dependent upon a person's goodness or badness. You weren't born yesterday. You know that there is a kind of randomness to life.

Unfortunately, such philosophizing had nothing to do with what Jesus says. When presented with two excellent examples of life's unfairness, his reply is not of Rabbi Kushner—well, these bad things happen, mostly as a matter of luck, life's a grand roulette wheel and when your number's up, it's up and you must learn to live with it—which is what I might have said. Rather, Jesus says, "Do you think that they were worse offenders than you? I tell you, No; but unless you repent you will all likewise perish."

I arrive, breathless at the hospital. Running down the hall, I come at last to a little knot of family members, leaning on one another, eyes filled with terror and tears. Yes, she is still breathing, but the accident has badly damaged much of her body. Was she driving too fast? Did she have her mind on something else? Was she wearing a seat belt?

And I, as Jesus' field representative, say, "No, do you think she is a worse offender than you? I tell you, unless you repent you will all likewise perish."

People, take note: Jesus knows how our questions deter us from *the* question. *The* question, it seems, is not about unfairness—how can bad things happen to good people like us? The Jesus question is not about justice: What do I *deserve*. *The* question is the cruciform—how do *we* stand before God?

When Bad Things Happen to Good People was a best seller not only because it is written so well, but because it flatters so well a self-pitying, narcissistic age. For us, *any* suffering is patently unfair and undeserved, *any* confusion, *any* unknowing or tragedy because so long ago we stopped trusting a God whose presence makes suffering, confusion, unknowing, and tragedy bearable.

They asked Jesus about life's fairness; but he wouldn't answer. He forced them to examine their own relationship with God.

We don't want God, we want answers. And God's answers had better not be too confusing or frightening or we'll look for answers elsewhere. We can find a God who demands less than repentance.

Why did this happen to me? Probably, for no good reason. Bad things happen to the good and the bad all the time. The notion that only good things happen to good people was put to rest when they hung Jesus on the cross. Now, this same Jesus takes our question—Why do bad things happen to good little me?—and makes it cruciform: can you trust God—in joy or in pain—to be your God? Can you love God without linking your love to the cards life deals you?

God's love carries no promises about good or bad save the promise that God will not allow anything worse to happen to us than happened to his own Son. There. Do you feel better?

So on Sunday we come to the Lord's Table, and you are given, not answers, but bread and wine which are, for us, nothing less than His broken body and spilled blood. *This* is the way God responds to our questions—not with answers which flatter us, or make the world simpler than it really is, but with his life given for us, that we might more fully give our lives to him.

12

Clean Hands

August 30, 1987

I walk in faithfulness to thee. . . . I will not sit with the wicked. I
wash my hands in innocence . . .

Psalm 26:3–6 RSV

*In an attempt to snag a few freshmen I invented "Orientation Sunday," the first
Sunday of a new school year when the new students had just completed their orientation to the university. The university—having instructed them in multicultural
inclusiveness, various methods of contraception ("How dumb are these people?" I was
heard to ask.), and how to consume alcohol, physics, and philosophy—handed them off
to us at the chapel. It was our turn to make our pitch for Jesus to the Freshpersons.
Here was my third attempt.*

*It is probably inappropriate for a Christian preacher to take a biblical text and
preach against it. However, students have a way of bringing out the inappropriate in
me so I took the bait and worked over Psalm 26. I'm sure I was influenced by Walter
Brueggemann in this sermon, probably his* The Message of the Psalms *(1984).
Walt has never been far from my preaching ever since I first met him in his 1982
commentary on Genesis.*

Here is someone whom you would *not* want for a roommate. Here is someone whom your *mother* might pick for your roommate, but even your mother
wouldn't want to live next door to the person who wrote Psalm 26. Hell
would be an entire Saturday night in the presence of this person. Would you
listen to him pray?

I have walked in my integrity,
     and I have trusted in the LORD without wavering. . . .
     and I walk in faithfulness to thee.
I do not sit with false men,
     nor do I consort with dissemblers;
I hate the company of evildoers,
     and I will not sit with the wicked.
I wash my hands in innocence,
     and go about thy altar, O LORD,
singing aloud a song of thanksgiving,
     and telling all thy wondrous deeds. . . .
But as for me, I walk in my integrity;
     redeem me, and be gracious to me.
                              (Ps. 26:1b–11 RSV)

Can you believe this guy? It's people like him who give religion a bad name. You have met him before. You have heard his prayer. Jesus tells a story about two men who went to the temple to pray, one a Pharisee, the other a tax collector. The Pharisee stood by himself, careful not to be defiled by these wretched sinners and prayed, "God, I thank thee that I am not like other people, extortioners, unjust, adulterers, or even like this tax collector. I fast twice a week, I give tithes of all that I get."

Mark Twain spoke of someone as "a good man in the very worst sense of the word." Here he is! Psalm 26. "God, I thank thee that I am so good. I have not wavered, have not sat with false people, evildoers, dissemblers, drug takers, heavy drinkers, adulterers, blasphemers, sodomizers, fornicators, or other people who do those things which are described in the Bible with big words which we're not sure of what they mean but that sound bad. God, I thank thee for me."

Here is cool, calm, calculating religion. It is religion of the covenant. "I will be your God, you will be my people." Obey my laws; all will go well for you. I have obeyed thy law, therefore all will go well with me. His "prayer" is thus an inventory of his virtues. He's in church to remind God of how well he has kept up his side of the bargain. God's job is to make rules. Our job is to keep the rules.

He doesn't ask anything of God. For what is there to ask? The relationship to God is fixed, settled, complete, finished. You come to church in order to reiterate the settlement, to go over the terms again each Sunday. We are God's cherished ones. Let's check each other out to be sure that we are still right with God, that our social attitudes are suitably progressive, that our hands are clean.

Who prayed this psalm? It is the psalm of an obedient person. It is the prayer of those who live confidently in the structure. It is the prayer of the older brother who always stayed home and did what Mother told him; not the prayer of the younger Prodigal Son who had a taste for harlots and loose living. It is the prayer of those whom the Duke admissions office blesses. I don't care what they say about a "well-rounded student body," the admissions office is out looking for the guy who prayed Psalm 26! They wish that all of you looked like him!

I was talking with a Duke student some time ago. I asked him, "Were you always a good son? Were you the perfect child, as far as your parents were concerned?"

He replied, "Look, I wouldn't be *here* if I were a slouch." Right. Lord, I thank thee that I have always done my homework. When the book was assigned, I did not go and purchase the "Cliff Notes." National Merit finalist. president of the debating club. Eagle Scout. Academically speaking, my hands are clean.

And it's only natural that, if we are the good little boy or girl, the perfect son or daughter, that we come to church the same way we came to Duke. Coat and tie. Mind your manners. No ambiguity here. Honor the contract and all will be well. Life is a symmetrical, neat equation of compliance/obedience. Here I am on Sunday, taking inventory of my virtues: Integrity? Check. Trust? Check. Faithfulness? Check. Innocence? Check. Chastity? Oh well.

Your job is to be obedient, right, to keep your hands clean and not to press God too much about things. God's job is to respond when we push the right obedience button. Our job is to study hard, take careful notes, play by the rules and life will reward us accordingly. My hands are clean.

Yet, if you push this sort of thing too far, you are on your way to an autonomous believer who really doesn't engage a transcendent partner. God isn't needed in this religion of clean hands. Look at Jesus' story of the Pharisee and the Publican. Listen to how often "I" is used: God, *I* thank thee that *I* am not like other people. Like this tax collector. *I* tithe. *I* pray. *I* give. My obedience, my virtue determines the shape of the divine-human relationship. The Pharisee assumes that the reward-obedience system works. Jesus said that the Pharisee, "prayed thus by himself." And why not pray by himself? He doesn't really need God for a religion in which "I" is the center of everything. God, I thank thee, for me.

Count the times that "I," "me," "my" is used in Psalm 26: I have walked . . . I have trusted . . . my heart, my mind, my eyes . . . I walk . . . I do not sit, nor do I consort, I hate, I wash my hands, I love, my life, I walk, redeem me, I will bless.

The end result of this dull, frozen faith of the I, and the me, and the my is the dissolution of the divine-human relationship. You don't need God for a religion where you are as good as God. When transcendence is closed, settled, unambiguous, and hands are clean you have the autonomous believer. Self-worship is inevitable. This is the dominant characteristic of much "religion" on the American scene—a kind of dignified atheism. I am the measure of all things. My nation, right or wrong. My nation is worth killing for because it is the extension of my god—me.

Religion always becomes a-theistic when it no longer needs God to make it work.

"This man eats with sinners and tax collectors," they said of Jesus. "Sure," Jesus replied. "If you're well, you don't need a doctor. I've come only for the sick." You don't need a doctor when you're all healthy, strong, well, and full—like you Pharisees. I've come for the sick, the sinful, the broken—not for big, strong, competent, good people like you!

We come to church on Sunday morning and busy ourselves with rituals of self-righteousness, plodding through the hymns, mumbling through the prayers—all of which seems a bit dumb since we're only talking to ourselves. I. Me. My. Church becomes like a decayed marriage in which the couple goes through the motions of love, the dry rituals of affection, when everything else is gone. There is no surprise in the relationship anymore, nothing to amaze, no mystery, or confusion. You gather up your things after service and go out. You come back next Sunday, you take off your hat and coat, like Mr. Rogers' Neighborhood. Yes, back in church. Altar still in the same place. Everything still bolted down. God up there. We're out here, inventorying our virtues. Let's get on with it. We must be done by noon.

Whose prayer is Psalm 26? You know. It is *the prayer of the successful and the righteous.* It is the prayer of the one for whom things have worked out right. I wanted to be captain of the team and I worked for it, and I got it. I wanted to get into Duke and I studied, and I got it. I wanted her for my wife, and I got her. I wanted the job. I showed them my Duke transcript, and I got it.

It is a prayer for times when you are young and have the world at your feet, and your barns are full, and the vineyards are productive. It is a prayer for bright, sunny, Sunday mornings with all of us here in dresses, hair tastefully styled, and coats and ties. God, I thank thee, for *me.*

And all will go well for you . . . as long as you don't mess up, and the sun shines, and your tie is straight, and your star is in ascendancy, and your hands are clean. You can pray Psalm 26 yourself, without God. You don't need God for that.

Early in my ministry, I became acquainted with a young man who was active in a conservative religious group on his campus. He was a biblical fundamentalist, always having the right Scripture verse or theological answer on the tip of his tongue to cover every situation. He was the epitome of the wholesome, All-American boy. But one Christmas he came home for the holidays. I thought that I noted a change in him. He seemed less self-assured, less confident that he always had the right answer.

I told him that I thought I had observed a change in him, a change which made him seem more accessible, more human. He confessed that, on a campus religious retreat, he had sexual intercourse with a young woman. He was shocked that he, a "born-again, biblical Christian could be capable of such sin."

I knew why I liked him better now: He was a real person rather than a stilted facade. His religion was now a way of dealing with the facts of life rather than a means of suppressing and denying those facts. He could no longer pray Psalm 26 with a straight face. But there were lots better, lots deeper, more real Psalms that he could now pray. Now he actually had something to say to God.

Jung noted that each of us wears a mask, a *persona*, similar to the masks that were worn in ancient Greek drama. The *persona* is the face we present to others. It covers our "shadow," our true inner nature that we regard as unacceptable, unmentionable. Jung felt that the brighter and cleaner the *persona*, the darker the shadow underneath. My hands are clean. My life is right. My world is together. What lurks behind the mask?

Sometime after graduation, a few years ago, he appeared in my office. He said that he had been suffering from depression. He had even required hospitalization on one occasion. Because of his bouts with depression, it had been difficult for him to apply for jobs. Yet his psychiatrist said that he was making progress.

"It's funny," he said, "when I came to Duke as a freshman, I was self-confident, more self-assured. But now, I don't know what I believe. I feel insecure, unsure. Funny, I was more confident and knew more when I was a senior in high school than I do now that I'm a graduate of Duke."

And I said, "Look, I can explain that to you. When you were eighteen you were more self-confident, more self-assured, because you were *ignorant*. Everybody feels right at eighteen. But now, with an education, you know what you don't know. You know that you are needy, vulnerable, weak. You know that you need others to help you get by. You've learned that you're not autonomous, not self-sufficient. Rejoice! You're a fast learner! Some men don't learn what you've learned until they are 45 and have their first heart attack. You really did get an education here."

13

Failure

Easter 1988

How to get a sophisticated, urbane congregation to entertain the notion that Jesus Christ is really, bodily raised from the dead?

More specifically, how to assert the resurrection as God's great victory among a group of therapeutic deists who assume that God has retired? I always regarded Easter with excitement. Here at last, on Easter, we lay our cards on the table. We assert before a disbelieving, Enlightenment-dominated world the scandal of the faith. We come to at last the heart of the matter—Christ is risen, he is risen indeed.

This sermon also shows my inclination to preach from Old Testament texts on Easter. One disgruntled congregant complained, "Are you aware that you preached from the Old Testament for three Easters in a row?" I wasn't.

After Easter, Christians look at the Hebrew Scriptures and see gospel almost everywhere.

The game was over. The roaring stadium was now silent, empty of fans, a forlorn place of crushed popcorn boxes and drink cups, trampled programs, and spent confetti. The coach entered a sullen, utterly quiet locker room. Helmets were down on the floor, jerseys pulled off and piled in a wash bin. "I just want you guys to know that I am real proud of the way you played this afternoon," he said. "Real proud. We didn't win, but we did prove to a lot of people what we could do. It was a moral victory."

On the way out that evening, with autumn sky now dark, the second-string tackle turned to the quarterback and asked, "What's a moral victory?"

And the quarterback said, "It's what a coach tells you when you lose the game. It's what a coach says to a team when he knows it's his last season."

If you can't fool a seventeen-year-old football player about failure, whom can you fool? When the scores are read on the 6:30 sportscast, nobody every talks about "moral victory." They put the numbers on the board. Those with the highest numbers are winners; those with the lowest are losers.

Oh, they'll tell you anything to get you to go back out and knock heads on another Saturday. "Moral victory." "The score didn't show what really happened." "It's not who won or lost, but how well they played the game." "If we had only made that second down in the third quarter, we could have . . ." No. Vince Lombardi was right. Show me a guy who really believes all that stuff about failure not being failure and I'll show you someone who has played too long without a helmet.

A coach remains a coach only when the win-loss record is in his favor. The corporate president stands up before a drooping sales graph and says to the shareholders, "Well, we lost six million this year but we're calling it a moral victory, a year of character building for our company." A week later, there's a new name on the front door.

I sit on the University's commencement committee. To my knowledge, we have never knowingly nominated anyone to speak to our graduates who has been a failure. We look for people who are tops in their field, the achievers and doers, shapers and movers. The graduates don't want to hear an address on "Reasons Why My Last Three Marriages Ended in Divorce," or "The Day They Came to Tell Me to Clean Out My Desk and Turn in the Key to the Executive Washroom."

And yet, the graduates know, just like that seventeen-year-old quarterback, that failure is built into life. I don't know whether or not they teach you how to go bankrupt gracefully at the Fuqua School, or if the chemistry department tells its PhD's what to do when you give ten years of your life to find a cure for a new virus only to have someone else get there six months before you, or if the divinity school tells its graduates how to stay alive in a rundown inner-city church where the roof leaks and the membership declines. But you know, don't you, that more of us spend our lives there than elsewhere?

Failure. It's that sinking emptiness in the stomach when you look down the list of grades on the exam. There are your initials . . . at the bottom. That breathless expectation as the figures are being added, only to be met with stunned realization that they will not tally in your behalf. It is the physician, returning from the operating room, surgical mask taken off to reveal a countenance which speaks without having to speak. Was the operation a success? No, I don't need to ask, do I?

It's packing up and moving from the house to separate apartments, packing last the book of wedding pictures that won't be viewed again because they are too painful.

It is the morning after the election . . . the unused boxes of buttons and bumper stickers, the balloons and confetti not needed, the desperate attempt to smile as if it doesn't hurt. "I want to thank all of you for all that you have done. We didn't win, but we made our point, I think. I'm sure that, if we had a few more weeks, we might have turned things around and I want to thank everyone for everything. Someday, we'll look back on this as a good experience."

Failure. Defeat.

What to do with defeat? Our response is cheap rationalization. It was a moral victory. I remember, as a young pastor, entering the home where her husband had just died and she met me at the door with a fierce look on her face saying, "Preacher, don't tell me nothing about how 'he's better off now,' or 'he's in a better place' or any of that other stuff. He's gone!" She knew. She wasn't up for any of this preacher talk. He was gone.

Today, in the face of failure, we have more skillful rationalizations. A typically modern response is to blame failure on some other person, or even to claim no knowledge or responsibility for the failure. Let Ollie North take the heat. "The woman whom you gave to be with me, she gave me fruit of the trees, and I ate." And she said, "The serpent whom thou created, he gave me the fruit to eat." Rationalization, blaming, is not new, you see.

What to do with defeat? It's in the Bible, in a story as old as Moses. "Who am I that I should go to Pharaoh, and bring . . . Israel out of Egypt?" Moses asks God (Exod. 3:11 RSV). Moses wasn't being humble. He was being realistic about the possibilities for success. One way to handle failure, we learn, is not to attempt anything too great, stretch ourselves too far, lest we fail. Life can be a series of successes, provided we don't ask too much of life. Insignificant successes are better than a big failure.

Go, God tells Moses. I'll be with you. I'll tell you what to say. Emboldened by God's promise, Moses takes charge and is rewarded by initial success in persuading the people to follow. "And the people believed; and when they heard that the Lord had visited the people of Israel and that he had seen their affliction, they bowed their heads and worshiped" (Exod. 4:31 RSV). Strengthened by the support of the people, Moses strides forth and tells Pharaoh, "Thus says the Lord, 'Let my people go.'"

Somehow, everybody got word of the exodus except Pharaoh. "Who is the Lord, that I should heed his voice and let Israel go?" There are negotiations, compromise. Pharaoh not only refuses the request but also increases the burdens of the Hebrew slaves. Moses' efforts to win freedom for his people end in failure with matters even worse than they were before. The people mumble against their would-be liberator. "Because of you, the Pharaoh will now kill us," the Hebrews tell Moses. "O Lord, why hast thou done evil to this people?

Why didst thou ever send me?" says Moses. Moses moves from complaint to outright accusation of God. "Since I came to Pharaoh to speak in thy name, he has done evil to this people, and thou hast not delivered thy people at all."

Harsh words against God. But think of the failure. And who is there to blame? Better that the people had not hoped at all. Better that they had been content to be slaves and not think of freedom. God has made us miserable putting such thoughts into our heads! Moses failed. God has failed. Hope has failed.

But in the next verses Moses is sent back to Pharaoh. Negotiations resume. Each time, the demand for freedom is refused. Each time, God comes up with some new attempt to soften Pharaoh's heart to let the people go. "Go back to Pharaoh, try this," God tells Moses. When everything else has failed, God comes up with the Passover. Pharaoh will not yield. Something drastic, terrible, new is demanded. The God of Israel is resourceful, persistent, creative, determined, even in the face of failure. The people pass over from slavery to freedom, saved by the resourcefulness of a God who won't be stumped by defeat.

In the wilderness, Moses fails again. The people turn against Moses and God. They rebel against Moses and threaten to kill him. When they grow hungry and thirsty in the desert, they say they were better off as slaves in Egypt and want to go back. God sends miraculous food in the wilderness. While Moses is up on the mountain receiving the Commandments from God, the people are down in the valley, bowing before a golden calf.

You couldn't have blamed God if he had stormed off in a huff, called it quits with Israel. But no, God is already telling Moses, "Go say to this stiff-necked people . . ." The story goes on. Moses died and Joshua leads the people across the Jordan into the land of promise. They take with them the ark of the covenant, a visible reminder of all that God has done for them. But again and again, says the story, they fall from that covenant. After Joshua come the judges, then Samuel, and also failure.

A radical new plan to meet the failure in the history of salvation emerges with the idea of a kingdom. David is God's specially chosen instrument. With King David, God would rule the world with justice and righteousness. Yet the ideal meets with harsh reality. David corrupts God's plans with his own infidelity with Bathsheba, his murder of Uriah. Then comes David's son Solomon, Solomon the wise. But at his death, his son Rehoboam shows absolutely no wisdom and this failure leads to a division of God's people into North and South. The story strains forward, looking to the horizon of history for a new David who could help make God's ideal a reality. Josiah hopes to renew the covenant God made with Israel, to take up the promise, but he meets an untimely death, a failure effected by an Egyptian king. In the face of so many failures, so many defeats, how could God also not be defeated?

There is then another Moses, a new David, a new prince arising out of the House of David, bringing at his birth hope for the world. Under the reign of Jesus of Nazareth, there will be peace for all. Yet, from the first—in the screaming of innocent children whom Herod kills, the taunts of a Nazareth congregation, the sneers of scholars and Bible-believing crowds—this new son of David meets failure. It gathers like storm clouds over all his ministry. "My kingdom is not of this world," he says. And yet what good does that do us? What other world is there for us to experience God's success, God's redemption, God's promised rule of peace? Other kings sell arms to two sides of a war, just to see how much destruction money can buy. Other kings get success by the clenched fist, the screaming bomb, the thunder of jackboots on the streets of weaker nations. This king works by other means. When asked to identify himself he replies, "The blind receive their sight and the lame walk, lepers are cleansed and the deaf hear, and the dead are raised up, and the poor have good news preached to them" (Matt. 11:5 RSV).

Five months ago we felt hope surge within us at the songs of angels telling us of God's determination to deliver this world from war, from enmity, and oppression; yet how quickly that angel's song is overwhelmed by the facts of the failure to have peace on earth. It was a short journey, from the songs of angels to the screaming of innocent victims and their mothers.

So, were we really surprised to stand on Friday on a lonely, windswept hill where the New David, the New Moses, the King, Liberator, Savior was dragged into the calloused hostility of a hostile people? They killed him, just as the Egyptians killed Josiah, just as the people wanted to kill Moses, just as Herod killed those innocent babies. We had become adept at killing the prophets before him. By mid-afternoon it was over and we could go back to our homes. So much for God's plan, the angels' songs, hope. Death, now omnipotent, undefeated, reigned. A losing season again for God. As he hangs there, let him stand for all the brick walls and dead ends and unfulfilled hopes and unkept promises which humanity must endure. Death laughed as his tomb was sealed.

Please, don't mock this Friday tragedy with preacher-talk of "moral victory," or empty consolation that "he will live on in our memories." Let's be honest enough to call defeat, defeat; failure, failure; death, death. And who would blame God if now, at last, in this death, God should desert us, leave us to our own devices? Who would accuse God, if at this failure, God should go?

Now, after the sabbath, toward the dawn of the first day of the week, Mary Magdalene and the other Mary went to see the sepulchre . . .

14

Get Ready for a Fight

August 28, 1988

EPHESIANS 6:10–20

Be strong in the Lord. . . . Put on the whole armor of God, that
you may be able to stand . . .
Ephesians 6:10–11 RSV

Sometimes people asked, "What was your inspiration for Resident Aliens?*" (my
1989 book with Stanley Hauerwas). Mennonites? I always responded, "No, that particular sectarian read of the church was given to me by young Christians at Duke."
To be a student, a practicing Christian on a college campus meant to know that you
were swimming against the stream, up against the powers-that-be. Thus I warned
new student arrivals in my first sermon of the 1988 school year.*

The next summer I preached this same sermon, auf Deutsch, *at the university
Chapel in Bonn, Germany (where Barth once held forth before the Nazis). I thought
it worked even better there. It was as if this student generation of Christians was
the advance wave of a vast disestablishment of Christianity. Young Christians were
beginning to feel like strangers in cultures where we thought we had at last created a
world where no one could get hurt for following Jesus.*

Today's epistle is not one of my favorite biblical texts; I'm sorry if it's one of
yours. I have trouble with military metaphors as descriptions of the Christian
life. "Be strong in the Lord. . . . Put on the whole armor of God . . . taking the
shield of faith, . . . the helmet of salvation, and the sword of the Spirit, . . ."
this mixing of the martial with the gospel is dangerous. Some of the darkest
days of church history occurred when Christians marched out with banners

76

unfurled to crusade, to make holy war. My church, the United Methodist, recently had an unholy row over whether or not to put "Onward, Christian Soldiers" into our new hymnal. I don't much care for the song, feel the same way about "The Battle Hymn of the Republic," which some of your great-great-grandmothers sang as your great-great-grandfathers marched down this way to rough up my great-grandparents. What have these military images to do with the religion of the Prince of Peace?

To be truthful about it, I'd have to admit that my objections to these Christian marching songs probably have less to do with my pacifist theology than with my experience during the summer of my junior year in college. That summer, as part of my R.O.T.C. training, I was the guest of the U.S. Army at an exclusive camp for boys called Fort Bragg. With help from mosquitoes, gnats, and drill sergeants, I became convinced that the best way I could protect my country was somewhere outside the U.S. Army.

I remember the day that I had to lead a platoon of other college-student-soldiers through an imaginary mine field. It was some sort of test of our military leadership ability. Well, I must have missed class the day we studied minefield crossing. I had not the slightest notion of what to do, so I told my platoon to march on across the field with a positive attitude.

When the exercise was done, the sergeant called me over and, with a tone of infinite contempt in his voice, said, "I hope you're happy, Mr. Joe College. According to my calculation, you just lost fifteen of the twenty men in your platoon."

I replied, "Sergeant, I'm not a professional military man myself but, in your informed opinion, would you say that was good or just average?"

What the sergeant said to me cannot be repeated.

"Onward, Christian Soldiers," and Ephesians 6:10–20 seem unworthy expressions of the Christian faith.

Or are they? When asked for their first association when hearing "Onward, Christian Soldiers," a majority of respondents said, "The need for the church to be in mission throughout the world." What do they think about when they hear "The Battle Hymn of the Republic"? The civil rights movement of the 1960s and the fight for racial justice. Perhaps we forget, in a time of tame churches, toned-down preachers, and timid prophets that there was a time when the church believed that there was something worth fighting for.

What do you first think about when you are urged to "put on the whole armor of God. . . . For we are not contending against flesh and blood, but against the principalities, against the powers, against the world rulers of this present darkness . . . take the whole armor of God . . . the breastplate of righteousness . . . the shield of faith . . . the sword of the Spirit"?

Is there anything worth fighting for today? Is there anything in your world so inimical to the way of Christ that you need some sword and shield to protect you?

I recall someone who proposed omitting the traditional Prayer for Enemies in the new *Book of Common Prayer* because, "Episcopalians are now so nice that we no longer make enemies." The writer to the Ephesians wrote these words "in chains" (yes, back then, Christians were given jail cells rather than TV shows). He told his congregation that, if you plan to follow Jesus, get ready for a real fight.

I wonder if this text from Ephesians 6, telling Christians to prepare for battle, means more to some of you than to me because of a difference between the generations. I was raised in a church where the main agenda of the church was to help Christians to adapt to the world as it is. Many of you, particularly if you are about the age of our freshmen, have grown up in a church where the agenda is how to help you to survive as a Christian. (Please note that the armament listed in Ephesians 6 is mostly of a defensive nature—helmet, shield, breastplate—the armor needed for survival rather than attack.)

I was born into a world where Christians seemed secure, confident, and powerful, the United States of the 1950s. My parents worried little about whether or not I would grow up Christian—it was the only game in town. The entire town was closed on Sundays. Everyone went to church. It was the American, accepted, normal thing to do. In that world the church did not have to bother itself too much about defensive maneuvers because, after all, we were fortunate to live in a basically Christian country. It was our world.

A few years ago I woke up and realized that, whether or not my parents were justified in believing this, no one believed it today. No one. American Christians, conservative or liberal, Roman Catholic or Protestant, no one believed anymore that we could stay Christian, or that our children would become Christian simply by living in the "right" neighborhood, drinking the water, and breathing the air. If our children grew into this faith, we would have to put them there. If we would hold to and live out this faith, we would have to do so with care and determination because sometime, sometime between 1950 and 1970, the world shifted. It was no longer "natural" and "American" to be Christian.

My last congregation, in Greenville, South Carolina, was next door to the synagogue. We shared a parking lot with them. The Jews parked there for their services on Fridays; we parked there for our services on Sundays. It was a good arrangement.

The Rabbi and I would often get together for coffee on Monday mornings. One Monday, the Rabbi said to me, "You know, it is tough to be a Jew in Greenville."

I said, "I can believe that. With Bob Jones running around free, if I were a Jew I wouldn't sleep well either."

The Rabbi said, "We are always having to tell our children, 'That behavior is fine for everyone else, but it is not good for you. You are special. You are a Jew. That language is acceptable for everyone else but it is not acceptable for you. You are different. You have a different name; you answer to a different story. You are a Jew.'"

I said to him, "Rabbi, you are not going to believe this, but I heard very much the same statement made right here in my own congregation. Yes. One of the young parents in my congregation said, 'It is becoming more difficult every day to raise a Christian in Greenville. We are always having to tell our children, "You are special. You are different. You are a Christian."'"

My neighbor the Rabbi had lived among a people that had never asked the wider society for special favors, props, crutches. His community knew that if they were going to be and stay Jews, they would have to intentionally make themselves to be so.

Paganism is the air we breathe, the water we drink. It captures us, it converts our young, it subverts the church. The writer of Ephesians did not have to be convinced that the world was a hostile, inhospitable place for discipleship. He wrote these words "in chains." His world recognized the subversive nature of the Christian faith and put him in chains. Our world recognizes the subversive nature of the Christian faith and subverts us by ignoring us. The world has declared war upon the gospel in the most subtle of ways, so subtle that sometimes you don't know you're losing the battle until it's too late.

For instance, a couple of years ago, on this same Sunday, Orientation Sunday, the text assigned to me by the lectionary was not Ephesians 6:10–20 but Ephesians 5:21. My heart sank. "Be subject to one another out of reverence for Christ. Wives, obey your husbands." I can't preach that, I thought. Only Jerry Falwell would preach such a text! Especially is it an inappropriate text for a university church. My associate would drag me out of the pulpit and puncture me all over with her spiked heels. Forget Ephesians 5. The word for our day is "liberation" not "submission."

But I decided to let the Bible have its say. I began my Orientation sermon by saying, "You despise this text. No one but Jerry Falwell or some other reactionary would like this text. What an ugly word! Submission."

And yet, we know that, taken in the context of the day, this is a radical word. Women had no rights in that day. The writer of Ephesians 5 expends more words giving advice to husbands, telling them about their duties to wives, than words to wives telling them what they are to do for their husbands. Scholars agree that this is not a text about women's submission in marriage; it is a text which urges mutual submission in the church. The tone is set by the opening verse: "Submit yourselves to one another" (5:21, my trans.).

And that is why we despise this text. Our word is liberation. In our day we have seen the liberation of just about everyone. And the sooner that husbands can be liberated from their wives, parents can be liberated from their children, individuals can be liberated from their community, and we all can be liberated from God, so much the better! Why do you think that we're all here at the university? To get liberated! To stand alone, on our own two feet, autonomous, liberated! And when we finish with you here at the university, and you have your degree, you will not need mother, father, husband, wife, children, God, anybody. We call it "education."

Yet the writer to the Ephesians says that is a way which leads to death, not life. And I tell you that's odd. That goes against conventional wisdom. In the oddest of ways, the gospel brings about a head-on collision with many of our culture's most widely held and deeply believed values. Being a Christian is not natural or easy.

Thus the writer to the Ephesians says that you had better not go out unarmed. It is tough out there. The world lives by different slogans, different visions, speaks a different language than that of the church. So we must gather to "speak the truth in love" (4:15) that we might grow up in our faith. Weak, childish, immature faith is no match for the world. Being a Christian is too difficult a way to walk alone.

Last year I was talking to one of our students who is a member of a dormitory Bible study group here on campus. (Did you know that, according to our calculation we have about 50 such Bible study groups that meet every week here at Duke?) He was telling me that he had never been in a Bible study group before, never felt the need of it back in Des Moines. "Why here?" I asked. "Have you any idea how difficult it is to be a sophomore and a Christian at the same time here?" he replied.

It's tough out there. Paganism is the air we breathe, the water we drink (and I'm not only talking about what they do in the dorms on Saturday nights—which is often quite pagan—but also what they do in the classrooms on Monday morning). You better not go out there alone, without comrades in arms, without your sword and your shield.

So we must gather, on a regular basis, for worship. To speak about God in a world that lives as if there is no God. We must speak to one another as beloved brothers and sisters in a world which encourages us to live as strangers. We must pray to God to give us what we cannot have by our own efforts in a world which teaches us that we are self-sufficient and all-powerful. In such a world, what we do here on Sunday morning becomes a matter of life and death. Pray that I might speak the gospel boldly (Eph. 6:20).

A couple of years ago, I was invited to preach in the congregation where a friend of mine serves. The congregation is located in the heart of one of our great cities. The congregation is entirely made up of black people who live in the tenement houses in that part of the city. I arrived at eleven o'clock, expecting to participate in about an hour of worship. But I did not rise to preach until nearly twelve-thirty. There were five or six hymns and gospel songs, a great deal of speaking, hand-clapping, singing. We did not have the Benediction until nearly one-fifteen. I was exhausted.

"Why do black people stay in church so long?" I asked my friend as we went out to lunch. "Our worship never lasts much over an hour."

He smiled. Then he explained, "Unemployment runs nearly 50 percent here. For our youth, the unemployment rate is much higher. That means that, when our people go about during the week, everything they see, everything they hear tells them, 'You are a failure. You are nobody. You are nothing because you do not have a good job, you do not have a fine car, you have no money.'"

"So I must gather them here, once a week, and get their heads straight. I get them together, here, in the church, and through the hymns, the prayers, the preaching say, 'That is a lie. You are somebody. You are royalty! God has bought you with a price and loves you as his Chosen People.' It takes me so long to get them straight because the world perverts them so terribly."

I'm glad that you are here this morning. I hope that this will be a time when you get your head straight, gain the equipment you need, see the visions you deserve, learn to name the name that saves because, it's tough out there.

15

Knowledge

October 9, 1988

GENESIS 3:1–19

PSALM 90

And he said, "I heard the sound of thee in the garden, and I was afraid, because I was naked; and I hid myself."

Genesis 3:10 RSV

Hoping that a few might join me in my love of the Old Testament I preached frequently from the Hebrew Scriptures during the eighties. Literary criticism of Scripture also made a big impression upon me during this period, thus my fascination with Scripture's narrative way with truth.

It's a story, primitive story, primordial, which means basic, deep; a true story. It's from Genesis, the beginning book of the Bible, beginning of humanity. Genesis means "in the beginning." In the beginning, God made man and woman and put them in the garden. God will keep the good garden. All man and woman must do is to enjoy, to "be fruitful and multiply"—which sounds enjoyable.

It's a story like the ones told to and by children—naive, fairy-tale-like, deep, true, like the fairy tales told to you when you were young, which Bruno Bettelheim says "speak the unspeakable and plumb the depths of our being."

Once upon a time, we had it all—with no business more pressing than "to be fruitful and multiply." Once upon a time we were like children, naked but unashamed, trusting and unafraid. We were a two-year-old after his bath, romping gleefully naked through the living room, free of the unnatural restraint called clothing. So we were. Undiapered and unashamed. The unself-conscious, trusting simplicity of children is the way God created us, so the story says, once upon a time. Let us assert what the story says and what it does not say.

Like any good story, this one doesn't explain, it narrates. *Contra* Augustine, this is not an explanation of how sin came into the world. The story does not say the man and the woman were at one time sinless. It just says they were naked and unashamed like children—they were only a few days old, remember. It is a story, not about sin, but about *self*-consciousness. And because it's a story about human life, it's a story about *limits*. You are free to enjoy the garden—only stay off that tree over there. The story does not ask, "Why that tree?" We're only told it's the "tree of the knowledge of good and evil." Therefore it's a tree of limits, for what makes us different from God is that we don't always know what is good, whereas God does. Because we're not God, we live with limits. Life has its limits. The story doesn't say why or how. It just states what everybody eventually learns—life, as good as it often is, has limits: (a) We don't know everything. (b) We shall die. It depicts rather than explains our first human testing, pushing at the limits. It's not a story about Satan (this creature is a "snake" who, in the first days of development, was smarter than man or woman). After all, we were only a few days old. Like most smart beings, the snake was good at raising questions.

"Are you sure that God said . . . ?" "Why would God create such a fine tree and not allow you to eat . . . ?" Socrates said that the purpose of a good teacher is to raise the right questions (just like the snake!). Good students will come up with answers (just like the man and the woman), though Socrates gave us little means of knowing right answers. We don't need Satan or Socrates to raise questions, given enough time. The snake is but a device to move the story along to ask the questions, deep and threatening. Are there really limits to life? Maybe those limits apply to everyone else but me? Could a good God really say that we shall die?

Herein is our human dilemma. God has created us, male and female, the highest of animals. We have a wonderfully contoured cerebral cortex. Since Genesis, we have bypassed snakes. We can reason, ask why, all on our own now, with no need of help from snakes. We can create and achieve, discover, invest. Can it be that creatures so marvelously endowed should also die? With all that we know, can it be that there is something left which we cannot or should not know? Did God really say that we should not eat of the fruit of the tree of good-evil, life-death?

Thirteen hundred on the SAT is a great achievement, but only average around here. If you can do that, then while you are here, we'll teach you to split atoms, clone genes, translate Sanskrit, macromanage the economy. And when you know that, we'll give you a degree and you'll be like unto—gods.

"Did God say . . . ?" "Did God say there are *limits* to life in the garden?" Surely not. Limits? Ah, that's the talk of primitive people, before science, in time B.C.—before computers.

The man and the woman, these wonders of creation, have been given the garden. But they are also given boundaries. They are human, but also creatures. Being creatures, there are things they won't know and they shall die. But having freedom, blessed with natural curiosity, they began to push against the limits. "Did God say you shall not eat the fruit of *any* of the trees?" asks the snake, grossly misrepresenting what God said. (The snake, by the way, appears to be the world's first theologian—asking questions, answering for God.)

The woman corrects the snake. "No, God said we are free to use all the trees, except for two." But the thought had been planted. The snake has suggested the possibility of an alternative way to God's way.

"Can it be that God, who has gone to such trouble to create us (and so wonderfully created, too), who has given us so many gifts, should also limit us?" The natural God-given boundary is now perceived as threat, a downright injustice. Death, the natural, expected boundary of life, has become the primary human agenda. What can we do about the preservation of our life? We must get organized and do something, take matters in hand, get moving!

"You will not die," says the serpent, moving from suggestion to outright rebellion. And why should we? It's not fair! So we take matters in hand. We were told that we were creatures destined to enjoy the Creator; that, as creatures, all we must do is trust. But *we wanted knowledge more than trust*. We were to entrust to God the meaning and significance of our lives, to let the Creator determine our destiny and worth as creatures. But that wasn't good enough. What good is a garden if we shall die? Not content to be creatures, we become creators. Look at what we can do and know if we just put our heads together! Go ahead, "a *little* knowledge is a dangerous thing." Eat up! Get wise.

Now, it's the Creator's turn to question. "Where are you?" And the creature gives a pitiful answer. "I was afraid. I was naked. I hid." We wanted knowledge rather than trust, and look what we got—a forlorn creature, shivering in the bushes, cringing in terror. We wanted to step over the boundaries, stand up and be free, and for all of this, we now know only one thing—namely, *we are naked*.

Ernest Becker claims that all culture, science, art, industry, philosophy arises as response to this primordial fact. We are naked. That is, we are (despite our marvelous brains) fragile, exposed, vulnerable creatures who die. And now that we have outgrown God, who is there to give meaning, purpose to our short lives? We must do it ourselves, says Becker.

So, lacking immortality, security, meaning beyond ourselves, we write books, do research, build houses, make clothes, endow chairs at universities, have children, make war, paint pictures—all as elaborate defense against the primordial awareness that we are naked and therefore afraid. Surely for creatures so wonderful as we, something must remain, endure, have eternal value. All our cultural attainments, Becker says, are the pitiful products of naked apes.

Our nakedness is no more apparent than in our pitiful attempts at self-justification through blaming. When asked, "What have you done?" the woman says, "The serpent beguiled me . . ." The man says, "The woman gave me . . ." We can't admit our actions. It takes secure, strong beings to be honest. The lying and blaming reveal the real truth about us: I was naked and afraid.

Dostoyevsky's *Crime and Punishment* tells of a bright student, Raskolnikov, who decides that he is smart enough to commit the perfect murder without being caught. He is intelligent, calculating, not like other weaker, less intelligent men. The novel is a story of his own self-destruction. Raskolnikov is punished, not by gods, but by the weight of his own offense.

So, in the birth of human self-consciousness and rebellion, man and woman are punished—not by God, but by the results of their attempt to secure their lives by themselves rather than through trust in God.

"You will be in terrible pain in childbirth," the woman is told. "You will have desire for your husband but he shall dominate you." This isn't God's will. God's will was for two companions in the garden, being fruitful and multiplying. Now, relations between men and women are confused, a matter of power plays, dirty tricks, domination, submission. Even the joy of children will cause much pain.

To the man: "You shall be at war with the earth. It shall bring forth as many thorns as fruit. You shall sweat and labor over the dusty earth your whole life and then return to it in your death." The dry, rocky, inhospitable land of the Near East stood in contrast to the once friendly world of the garden.

Now, in this topsy-turvy world out of joint, men and women are at odds with one another and there is no joy that is not mixed with much pain, and we die. We are naked now, more than ever, lonely, nothing to secure us against the onslaughts of mortality.

The story stands as an early critique of inadequate human attempts to overcome anxiety. It begins with man and woman losing their innocence, their childlike willingness to live as trusting creatures within God's creation. In the place of trust, we wanted knowledge. And look what we got.

You who are young may feel right now quite vulnerable and afraid. You have lost enough of your innocence to know that there's a world of things out there you don't know (midterms are only a week away), that relations between men and women are terribly conflicted. ("Nobody dates at Duke," somebody told me last week. "You plan to do a little more exploring on weekends before you're able to say anything definite about what is good or evil.")

You assume that your sense of vulnerability is a temporary by-product of being a student, that someday it will be possible for you, perhaps here at the university, to acquire enough self-understanding, enough knowledge, so that you'll know enough to be smart enough, adult enough to have overcome adolescent anxieties. By graduation, if all goes well, we will have succeeded in deceiving some of you into thinking that this has actually happened to you already—that is, "I'm all grown up now and can at last take hold of my life and stand on my own two feet because I got an A in organic chemistry." (The closest one can come, before the senior year, to being as wise as gods.)

And yet someday, if you live long enough, you come to see that this was a great deceit; that, in truth, you are not strong, wise, and self-sufficient but really quite small, finite, mortal—namely, *naked and afraid*. You will be sitting in your den, dressed smartly in Calvin Klein, a large house surrounding you, a martini in your hand, but you will be naked. Your heart will skip a beat, there will be this strange sensation in your chest and you can smell mortality. Then you will see yourself located, not in some restricted garden of Eden called "Westmont Estates," but in a weedy place where you are at enmity with the world, with other people, with life itself. And if asked "why?", you may blame your situation on your parents, an inadequate exercise program, a lousy doctor, your last spouse, or even Duke. Or you will say, if you muster as much honesty as Grandfather Adam, "I was naked . . . I was afraid."

Our attempt to know more is our effort to deal with our anxiety by circumventing the reality called God. If we can just know enough, get enough government research grants, build bigger and better systems of knowledge accumulation and dissemination, we can secure ourselves, carve out some enduring significance for ourselves.

"What you don't *know* about AIDS can kill you," says the poster on a bulletin board. See? Knowledge is power to escape anxiety.

The story, this old story, teaches otherwise. It is only God who creates, calls, permits, and prohibits and only God who can deal with our deepest anxiety.

It's a hard lesson for us to learn. We who have been told that our greatest need is for autonomy, liberation, and freedom are not likely to heed the call to *trust*. Most of the sermons you've heard are calls to action, to use your potential, to achieve, live up to your great talent. This story suggests that this way is the *problem*, not the *solution*. The story says that any freedom which doesn't discern the boundaries of human life leaves us anxious. Any exercise of our potential which is not at the same time an admission of our boundaries is demonic because it is based on a lie.

Our culture's attempts to resolve its anxiety are largely psychological, economic, or some form of narcotic. Our public life is largely an exploitation of our common anxiety—witness the current national presidential campaign. Our best politicians, theologians, advertisements, like the serpent seduce us into believing that security is to be had apart from the reality of God.

Therefore, I must call you to listen to an old, deep, mysterious, story of once-upon-a-time in our past. It is a story not about Adam and Eve, but about us because each of us, in our own lives, recapitulates this primordial act of rebellion and self-deceit. The story therefore has the power to shock us into recognition that our lives are constituted and have enduring significance, not because we have learned so much, but because we learn to trust the "one in whom we live, and move, and have our being."

Which brings us to the end of the story. Do you remember how it ends? (Those of you who are Baptists and have heard this story before this morning—do you remember how it ends?) The story ends, not with this curse of pain and enmity of thorns and dusty death. It ends by saying that the Lord God, the Creator, the Gardener, the Accuser, becomes the *Tailor*. God made, for the two creatures, clothes.

Creatures who know that they are naked need clothes, some protective covering as they go out into a now difficult and bewildering world. God gives them what they need. God will not abandon them to their destructive delusions' self-sufficiency. God promised to punish them by death. But God's grace wins out, as it would many times again in our story. God refuses to give up on these two naked, frail earthlings. God gives them clothes, thus promises to continue to care for them, even in their silly presumption. God gives us this holy good, even in our sin.

So, finite, frail, naked we are—yes, says the story. But also *loved*, preserved to live another day, clothed, fed, protected, in order to know not just the facts of life-death, good and evil—but also trust.

> So teach us to number our days
>   that we may get a heart of wisdom. . . .
> Satisfy us in the morning with thy steadfast love,
>   that we may rejoice and be glad all our days.
>   (Ps. 90:12, 14 RSV)

16

On Being Stuck with Your Parents

November 6, 1988

JOHN 15:16

Parents' Weekend packed the chapel. What a great opportunity to show the world what fun it is to think about the world in a Christian way. One of the challenges of being a college student is to achieve some modicum of freedom from parents. Yet the modern university also presents students with perhaps an even greater challenge—to acknowledge that our lives are gifts and not our achievements.

For the first time since I have been here, Parents' Weekend falls on All Saints. This is a happy convergence. The presence of parents reminds us of our indebtedness to others for almost everything that is important to us: our lives, our looks, our values . . . our Duke tuition. None of us is "self-made."

Saints are also reminders of our indebtedness. We began this service with thanksgiving for saints, some of the hundreds of parents in the faith who stare down from their stained-glass perches—Judas Maccabeus, Esther, Ruth. Their presence reminds us that faith is a gift. We believe only because someone lived the faith before us, told us the story in a manner which was worthy of our imitation. Saints are our great-great-grandparents and we are their children in the faith. None of us is a "self-made" believer.

Those of you who know something of the Bible and its stories of these "saints" may be less than pleased to have a Samson or a Sarah as your grandparents. They may look "saintly" now in the chapel windows, but in their day, few called them saints. People seem saintly after they've been dead a thousand years. But if you had to live with them, had to stare at them across the breakfast table rather than across a Gothic chapel, well . . . which reminds me that one thing unites these biblical saints in a funny sort of way—most of them had a lousy family life. I mentioned Samson and David—the mess they made of their marriages and families is legendary. Sarah, grandmother of a whole nation, was a conniving schemer who managed to pass on most of her psychoses to her children. If you knew their stories, as the Bible tells them, you might question why they are our saints. Of course, we don't choose our saints. *They are given* by the tradition of the synagogue and the church.

"Aw, leave them alone," you say. "It's bad taste for us to speak ill of our grandparents in faith."

And that pinpoints a major difference between us and the Bible. Today, when we speak of family, parents, children, we're apt to speak rather sentimentally, unrealistically, if not downright deceitfully—ours is the "happy family"—Ozzie, Harriet, June, Ward, Wally, and the Beaver. When the Bible speaks about parents and children in faith, it speaks honestly—Sarah, Samson, David, Bathsheba.

Our dishonesty about our families is surprising, considering the state of American family life. Never has the divorce rate been higher, never have we had more problems with spouse-child-elder abuse. Ask either presidential candidate. He'll tell you—families are in a mess, though there is disagreement on how to fix it. What on earth did politicians talk about before they discovered that American families are in a mess? (Though apparently not *their* families. We've certainly seen enough of their happy families during the campaign.) I doubt that either candidate knows what to do about parents and children in our families, not because the candidates don't care, or they don't have the happiest families in America, but because, when it comes to understanding what it's like to be a parent or a child today, the candidates, as we ourselves, don't know how to think about family.

In the name of freedom, we Americans created something called "the individual." Nothing is more important, to Americans of the political right or left, than maintaining the sovereignty of the individual and his or her options, freedom, and independence. As a result, relations between husbands and wives become a contract between two individuals who jealously guard rights and prerogatives. Relations in the family come to resemble the rest of our society—a conglomeration of friendly strangers. We've created a world where privacy is sought more than community, where no one is asked to suffer for anybody else, and where we want both to be intimate and still to be able to shake hands, say goodbye, with no bad feelings.

Such thinking makes relations between parents and children incomprehensible. The odd factor which makes being a child or a parent so unusual in our society is this: *You didn't choose your parents and they didn't choose you.*

Think about it. You don't choose relatives; they are given. Even if you adopt a child, that child will grow to be so unlike the baby whom you brought home from the adoption agency that you will continually know that this child is someone who has been *given* rather than selected. As parents and children in a modern world that worships individual rights and freedom, nothing is odder than learning to love someone whom we didn't choose.

To a surprising degree, this lack of choice extends even to the person whom we marry. Most people think that the toughest part of marriage is deciding whom we ought to marry, making the right choice. We say we are deciding whether or not we are "in love" with this person; i.e., are we emotionally attached.

Curiously, the church has traditionally cared less about our emotional attachments. What the church cares about is not who you have deep feelings for—how notoriously fickle are feelings—but rather *whether or not you are a person who is capable of sustaining the kind of commitment that makes love possible.* The pastor, leading a marriage ceremony, doesn't ask, "John, do you love Susan?" The pastor asks, "John, *will* you love Susan?" Love is here defined as something you promise to do, a future activity, *the result* of marriage rather than its cause.

I know that sounds odd. We think that the toughest part of getting married is choosing the "right" person. Well, for most of the church's history, marriage occurred among persons who hardly knew each other before the wedding. You are no doubt grateful that we have progressed to where, at least in our society, arranged marriages are passé.

Are they? Although they would loathe to admit it, one reason parents send their children to prestigious universities is so that they will meet prestigious people of the opposite sex. We all know that it's helpful for people to marry people with a similar social, economic, and religious background. Through piano lessons, summer camp, and a B.A. degree, parents give their children the illusion that the choice of someone to marry is not being arranged. I'm not being cynical here. Cultures which still practice arranged marriages (and are up front about it) have much lower divorce rates than ours. ("Who should be entrusted with such important matters?" asks a friend from India. "Someone who has actually been married and has fifty years of life experience, or someone who has never been married and has had no experience except school?" I didn't have a ready answer.)

Rather than be embarrassed, I think we should be more open about the arranged, unchosen aspects of our marriages because it enables us to think clearly about the peculiar ethical demands placed upon us in families as husbands, wives, parents, and children. You're probably conditioned to think that some action isn't ethical unless you have freedom of choice, unless you decide *for yourself* that this is right for you. The trouble with that point of view is that marriage requires, just as parenting, that we find some means of making sense out of being stuck with certain people for no good reason or justification. Most of us learn to make the best of it. Right there is a glimpse of us at our best. For right there is where we learn to be faithful, to love strangers even though we did not choose them as someone we might have liked to love.

Sometimes I ask fellow pastors, "What is the purpose of your premarital counseling?" Most of them say something like, "To be certain that the couple knows what they are getting into." Does a pastor know what people get into in marriage? Did *you*, those of you who either are or were married; did you know what you were getting into?

My friend, Stanley Hauerwas, has a wonderful essay in which he argues that *we always marry the wrong person* ("The Family as a School for Character," *Journal of Religious Education* 80, no. 2 [Spring 1985]: 272–85. See also his *A Community of Character* [University of Notre Dame Press, 1981], chaps. 8–9). That is, we never marry the one we thought we were marrying because marriage changes us. So you wake up one day and realize that the person next to you is not the person you committed your life to five years ago. But of course, you are not the same person either. So what do you do then? If marriage is the correct choice of the right person to whom you are emotionally attached, you are in big trouble. The person has changed, so have your emotions. Nobody ever chose to marry a person who is addicted to alcohol, or who develops a terminal illness. But lots of times you wake up in a marriage and that is the person you've got.

Being a parent is a lot like that, too. Parents never get quite the children they thought they were giving birth to. That's why I'm unhappy with the term, "Planned Parenthood," as if it's only good to have children if you have *planned* them, if you have *chosen* them. Who plans to have a severely retarded child, or a rebellious child, or a child who plays the drums in a rock band? Sometimes we get such a child. And what then? You can choose an automobile, but you can't choose a child. You must receive a child. The Bible says a child is a *gift*, not a possession or a project.

Nobody knows what he or she is getting into as a husband or wife, a parent or a child. Don't get me wrong. I'm all for marriage preparation, and we ought to do more of it. I'm in the marriage preparation business. But the trick is to prepare for a lifetime of commitment to someone who is always changing. How can you prepare for how annoying another person can be when he or she is so close to you so early each morning? How can you prepare for all the ways a child will challenge you, disappoint you, worst of all, come to look just like you only to desert you for college?

You can't. And because you can't, what you need is some means of being part of an adventure *that you can't control*, the end result of *which you do not fully understand*. Morally, we move into the future on the basis of the commitments that we made without knowing what we were getting into. Your parents sit here, thinking how much they have changed since they met you at the maternity ward twenty years ago. Twenty years from now, you will still be surprised at the ways your parents have been the most important people in your life even though you had absolutely nothing to do with their being your parents. Marriage, family are like that.

What you need, when you marry or have a child, is some means of turning your fate into your destiny. As Christians, our faith provides us the means to live together as parents, children, husbands, wives. Just as you didn't choose Samson or Sarah to be your grandparents in faith, so you didn't choose Jesus to be your savior. He came to us, not the other way around. John's Gospel makes this explicit: Jesus says to his disciples, "You did not choose me. I chose you so that you might bear fruit" (John 15:16, paraphr.). Life cannot be mainly about our choice and our decision since the Bible says that God must save us by what we cannot have by our efforts or striving.

The Bible, its stories of saints like Samson and Sarah, is a long story of God's continued determination to love us even when we are unloving and unlovable. It is also the story of God's continued commitment to make us into people who can be depended upon to love even strangers since we have learned, in Christ, what it's like to be a stranger and to be loved, even when we didn't deserve it. We come to his Table with empty hands and hungry hearts, needing God to do for us that which we cannot do for ourselves. And because he has chosen us and continues to feed us and to care for us here at his Holy Table, we are enabled to be free from our modern American obsessions with safety and control in order to risk being faithful. Even to those whom we didn't choose, faithful.

When God turns our fate into God's chosen destiny for us, that's what Christians call "salvation."

17

Harmless Hospitality

July 23, 1989

LUKE 10:38–42
2 KINGS 4:8–17

"Scripture interprets Scripture." This has long been an interpretive axiom of the church. Here a story of one woman's experience with a prophet becomes an interpretive key to another couple of women's stories with Jesus. I hoped this would be an evangelistic sermon, of sorts.

A few weeks ago I was to speak at the Lutheran Theological Seminary in Philadelphia. I took the last flight out of Durham. We landed late. A hair-raising, fifty-dollar, one-hour cab ride later, I was deposited at a now utterly dark, locked-up-tight, Lutheran Seminary. Had no idea where I was supposed to sleep. Wandered about, Willy Loman-like, bag in hand, trying this door and that, everything locked and dark. Midnight. Finally, I saw one last light in a house on campus. In desperation I knocked on the back door. A woman came, peered out. I told her who I was. She invited me in.

As it turned out, her husband was the only person I knew at the seminary—John Vannorsdal, the president. He wasn't home, but Pat graciously fed me, got me to where I was supposed to be. It's great to be on the receiving end of hospitality offered to a stranger.

"I don't usually open the door at night when John is away," said Pat. "It's a tough neighborhood. But you looked harmless."

I am! As a Methodist preacher wandering around Philadelphia at midnight, I am harmless.

But if you're a woman alone, be careful how you open your door to strangers. It is not always great to be on the giving end of hospitality.

Thus we come to our Scripture lessons for today, stories about women who opened their door to strangers and got surprised.

There was this wealthy woman over in Shunem. Any time Prophet Elisha happened to go through town, she invited him over for fried chicken, biscuits, gravy, and squash. It's in the Bible.

She said to her husband, "This is a *real* prophet, this bald-headed man of God who's always stopping by for lunch. Let's build him a special room so he can stay here whenever he likes."

My grandmother's house had a room called "The Prophet's Chamber" which was set aside for traveling Methodist preachers. This is where the term came from—the room which the Shunammite woman set aside for Elisha.

Elisha loved the room as much as he loved her cooking. So he says to her, "I want to repay you for your hospitality. Name whatever you need, it's yours."

Well, I told you she was rich. She tells Elisha thanks, but she's well fixed and doesn't need a thing.

"What on earth can I give an old woman who's got everything?" Elisha asks his servant.

"Well," says the servant, "she's got no son and, although her husband is a rich man, he's *old.*"

"Great idea!" says Elisha. "Call her over and I'll give her the good news."

"At this season, when the time comes around, you shall embrace a son," Elisha tells her.

"I'll embrace *what?*" she said (as she turned up the volume on her hearing aid). "Young man, do you know how old I am? Have you seen my husband? Who said I even wanted a son?"

Nine months later, the Thursday afternoon Book Club really had something to talk about.

Moral: *Be careful about being nice to prophets. A cup of tea perhaps, a light lunch, but be wary of overnight sleepovers.*

There were a couple of sisters over in Bethany—Mary (who loved to sit around and talk about great ideas) and Martha (who loved to throw big dinner parties and make cakes from scratch). Jesus was on the road traveling and Martha invites him in for a big meal. (Remind you of the Shunammite woman?)

Now put Jesus' visit to Martha in context. Were you here last week? Do you remember the story that Jesus told to the lawyer? The Good Samaritan (Luke 10:25–37). A man, on his way to Jericho, falls among thieves. They beat him up, leave him "half dead." Now, two men go down the road: a priest, a pious layperson. They both pass by the unfortunate traveler without helping. A Samaritan, a lousy Samaritan, was the only one who stopped and helped the suffering stranger, receiving him, bandaging him, risking his own life for the life of the wounded stranger. "Go, do likewise," says Jesus.

So maybe Martha heard that story of the Good Samaritan and took it to heart. Here is Jesus, out in the road. "Come on over to our house," she says. "In two hours I'll whip you up the best kosher meal you ever ate."

See? Martha is doing what Jesus said to do. She has gone and "done likewise"—received this hungry, needy stranger into her house. And she's in there working like a dog (before the days of Kenmore or Cuisinart). But there's her sister Mary, lounging at the feet of Jesus as he explains to her the finer points of the Nicene Creed.

"Hey," says Martha, wiping her dishpan hands on her apron, "Jesus, how about telling that egghead sister of mine to get in here and help? 'Go, do likewise;' right, Jesus?"

"Wrong, Martha," says Jesus. "Settle down and let's talk. Doing is OK. But there's much to be said for doing nothing, for listening. Mary knows. I'm not just passing through town on my way to Jerusalem. I'm on my way to Calvary, passing through life to death. A few weeks and I'm outta here for good. Then you'll need the Word more than food. Your fresh baked rolls are great, Martha, but as they say, 'You can't live by bread alone' (Deut. 8:3; Luke 4:4)."

He spoke these tough words to busy Martha just a few verses after he took his sharp left turn toward Jerusalem (9:51). The strange man of God whom Martha invited to dinner has a cross on his back. What's more, opening your door to Jesus, asking him in, is not just a matter of fixing up a few nice things for the preacher. It's a matter of Martha taking up her—cross—as well.

Remind you of Elisha and the Shunammite woman? Open your door to a man of God, you might get surprised. God's intrusions are rarely harmless.

"Look, all I wanted was a little food, polite conversation." What she got was a trip from the geriatric ward to the maternity ward.

"Look, Jesus, we were supposed to have a nice evening, a little activism, collection of canned goods for the less fortunate, old clothes for the poor. You have to go spoil everything by this depressing talk of death. How much is this meal going to cost me, anyway?"

Open your door to God. OK. Just remember: this is a *real* God, not some make-believe image of ourselves, not some tame deity you can have over for a chat. Break bread at the table of the *living* God, you don't know how you'll be surprised.

The Shunammite woman was like a lot of us. She was well fixed, yes. But her life was still *fixed*. Well fixed can be—well—*fixed*! The diamonds were nice, and the spring cruise. But at her age, with no child (which then meant no future) about all she could do is settle into what is, redecorate the den, add on a wing for the nice new young preacher. Her life was fixed.

Then she opened her door to the bald prophet and finds out that Rev. Elisha is more of a man of God than even she expected. He gives her more than her heart's desire, some gift she could not dare to ask for because she dared not to conceive it possible. God's presence intrudes, not always bringing what we asked for, but what God knows we needed.

Martha opened her door to similar divine intrusion. Conventional rabbis did not go to a single woman's house, much less waste their wisdom in teaching women. Jesus makes Mary and Martha disciples. Jesus will not spoon-feed them, patronize them with innocuous religious platitudes. He gives the truth of his way to them with both barrels, even though it be truth which is ambiguous, not easily defined, much less lived.

"Get out of the kitchen, listen, learn, follow me," he says.

Martha, like her Shunammite sister also receives a gift, but, like that given to the woman of Shunem, not the gift Martha expected. She, with Mary, is taken seriously, given opportunity to be a full disciple of the one who proclaims the intruding, barrier-breaking, living God.

Be careful to whom you open your door, and whom you invite to sit at table.

A pastor in Florida told me of how her congregation became concerned about the plight of the homeless in her city. They could see them, wandering the streets at night, sleeping in doorways.

"We've got this big fellowship hall downstairs," she told her congregation. "Why don't we simply invite these homeless men to come spend the night here?"

Why not? How nice of the church to do something for the homeless!

The first night, fifty-five homeless men entered the fellowship hall to spend the night. She said, "Now you take fifty-five homeless men off the streets and put them into a Methodist fellowship hall, you've got problems."

"First of all, we found out that there's a reason why many of them are homeless. Nobody wants them. Crazy, sick, offensive, malnourished, addicted. We had never actually met any homeless people. It was rough at first. Fights. A robbery. Somebody came down to distribute food one night and got roughed up. It was a mess. All we wanted to do was to be nice to some homeless men."

"So what happened?" I asked.

"So what happened was—we actually became a church. We had two choices. Either throw them out or else do what was necessary to be the sort of place that could show hospitality to fifty-five homeless people. By the grace of God, we chose the latter. Medical care, food, counseling, support, hand-holding, and listening were developed. Our congregation was converted from a friendly, ordinary, religious club, protecting its clubhouse, to a committed, bold—church. Because when we opened our doors to fifty-five homeless men, guess who else got in with them?"

"The one who said, 'inasmuch as you have done it to the least of these (surprise!) you've done it to me'?" I ventured.

"Right," she said.

I wonder if, in your life right now, there is a knock at your door. I wonder (I'm just asking) if where you are now living, there's a stranger outside waiting for you to open up. That tug at the heart, that tap upon the door, it could be you-know-who.

"Behold, I stand at the door and knock," he said.

Let's go ahead and let him in. You want to ask him in? What harm could he do?

18

The Unfettered Word

October 15, 1989

2 TIMOTHY 2:8–15

But the word of God is not fettered.

2 Timothy 2:9b RSV

When I went to Duke Chapel, some predicted I wouldn't be well received. "You get away with murder in the pulpit because you are such a conscientious, attentive pastor," Patsy said. "People allow you pulpit freedom because they are so indebted to your pastoral care. You won't be able to pull that off at Duke. No way for you to ingratiate yourself with that many of them."

At Duke Chapel, preaching to a congregation of well over a thousand each Sunday, it was as if all the normal pastoral props had been removed. All the pastoral tricks through which a preacher gains a hearing were gone. Nothing was left but the preached word.

I came to a new respect for the power of preaching. A number of listeners routinely drove many miles each Sunday to be there. Our radio audience was surprisingly large. Not every week, but often enough to keep me nervous, I received a letter reporting on some life changed, or some life lurched to the left or the right through a sermon.

Although he taught me most of what I know for sure about Jesus, I rarely bring my mentor Karl Barth into my preaching. He makes an appearance here. It's hard for me to speak about the power of the Word without reference to Barth and his Barmen Declaration against the Nazis. Barth's main objection to Hitler was homiletical. The nerve of the murderous little wretch to have the temerity to try to tell me or Barth what to preach!

He owned a hardware store and he was a member of my church. Someone had warned me about him when I moved there. "He's usually quiet," they said, "but be careful." People still recalled the Sunday in 1968 when, during the middle of the sermon (the preacher's weekly diatribe against Nixon and the Vietnam War), he had stood up from where he was sitting, shook his head, and walked right out. So I always preached with one eye on my notes and the other on him. He hadn't walked out on a sermon in over ten years. Still, a preacher can never be too safe.

You can imagine my fear when one Sunday, having waited until everyone had shaken my hand and left the narthex, he approached me, gritting his teeth and muttering something about, "I just don't see things your way, preacher."

I moved into my best mode of nondefensive defensiveness, assuring him that my sermon was just one way of looking at things, and that perhaps he had misinterpreted what I said, and, even if he had not, I could very well be wrong.

"Don't you back off with me," he snapped. "I just said that your sermon shook me up. I didn't ask you to take it back. Stick by your guns—if you're a real preacher." Then he said to me, with an almost desperate tone in his voice, "Preacher, don't you ever forget that some days, the only thing saving me from complete despair is whatever word of God you happen to speak in the sermon. Don't you dare take it back."

It is a heavy, awesome, well-nigh impossible task to preach this word of God. Sometimes, the only thing saving me from complete despair is your encouragement of me to dare to speak it. I think some congregations get the preachers they deserve.

Today's epistle is from Paul's Second Letter to Timothy. Paul writes his younger colleague from a jail cell—the source of some of the best Christian writing. He tells Timothy to "remember Jesus Christ . . . , as preached in my gospel." Paul, in jail, can't be with Timothy to guide him. All that Timothy has now in Paul's forced absence, is remembrance of Paul's words. Just words. It is this gospel, says Paul, "for which I am suffering and wearing fetters like a criminal. But the word of God is not fettered."

Paul is in chains, fettered in some Roman Alcatraz. But they can't chain Paul's gospel. You can chain a man, but you can't fetter words, the Word. So Paul encourages Timothy, "do your best to present yourself to God . . . , a workman who has no need to be ashamed, rightly handling the word of truth."

The only thing a Christian preacher has for which to be ashamed is in poorly handling "the word of truth." Tell me, after the sermon, "that didn't make me feel good," or "William Buckley would kill you," or "Teddy Kennedy would curse you for saying that." I won't take offense. Tell me I haven't handed over the unfettered word of God; I'm supposed to go home sick.

Paul is in chains. He can't be with Timothy or the church. All he can do is to smuggle out whatever unfettered word he can.

As a preacher, I too am in chains. Nobody has ever threatened me with jail because of my preaching. Iron bars do not a prison make. I like to be liked. Oh, I talk a good game of confrontation but, all other things being equal, I like to get along with people, adore their approval, pander to their praise. I didn't get to be president of my class from the seventh to the eleventh grade by being calloused to other people's opinions of what I say.

As a preacher, in this setting, I want to be academically approved. One mustn't be too simple or trite in speaking. Latest books read must be cited. When told, by one of our choir, after a sermon last spring, "That was a typical Willimon sermon—a rather profound idea disguised as triviality"—I went home and inserted footnotes in my next sermon.

I want to preach, to speak the word, but not in any unbalanced way, to overstate, to oversimplify complex matters, lean too far on one side or the other. This is a university pulpit, after all. I am chained.

"But the word of God is not fettered."

I've just returned from Germany. There, fifty years ago, the church went through a devastating test during the *Hitlerzeit*, the "Hitler Time," a test which, for the most part, the church flunked. As Karl Barth said, when it came time for the German church to say "No," it was about two hundred years too late, the church having said "Yes" to so much. The greatest theological minds of the German church had been enlisted to convince the church that the greatest task of contemporary Christians is to understand and to communicate with the "modern world." But in leaning over to speak to this "modern world," the church fell in. We had succeeded in preaching in such a way as to be accepted not only by Copernicus and Darwin but also by the Nazis.

Karl Barth was horrified that the church lacked the theological resources to stand against Hitler. But having spent decades telling ourselves that the Bible was just one book among others, that the Jewishness of Jesus was not really all that important, that Christianity is little more than one moment on the path of the forward development of all the world's great religions, there was nothing left wherewith to make a stand. We had lost the means to resist, lost the means even to know there was something worth resisting.

Jesus was not really, literally a Jew, they had said. The important thing about him was that he was an example of the brightest and the best of all humanity, the teacher of noble ideals. It was a short step from the liberal Christ-the-highest-in-humanity to the Nazi Superman.

But there were some in the German church who remembered. In 1934 Karl Barth wrote the Barmen Declaration, which began,

Jesus Christ, as he is attested for us in Holy Scripture, is the one Word of God which we have to hear and which we have to trust in life and in death.

We reject the false doctrine [that the church] ... would have to acknowledge as a source of its proclamation, apart from and besides this one Word of God, still other events, powers, figures and truths, as God's revelation.

See? When the church was bereft of leaders, power, protection, only one thing was left: The word of God, thank God, was not fettered.

It is a fearful thing to be abandoned to our own devices, left in a world with no one to speak the unfettered word. Powerful social forces conspire to make the church adopt, adapt, conform. Reinhold Niebuhr, as a young pastor, said that he thought there were so many tame, innocuous little preachers because pastors feared that, if they spoke, they would be fired. Later, Niebuhr learned the real truth. It is love of the congregation, rather than fear of them, that binds the preacher's tongue.

"It is hard to speak unpleasant things to people whom one has learned to love," said Niebuhr.

Yes, if I, as preacher, am silent out of love, it is a false love, for "the word of God is not fettered." Paul was in chains, but not his gospel.

I was serving in a little Southern town when the racially segregated schools were integrated. There was a meeting (attended by all the people of one color) at the town's high school to decide what to do to "save our schools." What could be done to keep "them" out of "our" schools? One by one, angry speakers rose to call for boycott, resistance, even violence to protect "ours" from "theirs."

There was an old, half-broken Baptist preacher in that town, who had baptized, married, or buried just about everyone at one time or another. He was old. His once clear bass voice was now reduced to a crack and a whine, ready to be put out to pasture. He came late to the meeting that night. Stood at the back and listened.

After an hour or so of the racist tirades, he asked for the microphone. The crowd made way for their beloved pastor. He stood before the microphone, eyes slowly swept the gathered throng in silence, then he spoke in measured, sure, certain cadence: "There is neither male nor female, Jew nor Greek, slave nor free, white nor black, for there is one Lord, one faith, one baptism. Go home, read your Bibles!"

The meeting was over. Slowly, people drifted out. The schools integrated that fall without incident. We have our chains.

"But the word of God is not fettered."

This summer, we drove down to somewhere between Lake City and Coward, South Carolina (do you know the place?), to hear my father-in-law preach his (third) farewell sermon as he prepared to retire from the Christian ministry (for the third time). After his first retirement, ten years ago, he was sent to tiny rural churches where no one else would go. But this year he told them that now, at last, he was going to retire for good and move to the mountains of Hendersonville to live among the Floridians.

The hot Sunday sun rose over green tobacco fields as the service began in the little church. He had asked a quartet of sweet, soprano voices to sing his favorite, "The Ninety-and-Nine." You remember, it's a song about the Lost Sheep: "There were ninety-and-nine, safe in the fold . . ." I don't think I'd heard it since I was a child. Don't think it's ever been sung in Duke Chapel.

After they sang, he preached. Before he set off for the mountains and Hendersonville, Carl Parker preached. His text? Something about the depth and breadth, the height and width of the love of God. It was Father's Day, so he talked a little bit about how we all love and cherish our children. God loves us even more than that, he said.

Then he spoke about the man who was to die in the electric chair in South Carolina the next day. I had seen his picture on the news the night before. Somebody had held a service of remembrance for this man's victims and their families. He had killed a couple of people, maimed others, in his rampage of terror. The preacher at *that* service had declared that he wished they would let him "throw the switch on this piece of refuse who destroyed these innocent lives." Mr. Parker went into lurid detail describing the crimes of this man. "And yet," he said, "today's Scripture, as well as the sweet song we have heard, says that God loves that man on death row, values his soul just as much as God values us."

The congregation got real quiet.

"Why, according to Jesus' story of the Lost Sheep, God will gladly leave us ninety-and-nine gathered in the fold here this morning and go to Columbia to death row just to get hold of that one lost sheep. And when God finds him, God's more happy to have him than to have all of us safe ones here in church."

I noted, at the end of the service, that congregation seemed a lot more willing to let Preacher Parker go on and retire to Hendersonville. He is old, long past time for respectable retirement. They've got him now safely stored among the Floridians in Hendersonville. You're safe. He won't be preaching too much any more.

"But the word of God is not fettered."

19

Religious Rage

March 18, 1990

PSALM 137

A preacher is ordained to be an advocate for the tradition, yet most of us contemporary preachers, products of modernity, are more skilled in criticism and defeat of tradition than in promotion of the faith once delivered to the saints. Universities that once saw as their main work to deliver the wisdom of the past to a new generation now teach the young the skills of disparagement of the past, even before they have attempted to understand the past. I therefore preached this sermon as an exercise in commending the tradition to a new generation of Christians.

Someday I may preach a series of sermons called "Bible Passages Too Hot to Handle." A preacher could get burned by getting too close to today's text.

Those of you who are regulars here know that we believe it a good practice for preachers to take, as their texts, biblical passages assigned by the ecumenical lectionary. This links us with the practice of the majority of the church, it provides for continuity, and (usually) preserves you from exposure to the pet peeves and hobbyhorses of the preacher. But there are passages that even the lectionary, in its three-year cycle of Scripture, consistently overlooks. Some omitted passages are boring, or trivial, or both. Some are simply too hot to handle.

Take today's Psalm for instance. It is a tradition to sing Psalm 137 this Sunday in Lent. And that's fitting. The children of Israel are in exile in Babylon. There they sing a song of grief, a song of mourning.

> By the rivers of Babylon—
>> there we sat down and there we wept
>> when we remembered Zion.
> On the willows there
>> we hung our harps.

103

For there our captors
  asked us for songs,
and our tormentors asked for mirth, saying,
  "Sing us one of the songs of Zion!"
How could we sing the LORD's song
  in a foreign land?

I say this is a fitting song for now because we're deep in the season of Lent, the forty days of fasting, penitence, and mourning. Psalm 137 is a dirge, a song of pain and grief. The Hebrews have been uprooted, deported into a strange, alien land, one of the many pogroms, deportations, and "final solutions" suffered by God's Chosen People.

"We wept when we remembered Zion. On the willows there we hung up our harps." The time for songs is over.

But the Babylonian captors taunted us: "Sing us one of the good old gospel songs of Zion. Let's hear one of y'all's Spirituals that you people do so well. Something of the 'sweet bye and bye.'"

And they said, "How can we sing God's song in a strange land? God's songs are about victory and salvation and triumph—which we feel little of here. How can we sing such songs in exile? If we forget Jerusalem, may God forget us."

When one is in exile, a stranger in a strange land, this is the typical response—mourning, songlessness. Where does this Lent 1990 find you?

"I'll be glad when we finally get done with Lent, these sad services and sadder hymns, all this talk of cross, and blood, and grief. Oh, to be at Easter's victory songs."

If you're well situated, comfortable, not suffering, at home, you will be impatient with these sad Hebrews and their laments.

"Can't we talk about something more pleasant? Something cheerful and upbeat? I want to feel good when I come to church."

I don't see anybody weepy on Sunday morning TV. Be Happy Attitudes; think positively; smile, God loves you; this is the day which the Lord has made, let us rejoice and be glad in it!

Come on, you Hebrews, get with it! Babylon isn't so bad. You could learn to like it here if you'll just learn some good Babylonian tunes, allow your children to intermarry, eat Babylonian food, accept Babylonian ways. Before long, you'll forget that you're in exile. It will seem like home.

Where does this Lent 1990 find you? Are you comfortable, at home with this best-of-all-possible worlds, victims of imperially induced optimism? Or do you sometimes, late at night or at the end of the day, find yourself grieving for something? Do you ever feel that you are out of sync, not in step, odd in a world and on a campus where everyone else seems to be happy, ambitious, goal-oriented, and on the way up?

At the party—with everyone else so very happy, so exaggeratedly happy, so relentlessly, often chemically induced happy—do you find yourself putting on the tape with the sad, melancholy songs?

"Kill it," they shout. "Put something on that's fun, happy, high!"

People in exile, strangers in a strange land, mourn, have to mourn even though all the others may laugh. It takes a kind of courage to admit sadness. Weeping can be an act of resistance.

I once knew a man who had come up the hard way. Because of his family situation, he never had a chance to finish school and was forced to work in menial jobs. In his mid-thirties he began the long process of earning his high school degree, finishing by the time he was forty. But when he got his degree, the company wouldn't promote him. Once a janitor, always a janitor, it seemed. Although he tried, he just could never get ahead. When he died in his mid-forties, some said he died of alcoholism, others said it was liver disease. His wife said, "I think he died of a broken heart. He so wanted to have a chance to make it."

There's a heap of mourning out there and in here this Lent. And every time the church tries to cover it up with our pretty vestments, and smiling preachers, and well-dressed congregation, Psalm 137 has said to all the brokenhearted, "Come on in here. Bring your mourning to church. Let God have your rage. Weep with us!"

"By the waters of Babylon, we wept when we remembered Zion. . . . How could we sing God's song in a strange land?"

And all might be well with this Psalm if we could end it there. Nearly all hymnals do. In our hymnal, Psalm 137 ends at verse 6. The exiles are in mourning, refusing to entertain their captors with song. But in the Bible, though not in the *United Methodist Hymnal*, the Psalm continues. It continues with verses I have heard neither quoted nor preached in a church until today:

> O daughter Babylon, you devastator!
>> Happy shall they be who pay you back
>> what you have done to us!
> Happy shall they be who take your little ones
>> and dash them against the rock!

Now what do you do with that? It's one thing to mourn, to weep, to refuse to sing; but here the feelings of exilic homelessness and lostness have moved beyond mourning to rage, white-hot, clinch-fisted, head-smashing rage. What do you make of that?

"It's not nice to say things like that in church."

That seems to be the attitude of those who edited our hymnals. John Wesley, founder of Methodism, said there are some Psalms that are "unfit" for

Christian ears. Nice people, Christian people, don't talk like that, don't clinch their fists and scream, don't rage. The Christian thing is quietly to acquiesce, patiently accept, distort the voice into a whine, resign.

"If only . . ."

"Wasn't it a shame that . . ."

Better end the Psalm at verse 6 because we don't want ugly, unacceptable thoughts like that in our church. We are so much more advanced than those primitive, backward, vengeful Hebrews. We have a religion of love, forgiveness, and acceptance. We would never think or say those unkind things about the infants of the Babylonians.

I once heard Father Roland Murphy, recently retired from the Divinity School, say, "It seems bad taste for the people who dropped the bomb on Hiroshima and Nagasaki to quibble over a few Babylonian babies." If we could muster the justification for the incineration of thousands of Japanese babies, we, of all peoples, ought to understand the rage of these Hebrews.

I, to my knowledge, have never wanted, even for a moment, to bash anyone's baby's head against a rock. But then, I've never had my children led into the gas chambers and I have learned to live quite graciously (although I do mourn sometimes) with a million abortions per year.

Rage. Can we feel it? Could we allow it in church?

"Oh, these were the words of human beings, grieving men and women, not God," you say. People feel rage. God is above all that. Read the Bible. God can rage. Besides, Psalm 137 is in the Bible and the Bible is God's word and you and I, even in our modern arrogance, ought to be a bit reticent to expurgate or silence God's word.

Here's another possible response to these baby-bashing thoughts of Psalm 137: This Psalm, like all of them, is a song of worship. Here, in Psalm 137, is the *public processing of pain*. Here, in church, before the altar of God, is strong, unrelieved anger, rage. I for one, am glad those Hebrews said it and I'm glad that they had the courage in the new *Hymnal* not to delete it.

Here's why. When we edit out this Psalm, we also edit out all the alienated women, and abused persons, and lost, homeless, angry people in exile. Where will they go to express their rage?

Some time ago, I had a woman in one of my classes. Scarcely had the very first class ended than she was up at the podium challenging me, not liking the way I said things, accusing me of sexism. She impressed me as one of the most angry people I had ever met. Frankly, I hoped that she would trust her instincts and drop the course. But she didn't. She stayed for the whole course, arguing, fighting, raging every step of the way. On the last day she gave me one of the most hostile, uncomplimentary evaluations I have ever received from a student.

Well, she had been abused in her earlier marriage, you say. Yes. She was having a rough time balancing school, child care, and all the rest, you say. Yes. But people like her are not pleasant to be around. I wanted her out of the class.

But, thank God, she is *not* out of the Bible, not out of the church. Read Psalm 137—*all of it*. Come, you hurting daughters of Zion, don't just grieve, rage with me. Did it ever occur to you that God may be as angry as you are?

I see here at least two possible religious responses to injustice, pain, and tragedy in life. One response is mourning: I will not sing. I will sit quietly and wail. Hang up the harp. Weeping Rachel won't be using it anytime soon. Mourning.

There is, by the grace of God, another response: rage. Babylon, you whore! I will not keep quiet, not submit, not bow down, cave in, give up. Rage. I don't say that it's pleasant. I say that rage is real, honest, biblical, and faithful.

In the book of the prophet Jeremiah, which also comes out of Israel's exile (as does, I believe, about a third of the Old Testament), you can detect two possible responses to the problem of exile, homelessness. The first is from Jeremiah 29:5–7:

> Build houses and live in them; plant gardens. . . . Take wives and have sons and daughters; . . . seek the welfare of the city where I have sent you into exile, and pray to the LORD on its behalf, for in its welfare, you will find your welfare. (RSV)

"Dear Lord, please help Babylon tonight. Help us Hebrews to be more cooperative with our alien rulers. Teach us to accept our lot in life and to try to be happy."

Yet in Jeremiah 51:63–64, there is another response which reminds one of Psalm 137. "When you finish reading this book, bind a stone to it, and cast it into the middle of the Euphrates, and say, 'Thus shall Babylon sink, to rise no more!'" (RSV). Clinch-fisted defiance. There is more than one song to be sung in a strange land.

"Do not go gentle into that dark night. . . . Rage, rage against the dying of the light" (Dylan Thomas).

In the Holocaust Museum in Israel, I am told by Ralph Klein that there is a shirt that is made from a Torah Scroll. It is a shirt which a Nazi SS Officer, as a joke, forced an unknown Jewish tailor to make, thinking it would be cute to have a shirt made from the vellum pages of the Hebrew Bible. The tailor, who knew Hebrew, made the shirt entirely of pages from Deuteronomy 28.

Look up Deuteronomy 28 when you get home. It is a series of vile, rage-filled, wonderful, life-giving—curses!

20

Some Way to Run a Farm

July 22, 1990

> The kingdom of heaven may be compared to a man who sowed
> good seed in his field; but while men were sleeping, his enemy
> came and sowed weeds among the wheat. . . . He said to them, . . .
> "Let both grow together until the harvest."
>
> *Matthew 13:24–30 RSV*

Summertime, particularly on a college campus, and things are more relaxed, less formal. The tone and tempo of sermons can change too. Parables lend themselves to a more playful presentation of the gospel. Thus this sermon on some of the agricultural parables of Jesus.

I would wager that the two predominate reasons modern people give for not being Christian, not associating with the church are: (1) People in the church seem just as lousy as everybody else in the world (here they cite some sin which they feel fairly sure they are innocent of like racism, or hypocrisy, or materialism, and ascribe it to people in the church); or (2) With so much evil and suffering in the world, belief in a good and righteous God is impossible (here they cite some evil which is then ascribed to God's ineptitude). If God, and by implication, God's church, could just clean up his act, think of all the wonderful, morally sensitive people who could get in the church!

From time to time we have tried to clean up both God and our act as the church, but we've never been quite able to pull it off. We have tried to clean up the church, removing from the rolls all the slackers, dead wood, morally impure. Let's get this church pared down to the truly religious, the really committed, we said to ourselves. Invariably, we ended up with a church which more closely resembled the people who crucified Jesus rather than the ones who followed Jesus. The old saw about the two Puritans chatting and one says to the other, "There is no one so righteous as me and thee . . . and sometimes I worry about thee."

I for one greatly admire the people in the tiny Mennonite church. I admire their tight discipline, their pacifism, their courage. I said this out in Kansas last year and, after I said it, a Mennonite pastor came up to me and said, "We Mennonites tend to look better at a distance. We're pacifist, except when in a fight with other Mennonites."

Such is the church, the messy, rather untidy, always only partly faithful church.

We have tried to defend God against the charge of ethical ineptitude. Against those who wondered why, if God were all powerful and good, there was still so much injustice, pain, and evil in the world, we have come up with a variety of defenses, theodicy, none of which is very satisfactory. Any explanation for the moral messiness of life invariable ends up sounding as if evil weren't really evil but good since God is allegedly going to use our evil for some greater good. Our theodicy doesn't work. Things are still a mess.

Jesus told a parable that, while it may offer not a bit of help to people who question the messiness of the church or of life, may be of some help to those of us who must live with the mess in the church, in life, and in ourselves.

[Read the Parable of the Wheat and the Tares, Matthew 13:24–30.]

What kind of farmer is this? Is this any way to plant a garden? This parable of the Wheat and the Tares is preceded by another agricultural fiasco. A farmer goes out to sow seed, says Jesus. And he plows his furrows and, in straight lines down each furrow he places seed after seed? No. He just starts throwing seed everywhere. Seed is flying in all directions. Naturally, some falls on rocks, birds have a feast on most of the rest of it. Some of the seed—surprise, considering this sloppy farming method—falls on good earth. You'd think the farmer would cultivate the good earth, be a bit more careful in the sowing. But no, seed slung this direction and that, falling on both good earth and bad.

If that parable didn't confuse you enough, Jesus follows with another. I think it's about the same farmer. He sows seed in his field. But when the seed germinates and the wheat appears, weeds also appear. Weeds. Darned. Looks like wheat at first, but later, when it matures, it bears nothing. Just weeds. "What happened?" ask the farmer's servants. "Sir, Lord, did you not sow good seed?"

"An enemy has done this!" says the farmer. "Must have come in the night and sown weeds in my perfectly good wheat."

Enemy my eye. You've watched this farmer at work before. Last field he planted, there were weeds there too, and birds. You get that when you start slinging seed at random. This farmer doesn't need enemies sneaking around at midnight to ruin his harvest. He'll ruin it himself.

When his servants then ask, "Master, do you want us to go out and try to pull up some of those weeds so the wheat can grow?" this famer replies, "No, just let the weeds and the wheat grow together. Too much trouble. You go weeding that garden, you might accidentally pull up wheat as well. Just leave it. We can sort it all out at the harvest."

Can you believe that? Of course you can. This is the same farmer who slung seed all over everywhere rather than take the time to do it right. As it turns out, he's not much better at hoeing than he is at sowing. Just let 'em grow together. We'll worry about it come September.

Jesus says the kingdom of heaven is like that.

Now, I'm a bit surprised that Matthew would tell a story like this. Matthew is the Gospel of judgment. No permissive pat on the head of Matthew. His Gospel is full of stories about the separation of good from bad trees, houses built on rock and sand, choosing God or mammon, pulling out the sheep from the goats, pearls and swine, the narrow gate as opposed to the wide, and wheat and weeds.

It's in Matthew that we meet Jesus through fire-breathing John the Baptist, "His winnowing fork is in his hand, and he will clear his threshing floor and gather his wheat into the granary, but the chaff he will burn with unquenchable fire" (Matt. 3:12 RSV).

Separate, purify, purge.

But it was also Matthew who told of the marriage feast in which the servants are told to go out and invite to the party "as many as you find both *bad and good*" (Matt. 22:9–10). It was Matthew who told of the great dragnet, pulled to shore between two boats, net tied to each boat so that it dragged in "*fish of every kind*" (Matt. 13:47–50).

You want to work from the *Social Register*? No, send an invitation to everyone in the Manhattan telephone book. You want us to fish just for the tuna? No, stingrays and sand dollars taste good too.

What kind of way is this to party or to fish?

I expect that these parables originally spoke to the messiness of the church. Jesus commanded his church to "make disciples of all nations" (28:19), to preach this gospel "throughout the whole world" (24:14), and look who showed up for baptism. The church cast its dragnet across the whole world, and look at the creatures we caught. The invitation was issued, and look who showed up for the party. It's a mess. But it's God's mess, this story seemed to say. When God gets to sowing, or inviting, or blessing, or calling, God just doesn't know where to stop. It is not for us to judge where the seed will take root, or to table the wheat in distinction to the weeds. That's God's business.

Yet, I also expect that these parables spoke to the larger, but not unrelated issues of the messiness within the world itself, life itself. If you think it's a mess in the church, then look at the mess in the world. If it's really God's world, one would think that God might have done a better job of making it seem more like God's world. War, injustice, pain, suffering, sickness, racism. Make your own list.

I think it's that question which is caught up in the servants' question to their reckless master, "Lord, did you not sow good seed in your field?"

Lord, when you looked on your creation and said, "That's good, that's real good, did you mean this world?"

Why are there weeds? Well, there was this enemy who slipped in at midnight and sowed these weeds. And that's possible. But rather improbable. Nowhere in Near Eastern literature is there any story of someone slipping around at night sowing weeds. There are quicker, cleaner, nastier ways to get even with somebody. How like us to try to pin the evil that we experience and especially the evil that we do on somebody else, some other force. "The devil made me do it." I don't think that rather lame explanation about the nocturnal enemy is very helpful.

I think this is a parable which struggles with the problem of evil. Perhaps evil does come from some supernatural force let loose in our world, some Satan or something who roves about the darkness, working mischief in an otherwise benign creation. Perhaps. But whether or not that be the source of evil and pain, of injustice and suffering, all we know for sure is that evil is real. The world is indeed a mess. The bad seed grows right alongside the good. Weeds germinate in good soil just as well as wheat. Often, one can't tell the weeds from the wheat until they are full grown and then it's often too late to do anything about it.

Out of this mess arises the ancient, anguished biblical cry: "O LORD, how long shall the wicked, how long shall the wicked exult?" (Ps. 94:3 RSV).

When Duke lost the national championship to a school somewhere in the desert, I wrote our coach asking him to look up Jeremiah 12:1 in his Bible. "Why does the way of the wicked prosper? Why do all who are treacherous thrive?"

It's no joking matter when, in your life, evil sometimes flourishes while goodness withers. When those cancerous cells spread and the good cells starve, when defenseless students in Beijing stand before the tanks and are crushed, or drugs despoil our youth who buy them and enrich those who sell them, we are apt to ask, "Lord, did you not sow good seed in your field?"

It is a mystery. And it remains a mystery. What is the farmer going to do about all that wasted seed? What about the weeds growing alongside the wheat? We'll have to wait until harvest, according to the story. Perhaps what the farmer does is right. Yet everything dear to agriculture suggests that he is taking a big risk, that he is headed for a tough harvest. He is putting a lot of good wheat at risk.

"Do you want us to go and gather the weeds?" ask the servants. And we suspect that makes the most sense. No, wait, says the farmer. I'll risk it.

Isn't that wasteful? Odd? Especially for conscientious, ethically sensitive, religious people (like us), isn't that odd? What kind of way is that to run a farm?

"Well," says the farmer, "one time I had this sheep that got lost. So I left the ninety-nine in the wilderness and searched for that one sheep until I found it. Then last year I gave this dinner party. I invited everybody I could lay my hands on. It was rough on the furniture, but, boy did we have a party! Then when we had those grapes to harvest, at the end of the day I said, 'What the heck? I'll pay everybody the same wage, no matter when they started work.' Besides, this is my farm and I'll run my farm the way I run my farm. OK?"

My last church, at the end of a long day. I was tired. Not much progress. Depressed. So few results, so little progress. So, at the end of the day, I'd pour a cup of coffee for the Lord and he and I would sit down and I'd say, "Now, Lord, let's go over this one more time. Why did you think it would be a good idea to have a Methodist church up here on Summit Drive in Greenville?"

And I'd listen, but I'd never really understand.

"OK," I'd say. "But why a church with these people? If I were making a church, I could certainly do a better job than you did in inviting people to join."

And the Lord would say, "Look, this is my farm. Right. I'll run my farm the way I'll run my farm. It's my farm."

21

More

December 16, 1990

The Spirit of the Lord GOD is upon me, because the LORD has anointed me to bring good tidings to the afflicted; . . . to bind up the brokenhearted, to proclaim liberty to the captives, and the opening of the prison to those who are bound; to proclaim the year of the LORD's favor. . . . They shall build up the ancient ruins, they shall raise up the former devastations. . . . The Lord GOD will cause righteousness and praise to spring forth before all the nations.

Isaiah 61:1–2, 4, 11 RSV

Christianity is a thoroughly eschatological faith, no matter what some contemporary would-be retrievers of the "historical Jesus" may claim. Yet eschatology has always been a tough topic for us preachers. Advent is the supremely eschatological, apocalyptic season. Thus my attempt to preach eschatology in this 1990 chapel sermon.

There is more to life than meets the eye. There is more in our past than history can tell. There is more going on in the present moment than we know. There is more to our relationships with one another than we are aware. And the more we explore the mystery of our lives, the more we learn about ourselves, the more mysterious ourselves become. Seldom have we been content with what appeared on the surface; we know there is more. Seldom have we felt fully at ease in the present moment, sensing, however inchoately, that no matter how full our present, beyond the now, there is more.

We tend, if left to our own devices, toward reductionism. Here in academia, we ought to be exploring possibilities, enriching our sense of what is not known, cultivating wonder. Alas, if left to our own devices, we reduce the cosmos to the periodic table. We explain human history by reducing it to two or three factors, the six causes of the Civil War, the main reason for the Great Depression, thirty true-false statements explaining the eighteenth century. In our better moments, when delivered from our own devices, when the modern analytic gives way to the eternal poetic, we know there is always more.

When life is reduced to technique, six easy steps toward sure success, flattened to a series of problems to be solved, we become numbed, anesthetized against either real pain or true pleasure. The body adjusts, in the absence of expectation, to its cage. But occasionally, someone manages to hit a nerve and we, twitching slightly in discomfort, suspect that there just may be more.

The audience for this Advent text from Isaiah are the afflicted, the brokenhearted, the captives, those in prison, and mourners. In short, your average Durham December congregation. The people to whom these words are addressed are those who come to church out of a sometimes barely felt, sometimes fervently burning hope for more. The words also speak, though we know not how they will hear, to those who have stopped coming to church because they have given up hoping for anything else.

Isaiah says that God has intervened, that God has anointed one to take action. That action announced is political—release of prisoners, reparation for the ruined cities, justice. The intervention is announced by the poetical. It's just poetry here. Poetry with dangerous (dangerous for the establishment, that is) political repercussions. The "year of the Lord" which Isaiah announces is jubilee time, when everything to which the established political order would have us adjust is turned upside down, set right, and the devastated, empty streets of downtown Durham are transformed into a great festival. When we were slaves in Egypt, God intervened and brought us out. We had learned to be content with our lot in Egypt. At least in slavery, our masters gave us three square meals a day. God intervened and led us toward more. Intervention is needed again, some decisive intrusion which will enable new life and halt our march toward death. Israel and church struggle to describe this intervention. Exodus. Bethlehem. Calvary. The upper room. The empty tomb. Without intervention, then there is no hope, for there is no "more." And, thank God, because there is God, in circumstances of the worst brokenheartedness, captivity, imprisonment, and mourning, there is always more.

Isaiah speaks of a world beyond present arrangements, a world where there is good news, liberty, comfort, garlands instead of ashes. This is biblical apocalyptic, Bible talk about the more beyond the now. It is daring, poetic, politically significant speech, speech pushed to the boundaries in description of what God is breaking open among us, breaking open in dusty little out-of-the-way places like Bethlehem or Soweto. Isaiah's words refuse to abide within the confines of the rationality of the dominate society, refuse to be limited by common sense, everyday experience. Isaiah taught Mary to sing apocalyptically,

> My soul magnifies the Lord, and my spirit rejoices in God my Savior, . . . he has scattered the proud, . . . he has put down the mighty from their thrones, and exalted those of low degree; he has filled the hungry with good things, and the rich he has sent empty away. (Luke 1:46b–53 RSV)

When we come to church and are exposed to such speech from Isaiah or Mary, we are beckoned out beyond the world of predictability into another world of thought and risk and gift, in which divine intervention enables new life to break our prosaic reductions, to subvert our tamed expectations, and to evoke fresh faith. Dangerous hope leads to daring resistance. Docility is no longer possible for those who hear tell of more.

Being interviewed on television, a group of Soviet Christian dissidents was asked by a reporter, "Well, what do you want? Why aren't Soviet Christians satisfied with the new freedoms which Gorbachev has given? Why won't you now soften your criticism and support the government?"

The Christian dissident responded. The translator explained, "He says they are not satisfied. He says they want more."

Anything less is trap and delusion. Sunday, at its best, is a summons toward more. But not just any old more. Our vague, frequently reoccurring, gnawing sense of need, which we so often attempt to assuage by mere buying, accumulating, getting and giving, particularly at this time of year, is articulated and reformed as a groping after God and God's will. The more we desire is given a name, named "The year of the Lord's favor." The year in which God gets what God wants, when earth more closely resembles that which God first had in mind when God began forming nothing into something, less into more.

Poetic, apocalyptic, prophetic speech as that of Isaiah, or Mary, or an Advent hymn, doesn't just describe the world, it re-creates, makes a world. It is a world made open, with old, comfortable certitudes broken by the advent of a God who makes all things new. In the world where God comes, we are allowed to roam, to redecide. Here is poetic imagination assaulting ideology. New configurations of life yet unformed, unthought, undreamed, now available.

> The Spirit of the Lord God is upon me, . . . good tidings to the afflicted; . . . the opening of the prison to those who are bound; . . . to give them a garland instead of ashes. (Isa. 61:1, 3 RSV)

Here is Isaiah's poetic protest against religion reduced to slogan, morals, bumper sticker proverbs, thoughts for the day, religion relegated to the conventional, the boring rehash of the obvious and the already known. Here is protest against Sunday as adjustment to what is seen rather than probing of the more. We came to church for certitude, to touch base with the known, but apocalyptic speech does not give certitude. In the poetic, apocalyptic, Spirit-anointed space, possibility overwhelms necessity in life and we can breathe.

So we go forth after church. There are the same quarrels in the car on the way home, same tensions over the dinner table, same blue Monday. Now, however, we are aware of a new world, new hope, new possibility, new dreams, new hunger for something else, in short, we are aware of more. We see how greatly reduced, how tamed has been our truth. We who have tasted new wine, now thirst for more.

The Prince of Darkness whispers, "Adjust, adapt." The Prince wants to keep the world closed, for a closed world is easier to administer, and people without a future are more manageable than those with imagination.

Sometimes, on Sunday when we gather, the Prince rules the roost. No new thing is uttered or heard. The pulpit is the place of platitudes and comfortable cliches, proverbs and slogans and nothing more. But sometimes, on a cold Sunday in December, we peek over the horizon, stand on tiptoes with Isaiah, and there is more than we dared to expect. Somebody goes home from church newly discontent with present arrangements, hungry. Someone gets ready for more than just another Christmas. Advent becomes adventure. And we dare to wish for ourselves more, more for our world, more for others, and Isaiah laughs and Mary smiles. Poetry has carried the day against prose, and the Prince knows that he has lost a little of his territory to its true Lord. The Lord's newly reclaimed territory is you.

> The kingdom of the world has become the kingdom of our Lord and
> of his Christ, and he shall reign for ever and ever. (Rev. 11:15 RSV)

Did you read in the paper about the man in a depressed region of Appalachia, a coal miner out of work for months, who caught his children on the back porch thumbing through a Sears Catalogue, wishing. He flew into a rage, switched their legs, tore the Catalogue to bits, and sat down in his yard and wept.

Did you read in the Bible about the young woman in a depressed region of Judea, a poor unmarried mother-to-be who was caught wishing for more? Singing, "My soul magnifies the Lord, . . . for he has done great things for me. . . . He has shown strength . . . , he has scattered the proud . . . , he has put down the mighty . . . , and exalted those of low degree; he has filled the hungry with good things."

22

Public Sex

October 6, 1991

GENESIS 2:18–24
MARK 10:2–16

> Therefore a man leaves his father and his mother and cleaves to
> his wife, and they become one flesh.
>
> *Gen. 2:24 RSV*

*This sermon shows the influence of my work as a campus minister. It also displays my
sense that we preachers have, as one of our tasks, to argue for the tradition, to open
up the riches of Christian scripture and the joy of believing for a new generation.* *

While you were away over the summer, the Presbyterians, PC(USA), discovered sex. They issued a big report on sex at their General Assembly, voted it down by a margin of 95 to 5, the report that is. But not before Presbyterians captured many headlines, so shocked was the media to see staid Presbyterians talking in public about a subject like sex.

The report advocated "justice-love" for Presbyterians who wondered what to think about sex. Justice-love. I couldn't figure out what they were talking about. Neither could their own church. A Duke student said it well: "Justice-love, I gotta remember that. Next time I'm in the back seat of a Chevrolet, I'll tell her, 'This is justice-love!' That's good, 'justice-love'!"

The same sort of talk about sex has gone on in many of our churches. That which was once unmentionable among Christians is being discussed quite

---

*Thanks to Duke's Stanley Hauerwas for many of the insights here. See Hauerwas's new book, *After Christendom?* (Nashville: Abingdon, 1991). Lamar Williamson's commentary on *Mark* (Atlanta: John Knox Press, 1983) was also helpful.

openly. Not long ago, a group of Catholic ethicists criticized the traditional Catholic view that sex should only be for the "procreation and education of children." Too legalistic, negative, and narrow for today's Catholics. They urged instead that modern Catholics have sex for "creative growth toward integration" (*Human Sexuality: New Directions in American Catholic Thought* [New York: Paulist Press, 1977], 86). "Creative growth toward integration."

My own denomination (United Methodist) has spoken of the purpose of sex as part of "the fullness of our humanity." Not much help in the backseat of a Chevrolet.

I knew that TV evangelism was in big trouble when a TV evangelist confessed to having "a sexual encounter." Whatever happened to "fornication"? Now there's a good word: Fornication. You don't know what it is, but you know it's wrong!

What *is* sex for? And why should we be talking about it on Sunday, in public, in church, on Parents' Weekend? Well, the Bible talks about it, Jesus talks about it in today's Gospel (Mark 10:2–16). Early on, right at the first of creation, first book of the Bible, Genesis, there is talk of sex. In fact, no sooner has the human being been created (he's not yet a man, a "male") than God takes a look and says, "Not quite right. Something else is needed. Oh, I have it. It's not good to be alone. I'll make another model, more complicated, more advanced." And in a stunning second act of creation, God makes woman. Now there is man and there is woman, male and female, meant for companionship. "Be fruitful and multiply," God tells them. The very first (and I daresay most enjoyable) of God's commandments.

"Be fruitful and multiply." That's why, says Genesis, a man leaves his mom and dad (I don't know why only men need to leave their parents) and clings to his wife and they become "one flesh." Do you know how men and women become "one flesh," boys and girls? Could it be . . . *sex*? Yes! God created sex. It's in the Bible, there at the first. God created male and female and told us to multiply, to let go of our loneliness and become one flesh. See? You thought I was going to come down hard on you, tell you "No!" Serve as your parents' enforcer. No, sex is a creation, a gift of a God who is opposed to loneliness and big into oneness. Be fruitful! Multiply! Become one flesh!

But a great deal happened between the playful exuberance of Genesis 2 and the grim questions behind Mark 10.

"Jesus, is it OK for a man to divorce his wife, write her a note of divorce and send her away? Is that OK? Moses said it was OK."

Jesus answers, "*No. From the beginning it was not so. Read Genesis 2. In the beginning, God created male and female, not for separation but for reunion. One and one = one flesh.*"

So what happened between Genesis 2 and Jesus, between this joyful divine invitation to become "one flesh" and the disintegration of so many of our marriages, the mess of our families, today's war between men and women?

All I know is, in the beginning, it was not so.

I agree with Duke's Stanley Hauerwas, who says that the greatest corruption Christian thinking about sex has suffered in our age is not that we think sex is fun, or dirty, or pointless, but that we have come to think of sex as *private*. Despite the Bible's up-front talk of sex as early as Genesis 2, despite Jesus' willingness to buck the trend in his own society in regard to divorce, we have bought into the weird notion that sex is private, my own business, a secret exchange between me and (usually) one other person, nobody's business but my own, thank you. (We even hope to discuss abortion as a "right to privacy issue.")

I agree with those feminists who say that *sex is always about power*. When a professor who is in a position of power, tries to have sex with a student who is powerless, it's not only a moral issue, it's a political power issue. And I'm glad that many feminist thinkers are willing to talk about sex as a public act with public, political consequences for the subjugation of women in a society where men hold most of the power. Something social, political is at stake in sex.

One of the worst legacies of political liberalism is the unbiblical assumption that sex is a purely private, personal matter. "Who cares how he behaves in a bedroom as long as he votes right on the floor of the Senate?" That kind of thing.

Was this what the church was getting at back in the fifteenth century at the Council of Florence when it condemned "private marriage"? Marriage, the church said, must be public, "in front of witnesses." The church only condemned one kind of sex—sex in private. In so doing the church declared sex in marriage to be a public, political matter, something with implications for the whole society.

In fact, it could be argued that the church never believed in the existence of "premarital sex," or "sex outside of marriage" because, in the church's view, *all* sex was marital, that is *public*. Nothing about the way men and women love was without power consequences, therefore sex was too dangerous to allow people to do it alone or without public promises. Therefore all sex is "marital," i.e., *public*.

In a weird way, our modern society seems to have recognized this. Sex has come out of the closet only to be hauled into the courtroom with palimony suits, sexual harassment suits, rules about sex in the workplace. It's as if we have found out that sex is too dangerous, too risky, too potentially damaging to leave it to private individuals. So now we do it with help from the government. Personally, I can't imagine anything worse than governmentally supervised and sanctioned sex, but at least give modern Americans credit for realizing that they can't handle it alone.

The church agrees. Sex is a public, political, power-laden act too important to be kept private. We may be skeptical that sex is better managed by the modern bureaucratic state, but Christians agree that the questions raised by our sexual mess are inherently political, namely, *how can our sex give life to one another rather than destroy one another?*

That is why we say that, whether people know it or not, all sex is marital. The issue for Christians is not, How to do sex? It is, How to be faithful disciples? Look at the Service of Marriage in most churches. Note that the pastor or priest never asks, "John, Susan, have you had sex?" Not one time have I ever asked a couple at the wedding, "Are you virgins?" At weddings, we don't say that much about sex or love. Rather, we talk about promises, faithfulness.

As Paul Ramsey said, "Because the words, 'I love you' can mean 'I love me and want to use you to love me even more,' we do well to test our love by the promises of marriage" (*Basic Christian Ethics* [New York: Charles Scribner's Sons, 1950], 330). Can our declarations of love endure the demands of fidelity?

So that's why Christians don't get that excited about questions like, "Should I have sex with this person or not?" Who knows? That question is impertinent without first asking, "Well, who do you hope to be at 64?" or "How capable are you of deceiving yourself about the real motives behind your actions?" So it's not so much a question of sex but rather one of fidelity, faithfulness. We've found that there isn't much way to be faithful, to get real close to someone sexually without destroying them, other than through public promises. We don't have sex with people to whom we have not yet gone public with our promises.

Interestingly, in Mark 10, about the only time they ever got Jesus off on a discussion of sex, he seems interested only in discussing sex as a promise issue. He doesn't say (though he probably would), "Don't have sex with people you're not married to." Jesus says, "Disciples of mine don't break promises to someone, especially promises about sex." Look up the context of Jesus' words about divorce in Mark 10. He has been talking, not about sex or marriage (two subjects of little interest to Jesus), but about discipleship (Mark 8:27–10:52), about the public cost of following him down a narrow way not taken by most ruthlessly privatized Americans. Sex is only interesting to us as a discipleship issue, as our way of fulfilling our public responsibility as disciples to witness to the faithfulness of Christ in all that we do. We've gotten hung up on talk about sex because it's easier to talk about than discipleship.

So I should not have been conducting classes for the youth in my last church on "Sex and Dating from a Christian Perspective." ("Look, Mommie, *even the preacher* can talk about sex!") I should have been teaching the kids about how to be faithful. How do you keep promises to someone even when you're having sex with them, raising children with them, making car payments with them? That's the question. Fidelity. How can we be as faithful to the people we sleep with as Jesus has been to us?

Frankly, I don't think you can do it by yourself, sex or discipleship. You need somebody to back you up. There are just too many corrosive acids in modern life, eating away at our ability to be faithful to our commitments. We name them individuality or autonomy, hedonism, or the old who-cares-so-long-as-nobody-gets-hurt? You have been so schooled in the notion that your genitals are your own private, personal business that it is tough for you to sustain a public commitment to another human being. The modern corporation needs mobile people who are always ready to break ties, leave spouse and family behind and move on. It's not a good environment for good sex. Our capitalistic, consumer economy is better at the politics of severing oneness than in joining together as one flesh and being faithful.

But Jesus reminds us. We are not our own. We are not called to be free but to be faithful. You now need the church, more than ever, to give you something significant to do with sex, to enjoy sex as a gift of God, used in the service of God, rather than as a personal possession to be expended in self-gratification. Don't just have safe sex, have faithful sex. Jesus didn't promise his disciples safety. He promised us adventure. A chaotic, superficial society has made even sex among Christians interesting once again.

I worry about you in a world that has given you nothing more important to do with your sex than personal pleasure. Such use of sex does not defeat our loneliness, it intensifies it and as Genesis says, God thinks it is not good for us to be alone. I worry about a church that offers no better help to you in your struggles to be faithful disciples than to tell you to think for yourself. I disagree with Professor Marvin Ellison of Bangor Theological Seminary who cries, "Our pews are emptying and our outdated attitude about sex has a great deal to do with it." I love the young adult who stood up at the Presbyterian General Assembly and pled with her church to give her the means to resist what the world was doing to both sex and to disciples. She knew. Rather than affirming her, her church was pulling the rug out from under her in her struggle to be faithful.

A few years ago I talked with a Duke student (a Presbyterian!) who had given a semester to go work with Habitat for Humanity in Americus, Georgia, to spend a semester volunteering to help build homes for the poor. I had lunch with her when she returned to Duke.

"Americus, Georgia, is really small," she said. "There's nothing to do there at night except to go to a gospel sing at some little church. The college students who are there with Habitat do a lot of sitting on the porch in the evenings. We just have a beer and sit and talk."

"Millard Fuller doesn't mind if you have a beer?" I asked.

"Well, I guess he sort of looks the other way. But you can't sleep with each other," she said.

"Really? Is that because Millard is a Presbyterian?" I asked. "Doesn't want people to have a good time?"

"No. I don't think so," she said. "Millard says that there are just too many poor people without adequate housing for us to be wasting time."

I love that. That's putting sex in its place! Sex is a good gift of God. Like money (Mark 10:17–31), power, knowledge, the goodness of sex is for us relative to our attempt to be faithful disciples of Jesus. It makes all the difference in the world *how and for whom* we do it.

23

Don't Think for Yourself

November 3, 1991

DEUTERONOMY 6:1–9

MARK 12:28–34

Hear, O Israel: The LORD is our God, the LORD alone. You shall love the LORD your God with all your heart, and with all your soul, and with all your might.

Deuteronomy 6:4–5

Ancient wisdom becomes present truth in this All Saints' sermon. Deuteronomy is put in conversation with the modern university. Here I am, once again, helped by Walter Brueggemann, who showed me how Torah can still show us the way, if we dare submit to its countercultural truth.

You've seen *The Dead Poets Society*. A young teacher at an exclusive prep school invigorates his hung-up young men by admonishing them to doubt everything and "to think for yourselves." He rips up the textbook to prove to them that they ought not to be bound to anyone's opinion other than their own. Think for yourselves, he tells them.

A friend of mine noted that, despite the movie's claim that this teacher was liberating his hung-up young men, it would be difficult to think of a more conventional and conformist message in our day than "think for yourself." If there were ever a day when such advice was radical, it has passed.

Here's how the president of Yale welcomed freshmen to Yale last year:

The faculty can guide you. . . . We can take you to the frontiers of knowledge . . . but we cannot supply you with a philosophy of educa-tion any more than we can supply you with a philosophy of life. This

must come from your own active learning. . . . Yale expects that you
will take yourself seriously.

In other words, the university is clueless about what you should be doing
here, so "think for yourself." We have this curriculum, this smorgasbord of
courses and professors, but it's up to you. Think for yourself. Whether it all
adds to up anything by graduation is mostly up to you. Think for yourself.

A few weeks go, a woman in her seventies wrote me, enclosing a clipping
from the Raleigh newspaper (I think the Durham paper protected us from
this story) telling how American troops had buried alive about seven hundred
Iraqis in their trenches during the war. One GI was quoted as saying, "It was
just hands and arms sticking up out of the sand."

"Why was there no outrage over this?" she asked. "Where is the moral
voice of our churches?"

One response. Look lady, it's called war. It's a nasty business. Rules don't
apply. Besides, I've got my views about war or burying people alive. You've
got yours. Think for yourself.

When I got her letter I was reading *The Day America Told the Truth* (James
Patterson and Peter Kim [New York: Prentice Hall, 1991]). Ninety-one percent of us Americans lie routinely. Thirty-one percent of us who are married have had extramarital affairs lasting over a year, 86 percent of youth lie
regularly to parents and 75 percent lie regularly to best friends. One in five
Americans loses his or her virginity before the age of 13. Two thousand, two
hundred forty-five New Yorkers were killed last year by their fellow citizens,
up 18 percent. By the way, religion plays no role in shaping the opinions of
more than half of those who were asked their opinions on sex.

So it's a lie here, an extramarital affair there, and before long it's "hands
and arms sticking up out of the sand." We really are thinking for ourselves.
An alternative epistemology is asserted in today's texts from Jesus and
Deuteronomy.

> Keep these words that I am commanding you today in your heart.
> Recite them to your children and talk about them when you are at
> home and when you are away. . . . Fix them as an emblem on your
> forehead, and write them on the doorposts of your house and on your
> gates. (Deut. 6:6–9)

The "words" of which Deuteronomy speaks are the words of Torah, the
"law" of Israel. A better translation of Torah is "teaching" or literally, "to
point the divine finger." Torah is not so much the "law" we should not break
as it is the finger pointing in the direction we ought to go. When asked about
life's big issues, Jesus, faithful Jew, simply referred to today's text from Deu-

teronomy. We have been commanded to love God with all that we have, in all that we do, to the very depths of our being, and our neighbor as ourselves. This is Torah.

You may not know a lot about Jesus, may not be that straight on all he did and said, but today's text says this is all you need to know now—love God more than anything else and your neighbor as yourself. Class dismissed.

People who follow Jesus are those, like Israel before, who do not bow down to other Gods, be they called Eros, Mars, IBM, Amway, or U.S.A. (We're peculiar about whom we worship.) We do not use labels like Faggot, Kink, Nigger, or Broad, preferring instead sister, brother. (We have an odd notion of neighbors.)

Love God with all that you have and your neighbor as yourself. Take these words, advises Deuteronomy, paint them over your door, brand them on your forehead, talk about them on your way to the cafeteria, teach them to your kids, tatoo them on your biceps.

Here's an alternative way of knowing, a culturally disruptive epistemology. You are the willing victims of a mode of education which urges you to locate a normative answer solely within your own experience, as though your experience, particularly your racial, gender, cultural experience yields insights on the spot. (Think for yourself!) Therefore, most of my sermons begin with your experience, groping for some point of contact with what you already know. Torah, on the other hand, begins with something you cannot know without its being told to you. "Hear, O Israel, the Lord your God is one." *Don't* think for yourself. Thinking in Israel begins as an auditory act. Hear. Listen. Speak. Tell.

Unlike Yale or many of my sermons, Israel did not expect her young to devise insight via personal conjuring. You need not be the author of your own faith, for here is a faith which lies outside the confines of the individual psyche. Israel's sons and daughters need not invent secrets of life. Their parents love them enough to tell them the secrets. It is no coincidence that this faith is depicted as an exchange between an elder and a child, as the giving of an intergenerational gift. Being nineteen is trouble enough without having to make up the world as you go. The stance you will shortly assume at the Table with hands outstretched, open, ready to receive the gifts of bread and wine— this is the predominant posture for the acquisition of Torah-type wisdom.

Alas, parenting and education in our day have become little more than the management of conflicting "truth claims," a process of cool consideration of diverse alternatives. But not here, not at the feet of Torah. When your daughter asks, "What do these stones mean?" (Josh. 4:6) Torah does not answer: "Well, it might mean that God brought us out of Egypt and thereby owns us, or then again it might not."

No, in this curriculum there is only assertion, nervy, passionate assertion of truth which is reliable, coherent, confident in the face of chaos, narcissistic subjectivity, "hands and arms sticking out of the sand."

Don't think for yourself. "Torah is not just for children. Anomie is not a danger only for the young; it may surface in what is now conventionally called the 'crisis of mid-life' or anywhere else. All persons face the threat of darkness. . . . All persons need these times of 'homecoming' when they can return to the sureties which do not need to be defended or doubted. And that is what Torah is. It is homecoming . . ." (Walter Brueggemann, *The Creative Word* [Philadelphia: Fortress Press, 1982], 21).

A Torah-less world, where there are many gods and no neighbors is a world of only idols and enemies. We rush breathlessly from one worship service to another. Before long our only posture is that of bowing down, so accustomed have we become at submitting ourselves to many gods—the nation, the corporation, our own ego—all the while pitifully asserting that we are free. Having learned to bend ourselves before so many altars, there is almost nothing to which we will not stoop. A lie here, a deceit there, until we are able to walk past the "hands and arms sticking out of the sand" without a twitch of conscience. The Durham City Council is us all over.

With no Torah-induced neighbors, the world is driven only by competing, savage self-interest. Everyone, even those under our own roof, are enemies. The office is a battleground in the war of the sexes. Chaos leads to immobility. Having nowhere to stand, we can't make big moves.

A recent Duke graduate asked his old man, late one night, to tell him about life. "Tell me what you know," he demanded. For this childlike request, the young man received a mess of childish ramblings about an affair the old man had ten years ago, his cynicism about his job, his desire to chuck the whole thing and go live in the woods.

"Man, you are messed up!" said the son. Now, he's reduced to thinking for himself.

Torah asserts a counter way of wisdom which is intergenerational, public, countercultural, historical. We do not bear the burden of thinking for ourselves. Every time you walk in this building, but especially today, All Saints, a great host of predecessors speaks to you, if you dare to listen. They stare down at you from the windows, wanting to show you the way. Saints are people who managed to love God even more than life and neighbor, even more than self, and thereby received true life. Saints are people of the past who push into our present and make the God question and the neighbor question the only interesting questions to be answered. Christians are those who learn to think with the saints. Thereby, we think much more creatively than we could if left to our own devices.

St. Francis, Martin Luther King, Teresa of Calcutta, Gideon, Mary. They help us to think beyond ourselves, despite ourselves. Thereby, in this act of holy remembering, options are envisioned, we are encouraged, a new world (not of our own devising) is offered. We get some big ideas.

Torah, and the saintly lives thereby produced, is a kind of intelligence by proxy.

Immanuel Kant once said, "I stand in awe of two things: the starry heavens above and the moral law within."

I still am awed by the "starry heavens."

24

Jesus Goes to School

December 22, 1991

LUKE 2:41-52

After three days they found him in the temple, sitting among the teachers, listening to them and asking them questions. And all who heard him were amazed.

Luke 2:46–47a

As a campus minister I spent most of my pastoral time with people for whom college and the allegedly "best years of life" were much less than good. College is great for some; grim for others. To be a student, particularly at a selective, prestigious university, is to have many opportunities to look small. So just before Christmas, when the Gospel reports the only event we have from Jesus' youth, I found myself thinking about school. I noted the curiosity of the central position of this pericope, carved in limewood over the Duke Chapel altar. I recalled what it was like to be in school.

I had a number of letters in response to this sermon. One was from a banker who said, "To this day I cannot even go to the PTA meeting with my wife because I become ill just walking in a public school—too many bad memories. I'm glad that Jesus is not afraid to go places where I never want to return."

I want you to look at a scene in the center, up over our altar on what's called the reredos. Only the choir can see it well. I invite you to come up and see it at the end of the service. Carved in limewood is an episode from Jesus' childhood. It's today's Gospel—the boy Jesus before the elders in the Temple.

I've traveled much, visited many churches, studied art history. I know of no other church in the world which has that not-too-well-known scene from Jesus' life in so prominent a place. I know of no iconographic parallels in churches either ancient or modern. There, as centerpiece of the scriptural program of the building, stands little Jesus before the big, adult scholars of the Temple.

We know nothing of Jesus' childhood except for this one episode. As a boy, did Jesus help out Joseph in his carpenter's shop? We don't know. Did he sometimes accompany his mother, Mary, on her trips to market? We don't know. The only thing we know of him as a boy was that he astonished the scholars up at the Temple with his knowledge of the Bible. He dared to debate them, dared to interpret Scripture to the interpreters. He looks to be about twelve, probably there for his bar mitzvah. How many of you are sixth-graders? Can you imagine yourself standing in front of the Duke Department of Religion debating, interpreting, exegeting? Well, there is Jesus. And there are the scholars. You can clearly see on their faces their amazement.

Now I know that many of you are on vacation from school and the last thing you want to hear discussed is school. You're here to forget school. But I want you to ponder this: We don't know anything about Jesus from his birth in Bethlehem until he's an adult except for this—he was a spectacular student, he amazed the teachers, knew more about the Bible than men who had spent their whole lives studying Scripture. And somebody had the bright idea to put that scene over our altar. Why is this all that we know about Jesus from birth until about age 30? Why, of all the scenes from his life, was this deemed to be among the most important for portrayal at Duke Chapel?

Here's what I think. I think that scene of Jesus before the scholars at the Temple was put there, at a university chapel, for everyone who's young enough, small enough, to remember what it's like to be in school. It's just for you.

Remember what it's like to be in school? I'm old, grown up, beyond the reach of education, but I can still remember a little bit about school. For one thing, I remember the smell. Schools smell like—schools—they have a special odor. Not a bad odor exactly. It's just an odor like—school. I remember smelling a similar odor when I visited a parishioner in the state penitentiary. A coincidence? You make the call.

Another thing. When I was in schools they didn't have telephones. In every school I've ever been in, there's only one telephone. It's up at the office. It's guarded by this person, the same one who guards the permission slips and the staplers. Even if you're a teacher, you have to go through this guard to use the telephone. For some reason schools believe that, if you let in more telephones some geometry teacher might try to use it without permission, and the whole place would explode into anarchy! Once they get you in school, they don't want you trying to make contact with the real world.

Many of my fondest memories of school involve being sent by the teacher to go look for a three-pronged adapter plug for the filmstrip projector. The teacher would come in on Monday, look us over, groan and say, "Class, today we're going to have a filmstrip on 'Rubber Cultivation in Borneo.'" Curtis Clinkscales would ask, "But isn't this a class in geometry?"

"Shut up, Curtis," she would explain.

She would get the film out of the can, have us move our desks back, struggle to get the screen hoisted, take the cord to the projector in hand, look at it and say, "Give me a break. Williamson, Williston, Willimon, whatever, go get the adapter plug."

The rest of the class hated me for it.

I'd go down the hall, down the steps, over to the principal's office to the guard dog stationed there, "No, you can't use the telephone," she would say.

"We need a three-pronged plug," I'd say.

So I was off to drama, then by the band room, a quick stop at social studies, glancing briefly out the third floor stairway window. "Look, there are people out there. Driving cars. Walking dogs." (It always comes as a shock, when you're in school, that there are people running loose who are not.) Fifteen gloriously wasted minutes later I give the news, "No adapter to be found, Miss Boggs."

"Sit down," she explained. She then did the only thing a person in her desperate situation could do. She went to the door of the classroom, looked both ways up and down the hall to be sure the principal was nowhere to be seen, turned her back discreetly to the class, and then ripped that third prong off that plug, shoved that plug into the receptacle and told us that this was our opportunity to know more about "Rubber Cultivation in Borneo" than anybody else in Greenville.

Remember school? It's hard to remember what it's like to be in school, hard to remember, until you leave a little one at the door, abandoning her to strangers and then drive away, or go to a parents' conference and you're told by the teacher why your child is not doing well in algebra, and then you say, "Now I remember how much I hated algebra when I was in school and why I had to become anything other than an accountant when I grew up."

I had forgotten what it was like to be in school, what it was *really* like, until a few years ago I went back to school. I decided to brush up on my German. I started over here at Duke. First year German. Eight freshmen and I. I had forgotten what it was like to be in school.

"Please tell us the prepositions which require the accusative."

"Well, let's see. There is *an, auf,* or is it *aus, ausser*?"

"We are waiting. Prepositions which require the accusative. Surely you know them. You had all weekend to prepare."

"But I was rather busy this weekend and . . ."

"We do not want to have to hurt you . . ."

"Oh yes, *aus, ausser, bei, mit, nach, seit, von, zu.*"

Homecoming weekend. End of class on Friday, professor said, "By the way, class, I will give you a quiz on Monday. Last six chapters." She brushed out the door.

"Are you people going to take that?" I asked the class (after the professor had left). "Don't you people have any plans for the weekend? I do. Tell her we don't want a quiz on Monday."

"*You* tell her," they said. It was a busy weekend.

I had forgotten, you see, what it is like to be in school, that is to say, *what it was like to be small.* School has a way of making you the smallest you will ever be in your whole life.

In my freshman seminar last year there was a person who sat through most of the semester and never opened her mouth in the class discussion. One night, she at last made a comment so succinct, so right, so to the point, made it in a marvelously melodically accented voice (similar to my own). After class I pulled her aside.

"I ought to wring your neck. Why didn't you speak up in class before now? You have a lot to say. We need you."

"Well, I'm from a tiny high school in a little town in South Carolina and all these people know so much and have been so many places. I was scared to speak."

"I'm from a little town in South Carolina," I said, "and look at me."

But you see, she was a student. She was still in school. Do you know what that's like? Small. Vulnerable. Not wishing to appear stupid. There are few things more horrible than the derisive, scornful laughter of a classroom, particularly when the laughter is led by the teacher. And I have been known to wake up in a cold sweat at night having dreamed that I was back in high school and I was staring at a black, abysmally black board, class to my back, chalk in hand, having been sent there to conjugate a Latin verb.

A little boy was sent home one day with a note pinned to his coat reading, "Thomas is too dumb to learn. School is a waste for him." His name was Thomas Alva Edison.

The judgments made against you in school can be the most devastating you will ever receive. School can make you feel the smallest you will ever feel in life.

And this Sunday's Gospel, this Christmas Sunday gift, is a story about Jesus in school. A little boy, from a poor, uneducated family, stands before the scholars in the Temple, toe-to-toe with them, instructing rather than being instructed by them. Can you see it from where you sit? You may be a little too big to see it clearly, but if you're small, I think you can see it fine.

The story is childlike, a kind of fairy tale right at the beginning of Jesus' life. It belongs with other such stories, told and retold by children. Jack outsmarts the giant. Little Red Riding Hood puts one over on the wolf. Little David gets the best of great big Goliath. It's a story about that.

It's a childlike snapshot of the boy, Jesus. Uncomplicated, playful, improbable, easy to remember. It is a story told with delight by little people, those who do not do well on the SAT, those who do not have access to powerful thoughts and big ideas. It is a story to be told again and again by those who can't get to the great books of the Western world, who don't even try to fill out the admissions application because they cannot endure another rejection, people who when you say "university" hear about a place they will never go, who when they hear "school" get a sick feeling in the stomach.

For whom was this story told? Who among us then or now would have heard it and exclaimed, "You tell 'em, Jesus!"

I believe it was the little people. This is the sort of story able to electrify the small, the weak, the vulnerable, by reminding them whose side God is on, who God's advent means to astonish. Mother Mary had sung, when told she would have a baby, "God is going to bring down the proud and lift up the lowly." You're seeing that here, live, before your eyes.

It is a story meant to unnerve the scholars, to make uneasy those who know the Bible backward and forward, who always have just the right chapter and verse on the tip of their tongue. It means to create a new world where deliverance is at hand for those who are small, and those on the bottom get to go to the head of the class, and little Jesus knows more than just people with a Duke PhD.

So in a way, it's everyone's story, this little story of little Jesus astounding the big people up at the Temple because in a weird way, *everybody gets to be small someday*. I wish I could tell you sixth-graders that the bigger you get, the more grown up you become, the more certain you are of the right answers. No. No matter how big and adult you get, there are still times when you feel small. It might be in school, or in a hospital, or in a family. Everybody gets to be small, someday.

And this story says, *he's been there*. He knows what it's like. Luke says that after amazing these scholars at the Temple Jesus obediently returned home with his parents, back home to where he "increased in wisdom and stature," which is a fancy Bible way of saying he grew up. But little Jesus never got so big that he couldn't remember what it was like to stand before the educational, intellectual, theological powers and be made to answer. He never got so educated, tamed, and refined that he got over his youthful tendency to stand before the educational, political, economic powers as a kid and to ask them tough questions.

Later in Luke, Jesus says, "They will hand you before kings and into law courts, they will test you, quiz you, force you to answer. Don't be afraid! The

Holy Spirit will tell you what to say. I'll give you the answer you need. I've been there. They're just the sort of bigwigs I love to amaze and astonish."

In two days we'll gather to celebrate the birth of baby Jesus. We're going to have a grand, glorious time because of a baby. When the great, powerful God of the universe came among us, he came *as a baby*. Ponder that. He came to us weak, vulnerable, and small. In a way, he never grew up. Bad news when you're big; good news when you're small.

And aren't we all, sooner or later?

25

Tears Today, Laughter Later

February 16, 1992

Blessed are you who weep now, for you will laugh.

Luke 6:21b

The upside-down spirit of Luke's beatitudes animated this 1992 sermon, preached on a cold February day hoping for Epiphany. I'm (again) indebted to Walter Brueggemann, Interpretation and Obedience *(Philadelphia: Fortress Press, 1991), 313–321, for the form of this sermon.*

I know that you do not feel nearly as good as you look.

I know that, though you may be dressed in your Sunday best, hair combed, seated in orderly rows of pews, not all of you are in order. And some of you have come here hoping that some voice might cut through the hymns of praise, the high-sounding cliches and name your pain rightly. Others of you have come hoping that the hymns, the prayers, the words will help you to forget, for fifteen minutes. I know because I know myself. I know all your tricks for denial, of evasion, because I play them myself as well as you—only better.

I am happy that I do not preach at the Crystal Cathedral. I would not want to be a preacher in one of those TV happy churches, where everyone looks so good, so happy, so successful, and they must bill their preachers when they get gray and reach fifty.

I would not want to preach before a congregation who measured Sunday on the basis of how good they grinned by the service's end. All it takes is one cancer diagnosis, or an anorexic child, or a lousy grade in Orgo or even Poli-Sci for that jig to be up.

134

In our better moments, we sense that our pain is interconnected, symptom of some deeper disorder at the center: the cancer a tip that our overly consumptive environment is poisoned; anorexia a possible revolt against a consumeristic culture, or at least evidence of the pathology of a world in which appearance is everything. A people who bomb babies in Baghdad need not be shocked at an epidemic of baby bashing in Durham. Our purely private pain may be indicative of more public pathologies. The secret, personal disorders which you brought in here this morning, the pain that you know not how to name, may be the inner aches and pains that tip you off that something is wrong, something is shifting, moving in the wider world; like an old man's aching knees that only ache when the weather is about to change.

Jesus came down with them to a level place and mingled with the crowd. When Matthew tells this tale (Matt. 4:23–25), he has Jesus go up on a mountain. Luke puts Jesus right down in the middle of us where he can feel what we feel. He saw their "diseases" their "unclean spirits" (Luke 6:18). Then Jesus said, "Blessed are you who weep now, for you will laugh" (6:21). Lucky are those of you who are enough in touch with reality to weep. Lucky if you've still got enough of your wits about you to be able to cry.

Jesus came down out of the pulpit and stood on a level place, among them, and summoned people to weep. Fortunate are those of you who are empty now, poor, who haven't got enough to make it, and know it. Blessed are you who suffer from gnawing hunger and can't be satisfied. Lucky are you who weep.

She told me, "I'm surprised by the difficulty I've had getting over his death. I do all right for a couple of days and then something will hit me, I'll open a drawer, see an old photo and I'm undone. I've got to make more progress on this grief."

"You *are*," I told her. I quickly learned, as a pastor, that grief is only dangerous when it is unable to grieve. The strong ones are those who are strong enough to weep.

When I went back into the parish after a stint of seminary teaching, I was surprised by how much of my time was spent with depressed people. Depression appears to have reached epidemic proportions in the average parish. I had one parishioner, had spent hours with her, trying to cheer her up, trying to help her think more positively about her situation. One morning she called me, "Can you come by today? I need help. I'm so down." I said I would. I had been studying a commentary on Jeremiah by Walter Brueggemann. (He'll preach here in two weeks.) Brueggemann says the prophets of Israel were poets. Through words, just words they incite people first to weep, for in weeping is relinquishment, letting go of an old order, that a new world might be offered and embraced. The first prophetic act of defiance against the status quo is tears. It takes great courage to weep.

That afternoon, I had different pastoral care to offer my chronically depressed parishioner. "I've been treating you as if you were sick or something, as if your depression were a kind of character flaw, a weakness. Now I wonder, maybe you're well and we happy ones are sick! A lot of people think this town is a great place to live. But you, being perceptive, have a hunch that we may be in big trouble. You're depressed, what the Bible calls grief. That's good. Your depression could be a sign that God is helping you to let go in order that you might be given something better. Tears are at least a beginning of health."

"Seeing the joy of a bubble-brained world," said the poet Auden, "I was glad I could be unhappy."

Or, as Jesus said, "Lucky are you that weep now" (Luke 6:21). Lucky if you've noted that something is dying. Fortunate, for the pain in your private life might be the foretaste of a larger dismantling.

For Jesus, there was something more dangerous than tears. It was the dangerous deception that our world is secure, stable, the best of all possible worlds. Don't worry, be happy. He warns of that deception, "Woe to you who are laughing now" (Luke 6:25). Woe if you feel too good, settled too comfortably with the way things are.

Against such self-congratulatory self-deception, Jesus hurls a prophetic word: "Woe to you that laugh now." "Lucky are you that weep." If you are twenty-two, thinking of graduation, you are possibly on the verge of tears. What's the matter with you? You ought to be happy to be at last getting out of here! Let me suggest that your disease may be an intelligent response to the present dilemma. We are gradually awaking from our great national daydream. If you're nineteen or twenty, you have been raised by the most selfish generation ever to rule America. In the seventies, eighties, and now the nineties we have squandered your inheritance, run up an unbelievable deficit, stolen from your children and grandchildren, and called that prosperity. And some of you know that the old world is ending, the old American, white male, Milton Friedman, George Will, Ronald Reagan, Robert Schuller world is going and you grieve because it feels like something secure and precious is being ripped off. You face commencement with a sense of loss, empty-handed, uncertain. We have two choices. We can either cry honestly or, in our mechanisms for denial, blame it on the Japanese.

Jesus offers another choice, a way spoken amid the ruins of Jerusalem, the wreckage of the Temple, the first demise of Western culture in the rubble of Imperial Rome. Jesus' word: Lucky if you embrace the loss, touch the pain, weep. Then he promised, "You shall laugh." You shall sing, rejoice, see a new world offered out of the ruin. You can't hear that hopeful word anywhere except out beyond grief embraced. To hope too soon, to laugh too easily, is self-deception, the reduction of Christian hope to November campaign fluff. Weep now that you may laugh later.

Our faith asserts that God gives life and hope, confidence in the midst of your chemotherapy or an IBM interview. We don't know *how*. We academic types are tempted toward an easy pessimism that masquerades as intelligence, willing to speak of the loss but without the guts to hope in the promise. Humor, laughter, is considered therefore to be inappropriate to serious discussion. Jesus says laughter is the fruit of serious admission of death, followed by bold embrace of God's life-giving promise.

"You will laugh," asserts Jesus. Not out of bubble-brained faith in some program of self-esteem, human betterment, or the productions of SRI. You will laugh because God is alive and busy, puttering about the ruins of the Reagan years getting ready to bring newness.

Of course, with the promise is a warning by Jesus: "If you laugh now, you will end crying." If you spend too much energy thinking positively about what is, you won't receive what will be. If you clutch too tightly what you have, your hands won't be open for my gift.

"You will laugh." I don't know which assertion of Jesus is more difficult to believe. "Lucky are you that weep now" or "You shall laugh." Is this true, that we must, like the recovering alcoholic in AA, hit bottom, cry it out, let go before we can be healed? Is it true that our future will not be brought by our own cautious retrenchment but rather the result of God's joyful gift?

Yes, says the church. The prophets have not lied to us. Yes, joy is a gift on the other side of grief, a gift of a God whose initiative is not limited by our myopic vision. Yes, Sunday morning is a move out beyond our tears, bold venturing forth beyond our present data. Without Sunday, all we've got is the hopeless grief of a bereft world left to its own devices, or the temporary diversion of the Super Bowl.

God wills the dismantling, works with the letting go. We will laugh later like Sarah, who first cried when told she was going to give birth at ninety, only to laugh later when she did; like the disciples who wept when Jesus told them that he was going away in order to come back better than before, they laughed on Easter when he did. The blessed, beatific promise: The way to laughter leads through loss, begins in grief, ends in joy, when God turns *tears to laughter, and the joke is on us.*

26

A Terrifying Tale

April 12, 1992

> ... others cut branches from the trees and spread them on the road. The crowds ... were shouting, ... "Blessed is the one who comes in the name of the Lord!"
>
> *Matthew 21:8b–9*

The liturgy of Palm/Passion Sunday is one of the most dramatic and rich of the whole year. The service begins in front of the chapel with the blessing of the palms. The great bells ring from the tower and all parade in waving branches and singing, "All Glory, Laud, and Honor." There are dancers and much loud music.

Then at some point the mood changes. The sermon sets a somber tone. After the sermon a student stands and recites the Gospel—the longest lesson of the year—the story of Jesus' passion, during which worshipers shout, "Crucify him!" on cue. After a wild rendition of "Lord of the Dance," all leave the chapel in silence.

It's the sort of Sunday when the preacher is able to say less, to leave much unexplained and unfinished, to be cryptic and let the liturgy do its work. The service is so rich that the sermon becomes a brief commentary on the liturgy, homiletical preparation for the rest of the week, a question that can only be answered in the unfolding events of the most mysterious of weeks.

On this day, crowds welcomed Jesus into Jerusalem by waving palm branches and shouting as he bounced into town on the back of a donkey. The waving of palm branches is usually interpreted as a biblical sign of welcome, hospitality. But recently I was reading an anthropologist who noted that, in some cultures, people wave branches to ward off approaching evil or terror. The branches are like an extension of our arms, an attempt to protect ourselves from impending horror. What if those waving palm branches were not simply an exuberant outburst of hospitality, but also a dark, unconscious attempt to ward off Jesus, to protect the inhabitants of Jerusalem from the invasion of this strange, terrifying intruder?

If that be so, then we ought to be waving palm branches every time we open the Bible. Terror is no stranger to the Bible. The Bible is a frequently terrifying book. On Sunday morning, read here, the Bible can sound less terrifying than it is. But on a Sunday like this one, it is hard for us, even with our urbane moralizing and rationalization, to escape the terror of the text, to evade the underlying, dark, sinister implications behind the events of Palm Sunday and Holy Week. An innocent man is about to be tortured to death, murdered before our eyes.

We were shocked when, in the Old Testament, God asks Abraham to kill and then burn on an altar his only son. And yet here in the New Testament, God is preparing another only son for a cross. How could a loving God do such a thing? Dare we speak of such horrifying reality in church?

To enter into this chapel on Sunday is to enter a dark, cavernous, overpowering place. Take this building, and how it feels to slide in on a Sunday morning, as a parable of what it is like to come face-to-face with this inscrutable God. People who follow this God are people who obey God usually without the least idea of how things are going to turn out in the end. Consider Jesus. On this day, Jesus bounces into town on the back of a donkey. But his Palm Sunday parade moves toward an end which he does not yet know. Take Jesus' entry into Jerusalem as a parable for how it often feels to follow this God. Oh, certainly, we may have faith that things will ultimately turn out according to God's will. But if we know anything about the God of the Bible, we know that God's will may be radically different from our own, so there is reason to fear along the way.

Recently, Barbara Brown Taylor, an Episcopal preacher (who preached here in the chapel last summer), spoke of "Texts of Terror" within the Bible. Among what she considered to be the most terrifying texts within Scripture, Taylor listed the killing of the firstborn of the Egyptians (Exod. 11:5); the ordering of Saul to slaughter the Amalekites down to the last woman, child, and donkey (1 Sam. 15:3); and those other texts in which the judgments of God serve to "separate me from my stuff." I assume Brown Taylor has in mind Jesus' command to sell everything we have and follow him (Mark 10:21) or perhaps the refusal to open the door to the foolish bridesmaids (Matt. 25:12). She says that these texts "are terrible to me because they expose my vulnerability. If God can condemn Amalekite babies for the sins of their parents, then is there no hope for me?" (She is from Georgia, so she has reason for this concern.) "Nor can I find safety in following Jesus, if selling all that I own is the way. So of course I will find myself on the wrong side of the door when the time comes, hearing my muffled sentence pronounced through the latch: 'Truly, I tell you, I do not know you.' These are terrible texts because they remind me how helpless I am, how frail and not in charge I am. While there are clearly things I can do to improve my life and things I can do to cheapen it, my fate is ultimately out of my hands. I cannot control God's disposition toward me, and that is terrifying." ("Preaching the Terrors," *Journal for Preachers*, Lent 1992, p. 4)

This Sunday, as we follow along behind Jesus, bouncing on the back of a donkey toward a fate he does not yet know, can we not feel the terror of being met by a sovereign God who is so radically different from us? Here is a God whose mind we cannot read, whose decisions we cannot predict. Are we prepared to go with *this* God?

As a preacher I am tempted to try to protect you from an encounter with this God. Rather than meditate upon the horror of a God who would ask Abraham to sacrifice his only son, I will quickly remind you that a ram was provided in the thicket, which, at the last minute, saved Isaac from his father's knife. Or rather than speak of the terrifying unknown that awaits Jesus on Friday afternoon at Golgotha, I will jump ahead to the raising of Jesus on Easter. Through such homiletical sleight of hand, I will attempt to reassure you that what at first appears to be so awful and terrifying is really not so terrible.

Even the form of my sermon, with its three points and attempted reasoning, deflates the awesome, dislocating terror before us in these passages. Just someone standing up and talking about these terrors, in a resonate tone of voice, can lead you to believe that biblical terrors are less terrifying than they first appear.

What are we to do after a thousand funerals for the Egyptian babies, the heaped, bloody bodies of slaughtered Amalekites, the awesome judgments of a God who slams the door in the face of procrastinating bridesmaids, who leads a good, innocent one like Jesus toward his appointment with bloody destiny on Golgotha? These terrible texts which remind us of how helpless we are, how frail and how out of control we are?

In a weird sense, there is some consolation just knowing that these texts are, in fact, in the Bible. A religion is no good if it will only speak on bright, sunny days, but has nothing to say for the late-night sweats, the 3:00 a.m. nightmares. A faith which is relevant only for orderly, placid, lives is little faith at all.

Every year or so, I take down the short stories of Flannery O'Connor and read them. Name me an author who looks so unflinchingly at life, particularly the underside, who portrays so vividly our mixed motives, inner inconsistencies, the absurdity and the tragedy of our goodness. Violence lurks beneath the surface in Flannery O'Connor's stories and few of her stories end without that violence bubbling over the top. Her stories do for me what Bruno Bettelheim said that fairy tales do for young children—they help us to see our worst fears acted out, to name our unnamed terrors. Oddly, this is redemptive.

The terror which lurks behind this story of Palm Sunday is recognizable to us. We recognize our faces in the faces of the crowd, those who first adoringly welcome Jesus into Jerusalem, only to turn against him in a frenzy of bloodshed and violence by the end of the week. We know the way in which we recognize our saviors, falling down before them in gratitude when we believe that they will give us everything our hearts desire, turning against them in angry resentment when they do not deliver what we expect. And somehow it is redemptive just to see that so honestly depicted in the Bible, present in the Bible even as it is in life. If the Bible were only about lilies of the valley and birds of the field, it would not be *our* book. But the Bible is our book. It is about us—the people we are rather than the people we wish in our fantasies we were. And because the Bible is truly about us, it is often a very terrifying book.

More than just accurately describing our terrors, the Bible depicts a God who embraces our misbegotten cruelty. God did not have Jesus stand over Jerusalem wringing his hands at the sight of mixed human motives, our evil, our sin. God beckoned Jesus into Jerusalem, through Jerusalem, all the way up to Calvary. God does not simply name and judge our terrors; God is present in them, working our redemption in ways that we are not equipped to see. The savior who rode in among us on Palm Sunday intruded into our lives the same way a surgeon's knife cuts into our bodies. If we are to be healed of what ails us, our healing will not be painless. The terrible events behind this week ask each of us: Are we prepared to follow God through *all* the events of our lives, or just the events which meet with our approval?

God does not mean simply to improve us but radically to save us, even though much to which we cling must be brought to death for that to happen. Last Sunday, the Gospel of John and the sermon spoke of Jesus' visit to the home of Lazarus. Jesus had just raised Lazarus from the dead, but no sooner had Jesus performed this act of life than Mary anoints Jesus for his own burial. There is bitter irony in that, as John says, by raising Lazarus from the dead, the religious authorities mark Jesus for death. The demon death stalks Jesus every step of his way. His very acts of life marked him for death. This suggests that the gospel itself is a terrifying story for all of us who wish to avoid suffering and death. Like a vulture perched in a tree, waiting for the last breath of life to be gone so it can swoop down and devour everything, death lurks in the shadows throughout every event of this week. And the story asserts: *God wills this.* Jesus does not begrudgingly give up his life unto the forces of evil. He offers it willingly. He wades into the bloody darkness alone, in quiet confidence that he will not be alone forever.

Of all the memorable moments of worship in Duke Chapel throughout the year, few are more memorable for me than today, Palm Sunday. As this long, violent, dramatic story is read before the congregation, tension builds. We know how today's story ends. We know, because this is always the way the story ends—in betrayal, violence, and death. As if to seal that terrible knowledge, there is that point in the story when Jesus stands before his accusers and is made to face the crowd. The same crowd who yelled, "Hosanna!" when he marched into Jerusalem a few days before, now yells, "Crucify him!"

The voices arise from out of the congregation. They are *our voices.* Spoken in our language, with our accent. They are the voices of fellow students, friends, faculty; the violent voices are our own. It is a stunning moment of terrible realization—the voices which scream for the crucifixion and death of Jesus are our voices.

But the good news is that our voices are not the last word on this week. Jesus did not flinch from the murderous mob. He did not sidestep the terror or miraculously escape deus ex machina into some divine world, hermetically sealed from human pain and terror. He came among us. He passed through the waving palm branches (branches waved either to welcome him or to ward him off, we know not) and marched with us up to death. The Place of the Skull. He embraced the terror, all the terrible, horrifying, painful ambiguity of human existence, and from the cross said, "Brothers and Sisters, I love you still."

27

I'm Saved, You're Saved, Maybe

May 24, 1992

ACTS 15:1–2, 4–11

One thing is sure about Jesus: Jesus saves. It was not just that Jesus saved, it was whom he saved that got him into such difficulty. The expansive reach of Christ was too wide for most of us, particularly when he embraced those who are not like us. Universities tend to be exclusive, selective, elitist places. Therefore a sermon on the rather reckless, inclusive, way Jesus saves rabble . . . like us.

I have been heard to say, about this time of the year, after commencement when the campus is serene, mostly empty of undergraduates, "We would have a nice little school year if it were not for these students!"

And being in the church, loving the body of Christ, would be much easier for me, if it were not for *you.*

One of you said it within my hearing the other day. "I prefer worship in Duke Chapel because, unlike a *real* church, I don't know anyone who is there with me on Sunday, and they don't know me."

Jesus told a story about us. Two people went up to the temple to pray (Luke 18:9–14). One was a disreputable scoundrel, a tax collector; the other, a Bible-believing, morally upright, church leader like us. The church person prayed, "God, I thank thee that I am not like other people—adulterers, fornicators, savings and loan swindlers, or even like this tax collector over there in the third pew."

I know that Pharisee's prayer by heart. Do you?

"Look, dear, in today's paper, it says that the Smiths' boy was arrested last night. DUI. Isn't that a shame. Yes, a real shame. Their son got arrested.

143

Ours has never been arrested. God, we thank thee that we are not like other parents."

And so, though it is a shame, it is also a comfort to be reassured by the morning paper that *we are not like them.*

Maybe that's one reason why we come to church, to be reassured, on a weekly basis, that *we are, despite our occasional foibles and peccadilloes, not like them.*

Take my last church. Please, take my last church. We decided to emphasize evangelism. Go out and get us some new members. We initiated a program for single young adults. A woman in the church began teaching a single young adult Sunday school class. We went out to get young adults.

I wasn't optimistic. This is a difficult age group to reach. They are single, go skiing on weekends, sleep until noon on Sundays, hang out at places called "The Red Armadillo."

Lo and behold, in two months, that little Sunday morning group had doubled in size. The evangelism worked! They were coming in, these single young adults, in droves! Good!

Well, not so good. My counseling load tripled. Turned out that lots of young adults come to our church because they have problems, want help with their problems. They were making decisions about whom to marry, what to do with their lives. My pastoral counseling load quadrupled.

"Preacher, somebody told me the other day, though I never go in that sort of place myself, that some group from our church was meeting on Fridays over at The Red Armadillo. You know anything about that?"

As things turned out, we did not want new members as much as we thought. From that time on, we limited our evangelism to those who gathered at Captain D's.

You could see it coming from almost the first chapter in the book of Acts. We were told that this Jesus Movement would spread, spread like wildfire, from Jerusalem, to Judea, out to Samaria, to the very end of the earth (Acts 1:8). But did we believe it?

Things went well enough in Jerusalem. Three thousand people converted after a five-minute sermon by Peter (2:14–42)! But they were Jews, people like us, Judeans. Six chapters later, we were out in Samaria where Philip preached and these Samaritans came forward saying, "How about us?" (8:4–12) Well, though they were Samaritans, they were at least first cousins of ours, almost like orthodox Jews, almost. And though Philip had some explaining to do when he got back to Jerusalem (8:14–25), we said, "Well, after all, Samaritans though they are, they are still in the family, *almost like us.*"

Next there was that Ethiopian eunuch (8:26–40). Ethiopian? Eunuch? Well, we said, although he was from the end of the earth, Ethiopia, he had an Isaiah scroll on him at the time so that makes him like family, sort of.

Jerusalem. Judea. Samaria. The end of the earth. Next thing you know, here is Peter, sheepishly showing up at Wednesday night prayer meeting, "I want you all to meet our latest convert, the newest Christian, Colonel Cornelius" (Acts 10).

"Well, I could have predicted it. You go out and baptize those Samaritans, the gate is open. I should have spoken up when you showed up with that Ethiopian. Now it's come to this. A Gentile. A Roman. A Roman Gentile soldier."

"Well, at least he's an officer. And there's only one of him. How much harm can that do?"

And thus we arrive at today's lesson from Acts. Since Cornelius, there have been more of these Gentiles. It was fine when there was only Col. and Mrs. Cornelius, but now they have brought their non-kosher friends and they have joined and now we have a full-scale Gentile problem on our hands. Some in the church said, "They can't be Christians until they first become Jews. Is not salvation of the Jews? Did not our Lord say quite clearly that he came for the lost sheep of the house of Israel? God has chosen only Israel for salvation. They cannot be Christians, until they are Jews."

The argument was the most serious since the birth of the church. It threatened to destroy the church. To admit these Gentiles without honoring the law of Israel would be to undercut everything upon which the church is based, for the church is based upon the promises of God to Israel. It would be like admitting that all of Scripture—Genesis, Exodus, through the prophets—is invalid.

On the other hand, can one only come to Jesus through Judaism? Is there no other way? Are there kindergarten Christians and graduate school Christians? First-class, circumcised Christians and then these Johnny-come-lately Gentiles?

Luke says, "There was no small dissension and debate" on this issue which is a polite way of saying, they had a knockdown drag-out church fight. And well they should have. Because the fight over what to do about the Gentiles was a fight over the fundamental question, *Who is saved and how?* How is it that God chooses us and loves us and remakes us, saves us?

These "men who came down from Judea" had their answer: circumcision and complete adherence to the law of Moses (15:1). Case closed. You must be a Jew to become a Christian.

During the debate, the Pharisees had their answer: "Circumcise them and charge them to keep the law of Moses" (15:5). God said it, I believe it, that settles it.

What do we do about these gentiles, these liberals, these fundamentalists, these homosexuals? Why, they must first all become like us. They must enter the same door through which we came. Go back, put on scratchy wool pants, be bundled into a blue Ford, driven to Sunday school every Sunday until they are twelve, attend Methodist Youth Fellowship, come down to the altar at sixteen, take two religion courses in college. They must be like us.

Then comes the grace of God. In another Gospel, another time and place, Jesus said, "The kingdom of God is like a fisherman who cast a net wide, out into the open sea, then pulled it in. And when he pulled it in, he found caught in the net sea creatures of every kind, both good and bad" (Matt. 13:47, my trans.). That's God's kingdom. He who has ears to hear, hear. The messy grace of God.

What are we to do with these, caught in the great net of God's grace, who are not like us?

"And after there had been much debate, Peter rose and said . . ." (Acts 15:7 RSV). "I preached to what had happened in Jesus and God chose to let these Gentiles hear. God then gave them the Holy Spirit, just like God gave it to us. God made no distinction between them and people like us'" (15:7–9, my trans.). As Matthew says, God sends his sun to shine on the good and the bad, his rain to fall on the just and the unjust (Matt. 5:45, my trans.). Or as Peter put it, "God makes no distinction between them and us."

Then Peter said something which, for me, goes right to the heart: "Why are you putting a yoke around the neck of these people that neither we nor our forebears could bear? *But we believe that we shall be saved through the grace of the Lord Jesus, just as they will*" (15:7–11).

Here we are, busy yoking them to a law that even we church types could not follow. How could they? We are saved by grace.

They have not kept God's law. But as Peter says, *neither have we.* We who have had every advantage to be good, to get it right, to do right, are not right. Surprise, they *are* like us, more than we like to admit.

The murderer awaiting execution on death row, abused as a child, addicted to heroine as a youth—he'll need God's grace to save him. I, child of a middle-class, loving home, president of the Methodist Youth Fellowship, will need God's grace to save me. The gracious, non-distinguishing dragnet of God has caught us both in its loving grasp. We are saved by grace.

In this or any other church, you meet mainly two kinds of people: Pharisees and publicans, or Jews and gentiles, or good and bad, or just and unjust, insiders or outsiders, newcomers or old-timers and both are saved only by grace. To the outside observer, the church's inclusiveness may look like mush affirmation of everybody. To the inside observer, our churches' struggles to welcome everyone whom the Spirit drags in here may be a real pain. Yet Peter reminds us: Having been caught in the dragnet of divine grace, we ought not to be surprised by the others whom God catches. If God made a distinction between the good and the bad, *we* wouldn't be here. We are saved by grace.

The worst I can say about the one who sits this morning on death row or about you who sit next to me here at Duke Chapel is that, when it comes to how God sees us and loves us, you are just like me. We may differ, in our disobedience and sin, in kind or in degree, but you are just like me—*saved by the grace of the Lord Jesus.*

28

Managing Our Miracles

August 2, 1992

LUKE 12:13–21

"I will do this: I will pull down my barns and build larger ones, and there I will store all my grain and my goods. And I will say to my soul, 'Soul, you have ample goods laid up for many years; relax, eat, drink, be merry.'" But God said to him, "You fool! This very night your life is being demanded of you. And the things you have prepared, whose will they be?"

Luke 12:18–20

It's natural that university people, such high achievers as we are, should come to think of our lives as our products. Jesus' story of the Rich Fool is almost too easy a sermon to preach to an affluent, powerful congregation like Duke Chapel.

A reading of Bernard Brandon Scott's Hear Then the Parable *(Fortress, 1989) got me into a thoroughly parabolic mood this year. The dislocating quality of parables really captured my homiletic imagination. When the Parable of the Rich Fool rolled around in the lectionary, I jumped at the chance. I decided that the preceding question about inheritance (Luke 12:13–15) and the moralizing conclusion (Luke 12:21) have little to do with the parable itself and decided to preach on the parable of the Rich Fool alone. How does the fool interpret his miraculous gift from God? That seems to me to be the key problem posed by the parable. The fool's soliloquy shows that he makes no connection between his good fortune and God's graciousness or his responsibility to that graciousness. He becomes the only voice in the story, the sole narrator. His problem is solved by his own self-satisfied action. Now he can "relax, eat, drink, and take ease."*

"But God said. . . ." Here is the unexpected infringement, an intrusive voice which disrupts the fool's complacency, not with active divine judgment, but rather

with the reality of the limits of life. His fortification crumbles and his false security is unmasked. Luther called the gospel verbum externum, *the "external word." Most good gospel preaching is that word we could not have dreamed up on our own, that discordant address that comes to us only because a preacher dares to say it.*

It was one of those blessed summer epiphanies. A marvelously cool and breezy summer night at the beach, after a wonderful meal, surrounded by family, relaxed, content, days left on my vacation, and all was right in my world. And I considered my family—healthy, happy, well housed, well fed, and it was good, it was very good. Summer contentment.

"Soul, you have ample goods laid up for many years; relax, eat, drink, be merry. Honey, bring me another cool one from the fridge and settle back in the hammock."

I hope that your summer has blessed you with similar moments of contentment. If not at the beach, then when you saw your child graduate from college in June, or when you romped with your grandchildren across a green yard, or you glanced over your portfolio and took pleasure in how much you have squirreled away over the years for retirement, or pondered your scorecard, pleased to be only four over par. "Soul . . . relax, eat, drink, and be merry."

This morning's parable begins not in contentment, but in a quandary. A rich man has a problem. He is the beneficiary of a spectacular harvest, a harvest so great that he has nowhere to store all of the grain.

Jesus said, "He thought to himself"—he deliberated within himself, had a discussion with himself—saying, "What shall I do with all this grain that I have harvested?"

Then, still talking to himself, he says to himself, "I will do this: I will pull down my barns and build larger ones, and there I will store all my grain and my goods."

Which seems like drastic action. He doesn't just build new barns to augment his old ones; he tears down his old barns and builds new barns, thus underscoring that this was some harvest. If he has made enough from this harvest to be tearing down old barns and building new ones his harvest must be nothing short of miraculous. He hasn't just done well, he has done *very* well. Miraculously well.

"And I will say to my soul [Note that when you're this rich, this spectacularly successful, you don't need anybody else to consult with; all conversation is monologue] And I will say to my soul, 'Soul, you have ample goods laid up for many years; relax, eat, drink, be merry.'"

And I know this story. Do you?

"Number three in your high school class? Wow. Take off the summer before college and have a good time. You earned it."

"Yes, we have two who have really done very well, one in law school, one just finished med school. We really are very proud of them." Soul, you have been an A+ parent. Relax, eat, be merry you're headed to a grand retirement.

"Number one receiver on the football team! That's great. At least *you* don't have to worry about how to pay for college."

"Soloist at the opera workshop? Man, do you have it made."

And I have a job, a good job, if I do say so. And my marriage is reasonably stable and my kids are good, never been in trouble. Soul, you have ample goods laid up for many years; relax, eat, be merry.

And all this stuff—the diploma on the wall, the monthly computer printout of my IRA, the pictures of the chaste and obedient kids on the wall, the two cars, the garage door with electronic opener—are such a comfort. They mean not only that we have done a good job of the job of life, but also that we have constructed a kind of fence around life—full barns, a fat retirement account, a 3.5 GPA, a happy family—all as insurance against life's vicissitudes. Thus are we able contentedly to say, "Soul, you have ample goods laid up for many years; relax, eat, be merry."

We call this parable the parable of the Rich Fool, but Jesus doesn't. Jesus begins the story, not with talk about the man, but with talk about the land and its bounty. "The land of a rich man produced abundantly." What first impresses Jesus is this miraculous, barn-bursting harvest. A gift.

But the blessing is a burden. The gift becomes a big problem. And then the story becomes, How do I manage my miracle? What should *I* do? *I* have no place to store *my* crops. *I* will do this. *I* will pull down *my* barns. *I* will store *my* grain and *my* goods. *I* will say to *my* soul. "My soul, relax, you have ample goods laid up for many years; eat, drink, be merry."

How do I manage my miracle? It's a story about that. How do I manage my miracle?

How do *I* manage *my* miracle?

A friend of mine taught at Notre Dame some years ago. He said the thing that impressed him was that Catholic parents (my friend is a Methodist) had not one ounce of parental guilt. "Tell me about your children," he would say to them.

"Well, Joe's a priest in Milwaukee, Mary is living out of wedlock in Cleveland, the other six are doing various things." No guilt! Why? "Because they really believe children are gifts of God. Protestant parents believe children are projects to be managed with the right parenting techniques, proper tutoring, the correct program. Catholics believe that children are gifts of God, mysteries to be received." That's what my friend said.

It was said that a major reason that Mr. Perot dropped out of the race for the presidency was that he realized that our country is going broke. The largest claim is Social Security. Apparently, the country is bleeding itself to death, paying for retirements we really can't afford, and Mr. Perot, it is said, was smart enough to know that, unlike children, older Americans vote. The main claims on the government are not the military, welfare mothers with children, it's retirement. We are retiring not on funds we earned, but on the federal deficit. And discussing this last week, someone said to me, "By God, we earned it, we deserve it."

I have seen it as a pastor, in the way people give to the church. There never was a correlation between a person's level of income and how much that person gave to the work of the church, at least in my churches. No, the giving is related to something other than income. It had to do with gratitude, a sense that what I have is not what I earned or deserved but rather a gift, a trust from God. That's my theory for why some people are givers and some are takers. It has to do with how they manage the miracle.

We have givers and takers in the university. Only a small portion of a student's education at any school is paid for in tuition. Most of the cost of education is paid for by strangers, people whom we will never know, benefactors from the past. An alumnus could give generously every year to the annual fund and never, in a lifetime of alumni giving, come close to what was spent on him while he was here at the university.

During our Martin Luther King observance a few years ago, one of the speakers said, "If you are black and if you have a good job and a secure family, you owe a fortune to the NAACP. When are you going to pay up?" And much the same can be said, in one way or another for all of us. Coaches, teachers, doctors, nurses, janitors, pastors, people whose names we will never remember. Why is it—as we sit contentedly and gaze with pride over the achievements, the accomplishments, the acquisitions of our lives—it's all I, my, me, mine?

A psychologist here was telling me of his research relating to our self-image. He gave people some sort of problem to solve and then asked them, after they failed or succeeded, to account for their failure or success. Does it surprise you to learn that he concluded, "We tend to blame others for our failures and to give ourselves credit for our successes"?

All of the talk in this story, thus far, has been the monologue of the rich farmer. He talks to himself, plans for himself, congratulates himself, celebrates himself. I manage by my and me. It is only at the end, at the very end that another voice intrudes into the story—the voice of God. The voice does not accuse the rich man of injustice, of immorality, or even greed. God calls him, "You fool!"

The one whom we might call prudent, farsighted, God calls, "fool." Why fool? He didn't get what he got unjustly. He didn't steal like Michael Milken or Charles Keating. He didn't work at GE. Why did God call him a fool?

"You fool! This very night your life is being demanded of you. And the things you have prepared, whose will they be?" End of story.

A friend of mine pointed out that, actually, in the Greek it says, "Fool, this very night they shall demand your life." They? Who is the "they"? I think "they" are *the things*. The story closes with the question, "And whose will they [the things] be?" He thought the things were his problem, his opportunity, his insurance to manage as he pleased. Surprise. The things managed him as *they* pleased.

Can we not understand the irony of a man who thought *he* had so many things, only to discover, too late, too late, that his things had him?

The gadgets, the machines, the things which were supposed to make our lives easier, make our lives unmanageable. Some days it seems as if I have no other purpose in life than to tend to, care for, and take to be fixed, these things. "I wait for the plumber to arrive, therefore I am." We thought we were managing our modern lives with all these gadgets and things only to discover that the things were managing us.

A recent PBS series on the dilemmas, the horrors, the by-products of modern medicine was titled *Managing Our Miracles*. We thought we had these things. Surprise—the things have us.

It's all monologue, as we pat ourselves on the back for our great material progress, our medical, technological miracles, our great work as A+ parents, our high SAT scores, our homes, our jobs, our health, our lives. And just when we get it all fenced in, hedged well about, insured, locked in, there comes that voice from the outside, that intrusive voice which is God's, that is, reality, "But God said to him, 'You fool! This very night they shall demand your life of you. And the things you have prepared, whose will they be?'"

This move from self-satisfied, fat, contented, self-congratulatory monologue to dark, intrusive, realistic address by God is somber but real.

The Psalm says, "The fool says in his heart, 'There is no God'" (Ps. 14:1 RSV). There is just me, myself, mine and my management of my achievements. There is no miracle, no food, family, future, as a gift. It is all mine, to be managed for me. There is no transcendent, external, higher claim laid upon me and my possessions other than my own comfort, contentment, and pleasure. No connection between my resources and my responsibilities. The fool says in his heart, "There isn't a God."

Please note that God doesn't punish anyone here—unless reality be considered punishment enough. The intruding voice of God states only the facts, just the facts. "Fool! This night they demand your life of you. And all this management and preparation, these big barns and prudent insurance, whose will they be?"

And once again (how many Sundays has this happened?), the voice intrudes into my false security, my smug contentment. I am addressed, called "fool," by the one who is the source of all that I am and all that I have.

29

Righteous Woman

September 13, 1992

GENESIS 38:1–27

A sermon series is a risky undertaking, as every preacher knows. What if they don't like the first sermon? Will they check out for the rest of the series? However, one of the disadvantages of using the lectionary as a resource for our preaching is that it sometimes chops up biblical narratives, abridges them, and disrupts their flow in a way that does an injustice. I therefore determined, a few years ago, to preach a run of sermons on the patriarchal narratives from Genesis, particularly the stories of Joseph. I called the series, "The Family," and interpreted the Joseph saga as a long, wonderful narrative of the perseverance and persistence, with God's help, of a chosen family, Israel.

Things went well, I thought, until I came to Genesis 38, the story of Judah and Tamar. It is a strange tale, never, to my knowledge, preached upon for Christian edification. Yet with the help of Walter Brueggemann's fine commentary on Genesis, I was led to a sermon on Tamar as a peculiarly "Righteous Woman." Say what you will about Tamar's tactics, she got the job done and, through her, the family persevered, the same family who was, one day, to give us Jesus.

As I recall, the only memorable response that I received for my sermonic efforts with Tamar was one from an undergraduate right after the service. "What's 'onanism'?" he asked.

"Ask your mother when you go home for Thanksgiving," I responded, courageously.

I have told you we were going to preach through the story of Joseph, right through from beginning to end. Genesis 37 to Genesis 50. Those of you who may have been following along in your Bibles know that I lied. We had a sermon on Genesis 37 (Joseph's coat and his dream) and then a sermon on Joseph in Egypt beginning with Genesis 39. What happened to Genesis 38?

154

I have never preached on Genesis 38. To my knowledge, after a thorough search in the library, no one has ever preached on Genesis 38. Get ready. You were there.

[Read Genesis 38:1–27.]

Of this text, Walter Brueggemann has said, "This peculiar chapter stands alone, without connection to its context . . . isolated, . . . most enigmatic. . . . It is not evident that it provides any significant theological resource. It is difficult to know in what context it might be of value for theological exposition. For these reasons, our treatment of it may be brief" (*Genesis*, Interpretation: A Bible Commentary for Teaching and Preaching [Atlanta: John Knox Press, 1982], 307–8).

Then Brueggeman adds, "The major problem in dealing with this chapter is that even close study does not make clear its intent." To which I say, "Good, then I don't have to study it closely. Perfect text for a sermon."

Into the wonderfully instructive, edifying narrative of Joseph is introduced this marvelously uninstructive story of a woman named Tamar who dupes her father-in-law, Judah, into having sex with her. I'm aware that there are many young people here today. I'm aware that many of you have come to chapel this morning fully expecting to be admonished, morally edified, ethically enlightened. Well, what do you make of this?

The story begins with a woman. At first the narrator seems uninterested in her as if she is just a casual bystander to the real story about men named Judah, his friend Hirah, Judah's sons, Er, Onan, Shelah. Did Judah have daughters? The story isn't interested in daughters or wives. It's about men, makers of history, doers of great things, heads of families. But that's the problem—family. Judah has given a wife named Tamar to Er, his firstborn. But Er dies before Tamar conceives. So, Judah follows the Levirate marriage laws (cf. Deut. 25:5–10) which say that if a married man dies without an heir, then the next male kin must marry the widow, impregnate her, provide an heir—it being inconceivable that the widow should inherit her husband's goods.

Nobody in the story lingers to mourn over Tamar's plight as a widow, alone, vulnerable. Nobody ponders what Tamar may think about all this shuffling around from unproductive brother to unfruitful brother. Judah tells Onan, next in line, to go take Tamar and have children. Onan disobeyed, commiting a "shameful act" of birth control because he "knew that the issue would not be his." Onan dies (and generations of little boys got confusing messages about "onanism").

After these two funerals Judah says to Tamar, "Go on back to your father's house, Woman. Maybe when my third son grows up. . . . Woman, you are bad luck."

Tamar has shuttled back and forth throughout the story, through a succession of funerals and husbands and now she is sent home. End of story. Tragic. Dead end. Yet, if you know much about the history of women in any culture you would have to say that it's not a particularly unusual or original story. Dependent, of value only as child-bearers and husband-carers, a mere backdrop for what men will or will not do. It's one of those stories. But because this is the Bible, where nearly anything can happen and often does, this story continues.

Judah's wife dies—Judah, the father-in-law whose sons weren't much help to Tamar. And Judah happens to be up at Timnah for the sheepshearing, and after the sheep are sheared old Judah goes out with the boys for a night on the town. (I really hate that you first-year students must be exposed to this, but it's in the Bible.)

Tamar at last arises out of her culturally imposed passivity and takes matters in hand. She throws off her mourning clothes, dabs on "Night of Ecstasy" behind each ear, puts a veil on her face and heads for the red-light district of Timnah.

Judah sees her but of course doesn't recognize his ex-daughter-in-law because of the veil. They haggle over a price and agree on one young goat. But Tamar, having dealt with men in this family before, asks Judah to leave his signet ring, his belt, and his staff with her until he pays up with the goat.

It's a done deal. A few days later, when Judah's friend shows up with the goat looking for the perfumed harlot to pay, he couldn't find her. Judah says, "Let her keep the ring, belt, and staff lest she make a fool out of me." He went home after his escapades at the sheepshearing convention with a hangover, without belt, staff, and ring, sadder but wiser.

Six months later, Judah hears the gossip that his ex-daughter-in-law is pregnant because she has been working as a prostitute. Well, Judah is utterly indignant. As an upstanding progenitor of God's holy people Israel, a patriarch of the church, Judah can't have his daughter-in-law, ex or not, embarrassing the family name. In a singular act of righteous indignation, Judah says, "Bring her here to be burned. It will teach her a lesson."

They bring back Tamar, who is now wearing maternity clothes rather than a black veil.

"Do you have anything to say before we make an example of you for all our womenfolk by burning you alive?" Judah asked.

"Just one thing," said Tamar. "The man to whom belongs this stuff is the father of my child." And she produces the ring (with a big "J" on it), the staff, the belt.

And Judah said, "Oops! She has taught me a lesson. Court is over. Put away the torches and the gasoline. She is within her rights rather than I." No, let's translate it more accurately as, "She is more righteous than I." And that's an amazing statement for Judah to make about Tamar.

Judah, as a man, father of the family, had all the rights. Tamar, woman, a widow, unmarried, childless, had no rights. She is outside the law, without legal recourse. That ought to be the end of the story, the legal, proper, appropriate end. Moral of story: all you disenfranchised, disinherited people on the bottom better obey the rules or you'll get burned—rules, which you will note, are usually made by people on the top.

But, as I said, this is the Bible so that's not the end. The story moves on to (in Brueggemann's words) a "fresh definition of righteousness" (p. 310). Who is guilty now? Show him the ring, the staff, the belt, it'll teach him a lesson.

In this story, Tamar is (surprised!) vindicated. She bears twins, Perez and Zerah. The family will be continued, but not in the respectable, middle-class way Judah intended. It will be preserved through the crafty chutzpah of a gutsy woman named Tamar. If there's a moral here, a point of edification for all us good churchgoing people, it is not the one we wanted. Tamar has committed those sins which good bourgeois church people condemn—deception, illicit sex. Judah reacts at once as the world reacts—indignant condemnation.

Reminds you of King David and the prophet Nathan (2 Sam. 12:1–7). "The man who did this ought to hang," says David. "*Thou* art the man," says Nathan. A woman was involved there, too. "She is more righteous than I," King David needed to say.

The story doesn't glorify Tamar or justify her action. But you do have to admire the way she takes matters (and Judah) in hand, the way she wrenches a future for herself out of the clutches of male oppression masquerading as religious propriety. She doesn't whine about her circumstances or quietly resign herself to her situation—she goes out and wheels and deals, recklessly risking all, and thus suggests a new sort of righteousness. You've got to hand it to Tamar.

One of you was telling me about your home church. You said it was conservative, you said it was a "Bible-believing" church, a church taking stands against abortion, immorality. But when the pastor's son got his girlfriend pregnant, and then confessed it and they married, the board of deacons met and fired the pastor. That's our righteousness.

And I know somebody who is a schoolteacher, teaching in one of the most poverty-stricken areas of this country. He doesn't go to church, doesn't feel comfortable there, he says because of his (how shall we say it?) "orientation." Recently, when he was home visiting his folks, he attended church with them. In the sermon the pastor ridiculed, lambasted, worse, made fun of those whose "orientation" did not fit that of the majority of the congregation. That's our righteousness.

Now why would we bring up such an embarrassing story? A story that doesn't even mention God—except as the one who killed Tamar's first two husbands? Why would we spend a whole Sunday discussing this woman? Forget Tamar. Savvy, yes. Wise to the ways of the world, yes. But for all that, still a deceptive, lying harlot? Why bring her up, and on a Sunday, too?

Well, because Matthew brings her up. Matthew, the first Gospel, first chapter, third verse, you can look it up: "This is the book of the story of Jesus, son of David, son of Abraham. Abraham conceived Isaac, who was father of Jacob, who was father of Judah, who with *Tamar* conceived twins, Perez and Zerah . . ." (my trans.).

Now it can be told. The great-great-grandmother of Jesus was Tamar. If we hadn't had Tamar, we couldn't have had Jesus. So when Jesus called forth a new family, based on new, risky righteousness, would not his grandmother have been proud?

30

Who's in Charge Here?

November 22, 1992

2 SAMUEL 5:1–5

COLOSSIANS 1:11–19

JOHN 12:12–19

I'm always hard-pressed to know which is the most "political" Sunday in the church year. Christmas? Easter? Good Friday? There's something to be said for each of these as an attack on the political establishment and, when anybody wants to mess with politicians, count me in. The most explicitly political, or antipolitical of the church's festivals has got to be Christus Rex. *Thus my joy at preaching on this Sunday each year.*

A few years ago, on this Sunday, Christ the King, in a desperate attempt to interest a disinterested congregation in the theological implications of the kingship of Christ, I began my sermon asking, "Do you need a king?" I admitted that they didn't think they needed a king or queen since we are Americans, democratically disposed, averse to monarchy.

"I'm not talking about some polo-playing playboy who dabbles in architecture," said I. "I'm talking about a real king. I'm not talking about a pleasant woman clutching a purse, wearing a small hat and sensible shoes, I'm talking about somebody to set things right, somebody who's in charge."

Then I went on to speak of the lordship, the kingship of Christ and its implications.

After service, as people were shuffling past me on their way out, mumbling, "Nice sermon," a woman, husband in tow, approached—a woman clutching a purse, wearing a small hat, in sensible shoes. "Did it not occur to you that you might have British subjects in the congregation this morning?" she shouted.

"O gosh, I guess we've even got people from Michigan," I said.

"Well, you are not funny. In fact, you are extremely disgusting. Our queen is ten times the Christian of your silly actor president," she shouted, threatening me with her purse.

"Gosh, I would hate to put that to a vote here," I said jovially.

"You are not funny. You are repulsive. I intend to report you to your superiors!" A crowd was gathering, a number of students delighted to see this British visitor take the preacher apart. Being from South Carolina, I had no idea who my superiors were.

As she finally led her husband out the door, one of you (you know who you are) said to me, "We broke away from those people for stuff like that." A comeback so wonderful, I wish I had thought of it myself.

Perhaps she got the point of the sermon. Christ the King is a Sunday to answer the question, Who is on the throne? Who rules? This is the Sunday we debate the question, Who's in charge here?

If I were to characterize the conversation in the dorm Tuesday evening, a week ago, it would be a question. The question on the minds of many of us on this campus—"Who's in charge here?"

A couple of rapes, an escaped prisoner taking hostages, shot to death by police, and now a first-year student killed by the bus she was riding to class.

"I feel afraid, unsafe here," confessed one student. And you can understand how she feels. Now, no more a Gothic wonderland, academic ivory towers in the midst of Southern pine forest, for her, Duke has lost its luster. Every student there on the sidewalk, everyone on the bus, all who heard the awful sound, saw the horrible sight, grew old in an instant, moved all the way from naive nineteen to the cold cynicism of midlife. If college students can be victims of such horror in their dorms, on a bus, for heaven's sake, what is happening to our world? Who's in charge here?

In the aftermath, it's fine to ventilate feelings to someone from Counseling and Psychological Services (CAPS), as far as that goes, to set up a safety commission, to search for technological flaws in bus doors, fire two deputies in High Point for letting their prisoner loose, install new lighting, carded locks for the dorms. As far as that goes. But people want more. People want to know, Why. We demand reasons. There was this sensor on the door. In some freak accident, the sensor was tripped, then it closed. But that's not a reason. We rush to pin the blame on "pilot error," upon "system malfunction," but none of this is a reason. CAPS has no answer sufficient to the awesomeness of the question, Who's in charge here?

And if you could manage to get through your life, hermetically sealed from chaos, safe in the neo-Gothic womb, insured, secure, then you would never ask, Who's in charge here, and therefore you would never need to sing the hymns we have sung today, never need to know Christ the King.

All of today's Scripture, today's music, depicts Christ as King. David is enthroned as Israel's greatest king. Colossians, a letter to a persecuted and threatened little church, somehow summons the faith to sing of Jesus,

> He is the image of the invisible God, . . . whether thrones or domin-ions or rulers or powers—all things have been created through him and for him . . . in him all things hold together. (Col. 1:15–17)

And the Gospel of John portrays Jesus bouncing into Jerusalem on a don-key, his followers waving palm branches to welcome him in triumph, calling him "king!" The authorities, the bigwigs, and people in power get edgy about his threatening challenge to their control saying, "Look, the world has gone after him!"

A claim is being made in all these lessons, a claim about power, about ulti-mate rule, an assertion of the one who is in charge here.

The feast of Christ the King is a latecomer to the church's year, a creation of Pope Pius IX in 1925 (in *Quas Primas*). While the church had always cel-ebrated images of Christ as King, it took the church 1925 years to need this feast in the way the church needed it now. On the first celebration of Christ the King, Mussolini had been head of Italy for three years, a rabble rouser named Hitler had been out of jail for a year, his Nazi party was growing in popularity, and the world lay in a Great Depression. In such a time, Pius IX asserted that, nevertheless, Christ is "King of the universe." The feast became the church's great *nevertheless* to the godlessness of the modern world. Despite the rise of dictators, despite the widespread modern notion that religion was now a "private affair," Christ the King asserted that nevertheless Jesus Christ is Lord and he shall reign for ever and ever.

And so a bedraggled, whipped Jew stands before the proud Pontius Pilate. Pilate sneeringly asks, "So? You are a 'King'?"

And Jesus responds, "My kingdom is not from here."

Jesus' kingdom is not from here. Not from here—with a grubby, ruthless, vacillating Pilate who has nothing to keep him in power but Caesar's legions. Here—with our self-centered democratic pushing and shoving that sees the government as a means of preserving our personal power. Here—where every state, democratic or not, is a killer. His kingdom isn't from here.

Christ the King stands as a critique of every form of earthly power, a vast relativization of all other kingdoms, powers, and princes. My word for you today is that it also stands as a great comfort. The kingdoms here in this world may totter and sway. Nevertheless, one realm endures. Utopian schemes for human betterment rise and dribble off to nothing or else leave piles of bodies in their wake.

Nevertheless, humanity is not without hope. We get up in the morning, gather our books, trudge to class by substantial looking Gothic buildings, then there is a screech of breaks, a scream, and suddenly the whole world shakes on its foundations, things fall apart, crumble to dust, and we are terribly dislocated. Nevertheless, it is a great comfort, in times when the world becomes unglued, and we feel exposed and very vulnerable, to know who sits on the throne, who's in charge here.

These past days, God gives Satan a mighty long leash. Nobody who has lived through the last few weeks on this campus disputes that. We live in a world where things do not always work out for the best, where the innocent suffer unjustly, and people don't do right, and humanity inches forward only to fall a century back, and there is a huge amount of unreasonable tragedy, unexplained pain, pointless suffering and God neither plans nor wills every single thing that happens to us. Nevertheless, Christians are bold to sing with the prophets and martyrs before us:

> He is the image of the invisible God, . . . whether thrones or dominions or rulers or powers—all things have been created through him and for him . . . in him all things hold together.

A man emerged from a London bomb shelter one bleak morning in the darkest days of World War II. Devastation was all around. Amid the rubble, he was surprised to encounter a newspaper vendor, hawking his wares on a street corner. Half in jest, he asked the newspaper salesman, "Who do the papers say won last night?"

"I don't know," said the vendor. "I don't read the papers. I don't have to know who the papers say won the battle last night, because I already know who has won the war."

So the church gathered at Amy's funeral last Monday, and sang, "The strife is o'er, the battle done, the victory of life is won, Alleluia!" We are able to sing such a defiant "Alleluia," because we know who won the war.

Let none of us deny the pain, the wreckage, ruin, and rubble that afflicts many in this life, in this world, on this campus. The pain is real, the questions are large, the answers don't come easily, and the defeat is more than merely apparent. Nevertheless, we have courage in the battle, we manage to go on even after our defeats, for we know who sits on the throne.

> He is the image of the invisible God, . . . whether thrones or dominions or rulers or powers—all things have been created through him and for him . . . in him all things hold together.

A year or so ago, Thailand was rocked by civil unrest in which the people filled the streets to protest the military government's installation of a prime minister who was not elected by the people. The government reacted with a brutal massacre of the unarmed protestors. Days of riots, destruction, and chaos followed. The people refused to relent and to return to their homes; the government refused to give in to the people's demands. At last the beloved king of Thailand called the disputed prime minister and the leader of the opposition to his palace. In deference to the king, to centuries of tradition, and popular affection for him, they both meekly knelt before the king. The king ordered the two parties to stop fighting, end the violence, and work things out. In less than a day, the disturbances were over, the ersatz prime minister was on his way out of the country, and peace was restored.

One news commentator said, "The events in Thailand this week are a great victory for democracy."

I, schooled by Sundays like this one, thought it a great victory for monarchy, a kingdom not from here, our last, best hope, here.

31

The Dangers of Fishing with Jesus

February 5, 1995

LUKE 5:1–11

It wasn't that Jesus saved people—it was that he saved the wrong people, people that no one thought could be saved, people that no one wanted saved. "This man receives sinners and eats with them," was one of the earliest and most persistent charges against Jesus.

This sermon contains one of my rare references to an issue that is causing much mischief in my church. I have always wondered how different our conversation might be if the issue of homosexuality had been enjoined as an issue of evangelism. Just how far is the reach of Jesus?

The disciples have been fishing all night. They have caught nothing. Jesus tells them, "Put out into the deep water, let down your nets for a catch."

Peter informs Jesus, "We've worked all night but have caught nothing. . . . But if you give the word, we'll give it another try."

And they caught so many fish that they thought the net would break.

End of Scripture. At least that's what I thought ought to be the end of what I ought to preach upon this morning. "You stop at verse 6," I thought to myself. "They'll love that verse about how many fish they caught after they had the good sense to listen to Jesus."

And well we should. Because, every time the church gathers, we're here to listen to Jesus. "At your word, Lord, we'll let down the nets." At your word.

"Stop at verse 6," I thought to myself. "That part about, after a night of fishing failure, when they did what Jesus told them, launched on out into the deep, they had such success, they could hardly pull the catch into the boat. You preach on that."

164

If at first you don't succeed, try, try again.

And well we should, because, if you've ever spent much time in the church, you know there's much failure around here. Jesus has called you and me to be "fishers of people." "Follow me," he promises his disciples, "I'll teach you to catch people."

But . . . so much is asked of the church, and yet we have so little to show for our efforts.

Master, we've worked all night long; we've caught nothing.

I've led this Bible study for two semesters now, without anybody ever saying, "Thanks."

I tutored that kid for two years, two years, every Tuesday, and she's still flunking out of school. Master, we've worked all night long; we've caught nothing.

"You stop at verse 6," I thought to myself, "the verse about their success. I want them to leave church this February morning less depressed than when they got here."

But, I read on. Verse 8. The story of Jesus' fishing trip doesn't end simply with the great catch of fish. Verse 8. "But when Simon Peter saw it, he fell down at Jesus' knees, saying, 'Go away from me, Lord, for I am a sinful man!' For he and all who were with him were amazed at the catch of fish that they had taken."

Here's my question: Why would Peter have said, "Get away from me, Jesus, I'm a sinful man!"? You'd think he would have been delighted, what with this huge catch of fish after a futile night.

Why this, "Get away from me, Jesus, I'm a sinful man!"

If you don't know why Peter said, "Get away from me, Jesus," then you don't know about the dangers of fishing with Jesus.

Let's be honest, there's something about us that knows how to handle fishing failure, which wouldn't mind if this story ended in fishing futility. Something about us is downright comfortable with fishing all night without a bite, being in church all day with little to show for it, something in you, something in me, content with Good Friday, but scared half out of our wits by Easter.

I told them, before the fall stewardship campaign, that it was crazy a church our size, with our record of giving (or, more accurately, our record of *not* giving) to increase the budget 18 percent. I told them. Economy's bad. Trouble making this year's goal, and you want an 18 percent increase? Are you kidding? I told them, from the pulpit, *you will never pledge that budget.*

By the end of October, they had gone over by two thousand dollars . . . and . . . *preachers hate congregations like that!*

"Preacher, wasn't it you who said we wouldn't be able to make that budget?" I acted like I didn't hear him.

"Yup, I think it was you who said, just a couple of weeks ago, 'You'll never . . .'"

"Shut up," I explained.

Now, why is that? You'd think I'd be happy. Well, if you think that, then you don't know much about the perils of fishing with Jesus, in deep water.

I tell you what we know. We know all about sociological determinism. "Americans aren't religious anymore." Amen. The ones who are religious all watch TV preachers. Amen. We're stuck in the wrong part of town. All students sleep in on Sundays. "Master, we've worked all night long, but have caught nothing."

"Put out into the deep, let down your nets. Don't be afraid," said Jesus. "From now on, I'll teach you to catch people."

After this year's Martin Luther King Service here, I was talking with this student. "Great service!" I said.

"Yea," she said. "Great. But what good, all those words? I just think that there's too much water over the dam, in our history. Too much hurt. Too many disappointments, black and white. Too much stored up hate. I don't think we'll ever change." Amen.

We can handle Good Friday. It's Easter, the deep waters of God's unmanageable, mysterious, powerful grace that scares us, makes us want to cry, "Get out of here, Jesus."

"We are sending you to this old, inner-city church," said the bishop. "Some wonderful people there. Yet, they are old, been in decline for the last twenty years. Just a handful of them left. They won't expect much ministry from you. Just go there, visit them, and do the best you can."

She gulped. Her first parish was to be like this. So be it.

In her initial meeting with her board, she could see the reality of what the bishop had described—mostly older women, a room full of white hair and pastel dresses.

"I have previously thought I had a gift for working with children," she told the board when they asked about her interests.

"Then the bishop has sent you to the wrong church," responded one of the women on the board, bluntly. "We are long past those years here."

Yet in the days that followed she noticed many children passing each afternoon outside her pastor's study window, children on their way home. They weren't the congregation's children, but they were children. "God, show me a way to ministry here," she prayed.

One afternoon she was visiting with one of her parishioners, an older woman. "Tell me about yourself," asked the young pastor.

She told a story about an earlier life, a career as a pianist in vaudeville in her youth. "I played some of the best clubs on the east coast as well," the old lady said with pride. "Count Basie, the Dorsey Brothers, I knew 'em all."

A light went on in the young pastor's brain. "Would you play for the church . . . on next Wednesday afternoon?" she asked.

"Sure, if I can get these poor old bony, arthritic hands to work," said the woman. "I'll take an extra dose of aspirin and I think I can be ready."

The pastor asked two women to make peanut butter sandwiches. On Wednesday, the four of them rolled the old piano out the double doors of the fellowship hall, doors which had not been opened in a decade. Gladys sat down at the piano, out on the front porch of the fellowship hall, and began to play. She played a medley of hits from the thirties then moved into a little ragtime.

By 3:30 a crowd of children had gathered. The pastor passed out the sandwiches. Gladys moved from "In the Mood," to "Jesus Loves Me." The children clamored forward. The pastor told them a story about a man named Jesus. They promised to come back next week.

That was a year ago. Today, nearly a hundred children crowd in that church every Wednesday afternoon. On Sundays, Sunday school rooms are full, being taught by a group of older women who thought that they were now too old to have children. Those children brought their parents. Where there was once death, there is now life. Easter.

And the administrative board met the next year and asked the bishop to move their new pastor. "It's just not the same church," they said.

Jesus said, "Come on out in the deep water, cast your nets."

And we said in unison, "Get out of here, Jesus . . ."

It was a big church, downtown, Episcopal, Memphis, Tennessee. Get the picture?

I had been speaking there, speaking for their Noonday Lenten Series. I had just preached, rather eloquently I might add, on Ephesians 3:18–19 where the writer prays "that you may have the power to comprehend, with all the saints, what is the breadth and length and height and depth, and to know the love of Christ that surpasses knowledge, so that you may be filled with all the fullness of God."

After the service, at the lunch prepared and served by volunteers in the church fellowship hall, our table was served by a young man who wore a name tag saying, "David—Integrity." I immediately recognized him as a member of Integrity. He had on this pink triangle. The rector spoke jovially with David as he served us. David volunteered that the congregation "has been an answer to my prayer. I *love* this church and these people!" he exclaimed.

"David gets thirty dollars an hour to wait tables in the best restaurant in town," bragged the rector, "but we get him for free here at these lunches because he loves us so much."

During the meal, I couldn't help but ask, "Did you get any resistance to their meeting here?" I asked.

"Resistance?" the Rector responded. "Of course, they'll complain about anything, won't they? So, what, I say?"

I persisted. "How did you come to the idea that it would be good to have a group like this meeting at a church like this?"

"My idea?" asked the Rector sarcastically. "They weren't *my* idea. *I* didn't invite them. Why on earth would *I* want them? This is *God's* idea of a good time, not mine.'"

"Come on out in the deep water, cast your nets."

And we said in unison, "Get out of here . . ."

And Jesus said, "I'm going to teach you to catch people . . . or I'll *die* trying."

32

A Party? And during Lent?

March 26, 1995

LUKE 15:1–3, 11B–32

Why do we call Good Friday "good"? Why do Christians look upon the greatest injustice in the world, the crucifixion of Jesus, as the most joyful event in which God's justice was achieved. This paradoxical quality of the faith motivated this Lenten sermon.

She asked if she could make an announcement at the close of the funeral, at the close of her husband's funeral. I said yes, though it was not our usual practice. I figured that she wished to thank everyone for making the effort to come to the funeral. As the service ended, just before my benediction, I said, "Now Gladys wants to say a word."

She stood. "I want to say that everybody is invited over to the house, right after the burial, for a good time. I've got plenty of food, lots of beer, and we are going to tie one on tonight that will send John out in style. John would want it that way."

What? I told her to sit down. The utter inappropriateness! At a funeral! A party?

There are things that we do in life which are wrong, not because they are immoral or illegal, just because they are inappropriate. The same action, at another time, would be fitting.

This father was telling me that he had just presented his daughter with a new BMW. (Those of you who've heard me before know that I'm down on BMW's—principally because I don't own one.) This is the same daughter who, last semester, nearly flunked out of college.

"Let me get this straight," I said, "your daughter nearly flunks out of school and you reward her with a BMW? What gives?"

169

"Well, she's had such a struggle. And she was so upset over last semester. I didn't want her to take her failure the wrong way. I thought she needed a boost, so I got her the car."

Now, there are times and places where such a gift would be . . . appropriate. But a parent who rewards failure is asking for trouble. It was the wrong action at the wrong time.

Our time is Lent, the Christian season of penitence, confession of sin, mourning, and sober self-examination. The hymns are solemn, somber in this season of the cross. There are no flowers on our altar, and we wear purple, color of repentance, contrition.

Here, deep in Lent, the Gospel is the story of a young upstart ne'er-do-well who ungratefully demands his inheritance, takes the money into the "far country" where he quickly blows every cent on booze and bad women. And when this prodigal comes slithering home, reeking of Ripple and "Night of Ecstasy," his father . . . throws the biggest party ever seen on west campus.

Now, despite what they will tell you about me on fraternity row, I am not opposed to parties. BYOB or not. Quite the contrary, I like a good blowout . . . *if it is at the right time, in an appropriate context.*

When a prodigal daughter or son returns, homecoming ought to be done in sackcloth and ashes, not patent leather pumps and a tux. Throw a party for a prodigal, he'll think his getting wasted was okay. He'll do it again.

And why tell a story like this in Lent?

Deep in Lent, season of penitence and pain, the cross, there is a party. The church, in its wisdom, forbade the singing of "Alleluia" during Lent. Why this Gospel party story now?

We are not the first to ask.

Our question is that of the older brother when he heard the music coming from the house. "What's going on here? Music? Dancing? Levity? And in Lent?" Is this liturgically fitting? Morally appropriate?

It is not inappropriate for a father to receive back a wayward son, any of us would do the same. What is not fitting, meet, or right to do is this party. The older brother never questions that his father should receive back his hell-raising little brother. What gets him is that *party.* The older brother asks our question: "What is the meaning of this?" Luke expends more verses describing that party—shoes, ring, fatted calf, music—than on any other aspect of the story. A party! What is the meaning of this?

I recall the preacher, preaching from this pulpit on this parable, describing this party, in great, glorious detail. Then, as if coming to her senses, she said, "Now you students, this does not mean that it is appropriate for you to act irresponsibly in your academic work, for you to take mind-altering substances." It would be highly . . . inappropriate . . . for a minister to end a narrative of youthful indiscretion with a party.

What is the meaning of this?

The party means forgiveness. In a number of places in Scripture, the forgiveness of God is rendered as a celebration, with party clothes and refreshments. In Zechariah 3:1–10, the prophet says that Israel stands in dirty clothes before God, because of Israel's sin. "Take off his dirty clothes and dress him in splendid robes and put a turban on his head [sound familiar]. 'You see, I have taken your guilt away.'"

"Quick," says the father. "Pull out all the stops, spare nothing in this party for my wayward son. In his sin, he was lost to me. Now he is found. He was in rags; put him in a robe. He was dead. Now he is alive." And they began to make merry.

John Wesley, in his commentary on this story, says that the word "merry" here "implies nothing of levity, but a solid, serious, religious, heartfelt joy." Poor John Wesley. No, "making merry" meant then what it means on west campus on Saturday night. But you can see Wesley's worry. A party! And in Lent! It was inappropriate.

There's a heap of partying in this chapter of Luke's Gospel, much making merry. The shepherd finds the lost sheep, comes home crying, "Rejoice with me, come party, my lost sheep has been found." The woman cries to her neighbors, "Come rejoice with me, the lost coin has been found." The father says, "This son of mine was lost and is found."

The older brother's question is ours. What is the meaning of this?

Put this party in context. This chapter of Luke's good news begins with grumbling, "Now even tax collectors and sinners were drawing near to Jesus. Jesus' critics cried, 'This Jesus befriends sinners and . . . *eats* with them.'"

It is appropriate for a man of God to reach out to the lost, to demand that they change their sinful ways, straighten up and fly right. But this one *eats* with them, *parties* with them. It is inappropriate.

Jesus replies, "In heaven, there is more joy, more partying over one lost Sigma Nu who repents, than over twelve hundred of the righteous gathered in chapel during Lent."

He was always partying, eating, and drinking with tax collectors and sinners. He was guest at the table of many a sinner, some religious sinners, some nonreligious. The only party he ever paid for himself was, interesting enough, during Lent, Maundy Thursday to be exact, a meal in an upper room. (He never had an appropriate sense of timing.)

At that party, after the wine was poured and around, he shocked us saying, "This is my blood poured out for you."

"How much does this meal cost?" one of us whispered to another.

He took the bread, and passing it said, "This is my body, take, eat."

"Drink up. Eat your fill because I will not eat or drink with you, there will be no more parties, until the time is more . . . appropriate, until I party with you in the kingdom" (Matt. 26:29, paraphr.).

That is what he said there in the upper room. At long last, the party was over. I will not eat or drink with you again until the kingdom comes.

Earlier critics had said, "The disciples of John the Baptist fast and offer somber prayers, but your disciples eat and drink." In other words, "We can tell the disciples of John the Baptist are religious, they look so miserable. Your disciples, on the other hand, are always at a party."

Jesus replied, "When the bridegroom shows up for the wedding, do the wedding guests look sad?"

But then, in the upper room, at Maundy Thursday, on his way to death and the cross, he at last relented saying, "I hope all of you stuffed shirts and members of the World Wide Undergraduate Judicial Board are pleased. You wanted to fast, fast now. I will not eat or drink again, until I party with you in God's kingdom. The party is over."

He came to us. We did not say, "This man's theology is unorthodox." We said, "This man receives sinners and eats with them." He came to us, telling us that the time was full, ripe for revolution. But we said caution is the word, prudence is best, the time is not right for redemption. Finding that his inappropriateness knew no bounds, eventually we were forced to strip him, mock him, beat him, and nail him to the tree. Nails split sinew and flesh, blood dripped down, caught in a chalice, a bloody cup he pronounced as "poured out for you."

And from the cross he looks down upon us tax collectors, prodigals, whores, faculty, and students, sinners all, and with his last breath says, "Father, forgive."

Now. Let the party begin.

33

My Sin

April 9, 1995

What does the trial of O. J. Simpson have to do with the trial of Jesus? Leave it to
a preacher to attempt to make the connection. An editorial by Lewis H. Lapham,
"Notebook," in Harper's *Magazine (November 1994) propelled me into this ser-*
mon. I was embarrassed by a secular magazine editor who told the truth more exu-
berantly than I did in my sermons. I was betting that my sin—the sin of thinking that
I'm not sunk in sin—was their sin as well.

After service this Sunday a dean emerged from the chapel muttering, "Just once I
would like to see an academic or intellectual appear in one of your sermons and not be
an object of derision and ridicule."

Mea culpa.

By a happy confluence of events, Lent has fallen this year during the same
period as the O. J. Simpson trial. I say "happy" because around here, Lent is
one of my greatest challenges. It isn't easy for the preacher to convince mostly
young, upwardly mobile, and oh so very smart politically correct people—
people like you—that you are, despite your high SAT scores, fallen, sinful,
and in need of salvation. ("My Lord, I got out of bed and came to chapel,
and on a big social weekend, does that count for nothing?") Lent, Christian
season of sin and the cross, repentance and confession, always seems out of
place—among people like us.

But, happily, not this year. Not with your rushing home every afternoon
to watch the latest episode of the "Trial of the Century." And don't lie to me;
you know that you can't get enough of it. All of you are watching it, hooked on
it like heroin. You love O. J. with its mix of Lear, and Othello, The *National*

Inquirer, and daily parade of Hollywood sleaze (and not just the attorneys). A celebrity hood who dabbles in cocaine between Avis commercials. A woman abused, but too hooked on the lifestyle of the rich and famous to leave, all presided over by the oiliest collection of attorneys since the Inquisition who, for five million in legal fees might win you the right to do anything you want to your wife. And it's all during Lent.

So the preacher in me can say, See, boys and girls? If you don't straighten up, repent, and get saved, you will grow up to look like Bob Shapiro, or Johnny Cochrain—maybe even F. Lee Bailey, if you're especially bad. Marine-to-marine.

There are many reasons why you are hooked on O. J., not the least of which is that *here is a trial with which few of us can identify.* Drama teachers will tell you that, for us to be engaged by a play there must be a certain amount of distancing. We often think that the reason we love theater is that a play has characters to whom we can relate. But if we too closely identify with the characters, if from the moment they walk on stage we say, "Hey, that's *me,*" we are so busy defending ourselves that we can't get into the drama. So Bertolt Brecht always encouraged a certain amount of distancing, "defamiliarization" in his plays (See Walter Benjamin, *Understanding Brecht,* trans. Anna Bostock [London: New Left Books, 1973]). Sin is always more interesting when it appertains to other people, when there's some distance. Surely this is partly the basis for the current Republican assault upon unwed mothers and "food-stamp frauds." Most of the fulminations of Messrs. Gingrich, Bennet, and Buchanan against American "ethical chaos" tend to be aimed at the ethical afflictions of the poorest Americans. Their sins are safely not mine.

The virtuous few, those of us who compose the present company, we happy few here in this room, or by the pool at this club, or around the table at this faculty meeting always know ourselves to be innocent of the ethical chaos that causes us concern. It is other people who stand in need of correction, other people who don't like Woody Allen movies or didn't go to Duke. Note, if you will, in the strident moralism that infects political discourse today the fairly precise correlation between peoples' net worth and the extent of their ethical alarm. The more well-off the commentator on the world's corruption, the more earnest the commentator's indignation.

A woman I know just returned from visiting her father in his retirement in some golf commune in Florida. "He spent the whole time talking about how nobody in America wanted to work, welfare moms were bearing scores of bastard babies to burden the future, and the world was going to hell. This," she said, "from a man who has spent the last ten years, and maybe the next thirty living off a Social Security system he will take more out of than he will put in, whose plush retirement was purchased mainly through his sleazy sellout of his company, and who spent no more than a third of his entire life actually working."

Moral condemnation appears to work like binoculars. Look through one end, at somebody else's trespasses, at a safe distance, things are magnified. Look back at yourself, through the other lens, everything is tiny, insignificant, mere peccadilloes.

When we moved to Durham, we noted how real estate prices were lower in the city than in the county. Why? we innocently asked our realtor. "Simple. Lots of black kids in the city schools; fewer blacks in the county schools."

Perhaps sensing a glimmer of intellectual indignation growing in my eye at the nerve of a real estate person to make such a racist remark in front of a liberal professor like me, he added, "Funny. Lots of Duke faculty worked for the integration of the Durham schools, but once they integrated, they did anything to avoid sending their own kids there."

In such moments defamiliarization begins to move for me in a different direction, is it the same for you?

And I remember the professor who jetted about the country, lecturing upon the need for the liberation and equality of women while his wife stayed in Durham raising, fairly much on her own, the kids he had fathered.

Isn't it interesting in our current public policy debates that there are no "unwed fathers"? Poor American women appear to be having babies by parthenogenesis!

Give me O. J. on the tube! O. J., Marsha, Nicole, Johnny, F. Lee, and dear Cato, we need you now more than ever to lead us in the rituals of national self-delusion and sin denial. You graciously bear the sins of a nation, you and the welfare moms, the homeless men, and the food-stamp frauds.

Last summer I saw this exposé on bank robberies in L.A. Los Angeles is suffering a plague of bank robberies. You could see the whole thing on the bank's security camera. Masked people blow into a bank, ski masks, guns, demanding money. There's a bank robbery every hour in some bank in Los Angeles.

"It concerns us," said the FBI person being interviewed. "One of these robberies is going to go bad. Innocent people will be hurt. The average bank robber is a person on drugs. Our last three arrests have been women with children."

My indignation rose within me. I could be one of those folk in the bank, making a deposit in my tax-sheltered IRA. Any of us here could be caught in the crossfire. It's an outrage!

Then the FBI agent added, "When you think about it, bank robbery is a stupid crime. We catch about 80 percent of them. Get back most of the money. Bank robberies are much easier to solve than any other crime. We get the whole thing on tape."

Then the FBI man made just a little throwaway remark, "We lost about $120,000 to bank robberies in California last year. Funny, we lost over a billion in the Savings and Loan frauds, and none of those guys has gone to jail. Of course, all of those guys wear business suits."

And gradually, I get defamiliarized, discomfort grows, and I wonder . . . Was C. S. Lewis right, when he said of himself, "For the first time I examined myself. . . . And there I found what appalled me: a zoo of lusts, a bedlam of ambitions, a nursery of fears, a harem of fondled hatreds." My sin, *my* sin.

Now before you continue in this service of Palm/Passion Sunday, I have for you a warning. This service begins with the waving of palms, archaic dance, and ancient music. The stories are of other people—Jews of another time, another place. We will hear shortly a sad story of betrayal, as those closest to Jesus forsook him and fled into the night, as Caesar's soldiers led Jesus away to capital punishment. Don't worry, the ancient words seem to say, relax, this isn't your story.

Tension builds. The pace quickens as we move from Pilate's praetorium and the trial of the ages is taken to the streets for a verdict. We the people, democracy in action, in unison, are about to have our say in the matter. What will we do with this Jesus, Jesus of Nazareth? How answer we?

Listen for the voices, the voices which cry in unison, "Crucify him!" And again, "Crucify him!"

It is a stunning, unforgettable moment in the worship of this chapel. Listen. The voices which cry out for his death are *our* voices. They ricochet off the walls, bounce back into our brains. Our voices. Our sin. My sin.

The old spiritual asks, "Were you there when they crucified my Lord?"

Yes. The sin which hung him there, the well-organized national self-deceit which nailed him to the wood is my sin. My sin. So G. K. Chesterton, when asked to write a magazine article on "What's Wrong with the Universe," responded to the editor's request, "What's Wrong with the Universe" with one sentence, "*I am.*"

A service which begins with such joy and exuberance will end in somber, confusing cacophony. We leave this drama, this trial, confused, defamiliarized, encountered, stripped naked of moral pretension, asking, "What shall he do, this week, with my sin?"

My sin.

34

You Are the Christ. . . .
Now What about *Them*?

August 25, 1996

MATTHEW 16:13–20

I had the privilege of hearing Eberhard Bethge, friend and biographer of Dietrich Bonhoeffer preach on this text in Duke Chapel. Bethge called Matthew 16:13–20 "one of the top texts of the church." It has been the text which has consoled the church during tough times—we cling to Jesus who is the long-awaited Messiah, the very Son of God. On the other hand, as Bethge painfully noted, this text has also been abused by the church as an authorization for persecution of non-Christians.

Knowing this, I decided to attempt to use this text as an occasion to reflect with the congregation upon our Christian encounter with other faiths.

I'm a Christian. But last week my cantankerous car was finely fixed by a Muslim mechanic. My hunger was handled by food prepared by Hindu hands. A Zoroastrian solved my software problem and a Jew persuaded me to be on a citizens' committee to build a better Durham.

Welcome to multireligious America.

I'm not sure that we mainline Protestant types know how to live in such a world. After all, our major project, well into this century, was to make a "Christian America," to concoct a country so uniformly Christian that we would never encounter anyone who was unable to confess with, Matthew 16, "You are the Christ, the Son of God."

Have you noticed? Even in "God We Trust" America, Christians are increasingly feeling like a minority in the very culture we thought we had made Christian. Although 82 percent of Americans claim to be Christian (Gallup, 1993), increasing numbers of us are asking, How are we to live as Christians in communities which are bubbling with the vitality of other religions? What do you say (should you say anything?) to the person who sits next to you at work and is a Muslim? Your Hindu dermatologist . . . what about her? Is she going to hell because she doesn't believe Matthew 16?

Of course, Matthew 16 comes out of just such a time as ours. When Jesus asked Peter, "Who do people say that I am?" followers of Jesus were a tiny minority on the margin of Judaism. When Peter said, "You are the Messiah, the Son of the living God!" he said so amid dozens of vibrant, counter religions. Not one verse of the New Testament was spoken for a time when Christians were the majority.

I say that because sometimes it's difficult for American Christians to remember that our faith originated in a conflicted religious marketplace where encounter with folk of other faiths was a daily, even hourly reality.

So how could Peter, knowing full well that the response of most people to Jesus' question, "Who do people say that I am?" would range from, "You are an inspired and wonderful teacher," to "You are a charlatan and a complete quack," but few would say, "You are the Messiah, the Son of the living God!" how could Peter make such bold, exclusive confession of faith in Christ?

Now, in one sense it's odd to expect guidance for our encounter with other faiths from this text. From one perspective, this text in which Peter says, "You are the Messiah, the Son of God," kills interreligious dialogue rather than encourages it. After you have said, "You are the Messiah, the Son of God," what else is there to say? You can't say something silly like, "And Buddha is also the only Son of God." Therefore, this text has a long history of usage by the church as validation for Christian persecution of other faiths.

Such usage is misusage. Because it's not just that Peter says to Jesus, "You are the Son of the living God," but rather that Peter says, "*You* are the Son of the living God." You. Jesus. In Jesus, God comes among us not as a crusading warrior but as a suffering servant. You are the Son of God, come among us not as the caustic, condemnatory denouncer of other religions but as one who says simply, graciously, "Follow me!"

To my knowledge, Jesus never said anything against anybody's religion, except his rather fierce criticisms of his own followers!

Therefore, to say of Jesus, "You are as much of God as we ever hope to see" (which is what Christians say of him), is to say that, in our encounter with other faiths, we must speak to others as Jesus spoke to us. As Christians we believe, not just that we have met God, but that we have met God *as Jesus.*

Other faiths believe they have met God in the words of Mohammed, a wise and righteous warrior, or as the Buddha, an introspective mystic. That will make a difference in how they view us Christians. And Jesus makes all the difference in how we view them, how we talk to them, how we listen to them.

As we see it, when Peter said, "*You* are the Messiah, the Son of God," he set the rules for our encounter with folk of other faiths.

Jesus is judgment upon some of the ways we Christians have attempted to relate to people who believe differently from us.

The well-meaning soul who says, "Hey, you're Hindu, I'm Christian, but that's not really important. After all, we're all saying fairly much the same thing," is wrong. If you will sit down and actually listen to the Hindu for more than five minutes, you will see that she or he is *not* saying the same thing as Christians say. For you to say otherwise is an affront to Hindus.

What first appears as graciousness—"Hey, we're all heading in the same direction after all"—is actually the height of arrogance—"Hey, your Hinduism is really unimportant and insignificant."

No. When Peter confessed of Jesus, "You are the Messiah," he was saying something singular, different. Jesus is not the embodiment of a mess of vaguely religious emotions and pious platitudes, a la Leo Buscaglia. He is Jesus, someone who lived, spoke, and died in a very specific way. It was possible to get him wrong, as this episode demonstrates. Everything nice that folk said of Jesus ("He's a great prophet, a wonderful teacher of wisdom, a fine moral example") was not accepted by Jesus as truthfully describing him.

Statements like, "Well, you're Jewish, I'm Black Muslim, but what really matters is that we're all just human beings," shows, not that someone is open-minded about religion but just the opposite. One is so closed-minded about religion that one cannot even conceive that a person's religious belief is the most important thing in that person's life.

You do a Jew no favor when you say something which implies that Jewishness is insignificant, a mere quirk of the personality, a premodern vestige which can be overcome by appeals to common humanity, or universal feelings, or some other pagan drivel.

This is why many Jews and Christians have learned to be suspicious of intellectual vagaries like "Judeo-Christian." There's no such thing as "Judeo-Christian." There are Jews. There are Christians. But there are no "Judeo-Christians." Jews really do not believe that Jesus is, in Peter's words, "The Messiah, the Son of God." They really do not want to be baptized by us, even baptized into something called "Judeo-Christian." They want to be Jews, to be listened to as Jews, to be respected as Jews and not demeaned by being subsumed by some allegedly neutral blob called "Judeo-Christian."

So I'm saying that the first step toward learning to live with our religious differences is learning *to respect those differences*, allowing one another to live in our differences.

American democracy claims that it practices "freedom of religion." Too often, modern American culture allows people to be religious only after we have promised to keep our religion private and unmentionable, safely sealed off from public discourse, in other words irrelevant, unimportant, and insignificant. That won't do.

A Hindu on campus was telling me that she felt much in common with conservative evangelical Christians, not because, after all, their differences were only apparent, but because the conservative evangelical Christians, believing so deeply in their faith, constantly under assault by the benign paganism of this campus, could empathize with her as a Hindu when she felt excluded and under assault by the dominant modes of discourse on this campus.

Or as a Jewish friend told me, "You Christians are beginning to learn what Jews knew a long time ago. Your worst foe is not Jews who won't become Christians but rather pagans who teach that all religion—Jewish, Christian or any other—is an outmoded vestige of the past which enlightened people have at last outgrown."

We Christians have much more in common with the Muslim who says, "There is no God but Allah and Mohammed is his prophet," than we do with the happy American pagan who says, "Well, all religions are saying fairly much the same thing."

As Christians, we are to relate to people of other faiths as Jesus related to them: With respect and love, knowing that they are beloved children of God. With humility, knowing that we didn't come to Christ, he came to us. With joyful curiosity in learning more about what they have learned of the ways of God, hoping that one day they may in turn ask us to share what we have learned of God in Christ. With the awesome responsibility of knowing that they are quite right in judging the claims of Christ by watching how we live. From what I've seen, most people do not believe in Jesus, not because they think Jesus is a fraud, but rather because they see so little of Jesus in the lives of those of us who profess to be following Jesus!

One last thing to keep in mind in your encounters with people of other faiths: When Peter makes this stunning confession, "You are the Messiah, the Son of the living God," Jesus doesn't say to Peter, "Great! Now you have got the point, go out and arm wrestle everyone else into seeing things the way you now see them."

Jesus says, "Blessed are you, Simon! Flesh and blood has not revealed this to you, but my Father in heaven." In other words, Peter, you believe in me, not as a personal intellectual achievement, but rather as *gift*. Grace.

If this morning you can say, when asked, Who is Jesus? "The Messiah, the Son of God," it's only because it has been given to you. No place for smugness, self-righteousness here.

Note that first Jesus asks about them, "Who do others say that I am?" That mechanic who worked on my car last week, the chef who prepared my lunch, who do they say Jesus is?

But then, quite quickly, Jesus moves to the heart of the matter. "Who do *you* say that I am?" That's the question. The ultimate fate of others who do not believe in Jesus, the significance of their relationship to God, that's a matter between them and God. Your greatest concern is not, "What about *them*?" Your care should be, "What about *me*? What do *I* say about Jesus? How does my life—in the way I go about the world, in the manner in which I relate to others—how does my life demonstrate that Jesus really is the Christ, the Son of the living God?"

35

Retirement: A Whole New Life

July 13, 1997

Vanity of vanities, says the Teacher. . . . All is vanity. What do people gain from all the toil at which they toil under the sun? A generation goes, and a generation comes, but the earth remains forever. . . . There is nothing new under the sun.
Ecclesiastes 1:2–4, 9

Then I saw a new heaven and a new earth; for the first heaven and the first earth had passed away. . . . And the one who was seated on the throne said, "See, I am making all things new."
Revelation 21:1, 5

Most of my ministry I've attempted to defeat the type of preaching on which I was raised—topical preaching in which a preacher picks a topic, rummages about for some biblical text that justifies whatever it was the preacher wanted to say in the first place, and preaches that. However, on some rare occasions I've committed topical sermons myself. Deep in the summer of 1997, in my fifty-first year of life, I preached a sermon on retirement. Not much gospel here, but I hope at least some relatively wise advice.

My text is from Ecclesiastes, one of the Bible's most depressing, cynical books. "Vanity of vanities, says the Teacher. . . . All is vanity." Have you ever felt like that, looking back on your life? Your accomplishments crumble in your hands as dust. Your great achievements seem as so much chasing after the wind.

No wonder the writer of Ecclesiastes feels this way about his life. "There is nothing new under the sun," he says. Life is just one thing after another, a great wheel in which there is no beginning, and no end. Life is, in Shakespeare's words, full of "sound and fury, signifying nothing." Ecclesiastes is one of the only books in the Bible with a cyclical view of history. History doesn't begin or end, it's not going anywhere. History is a great cycle, a circle. There is nothing new under the sun. When there is no ending or beginning, no real newness, life is depressing.

I want to talk to you about something that nearly everyone here will do, some of you sooner than later. I want to talk about retirement. I have a problem right from the start. When I preach, I like to preach from the Bible, take a biblical text and work from there. Trouble is, it is only until recently that humanity lived long enough or had enough stored up goods to "retire" in our sense of the word. The Bible, particularly the Hebrew Scripture, considers old age, a long life, a great gift of God. But retirement, what to do with our old age or our now widespread long life, is a relatively recent problem.

I'm unhappy with the word "retirement." It's a cousin of other similarly uninspiring words like retreat, remove, regress. "Retirement" makes it sound as if, in our last years of life, we withdraw from the fray, settle in, settle down, quit moving, quit living for all intents and purposes. Yet we're learning that each stage of life has its challenges, its different demands and new adventures, including retirement.

I recall a student whom I was teaching in seminary. He was serving his first little church as a student pastor. One day he complained to me about his congregation. "The median age of my congregation is over sixty," he declared. "And you know how old people are."

"How are they?" I asked.

"You know—set in their ways, creatures of habit, slow to change, stuck in their ruts. They don't want any innovation or change in the way we do things at the church."

Not two days before I had read an article on retirement which noted that, of the six or eight greatest transitions you must make in life, the most traumatic changes, four or five of them will occur after sixty-five. Transitions, radical moves like declining health, loss of independence, unemployment, the loss of a spouse are among the major moves of this stage of life.

I noted this to the young, student pastor adding, "Which suggests that it's not fair to say that these older people are refusing to change. They are about to drown in some of the most dramatic changes life offers. When you've buried the man you have lived with for forty years, or you are forced out of your life work, about the last thing you want is to come to church and have some upstart young preacher say, 'Let's do something new and innovative today.' They're sinking in a flood of innovation!"

We once thought of adulthood as that time in life when you at last put down roots, hunkered down, burrowed in for the rest of your life, and stayed there. The really important developmental events occurred in infancy, childhood, or youth. We now know that adulthood is best construed as a series of passages (thank you, Gail Sheehy), of life challenges, which is far from stable.

For some years I have taught a course to first-year students at Duke called "The Search for Meaning" (Thomas Naylor and William H. Willimon, *The Search for Meaning* [Nashville: Abingdon Press, 1994]). We study the ways various people have found meaning in their lives, a reason to get out of bed in the morning. We also push the students to articulate their own sense of meaning in life, to write down where they are headed and who they plan to be when they grow up.

I have noted that most of them think to themselves, "I'm all confused and in flux now but, when I am twenty-five, I will have decided who I want to be, I will settle down, settle in, and be fixed."

It doesn't take much insight to see that life is not at all like that. For instance, I note how odd it is for us to ask students, "What do you plan to do (or be) when you graduate from Duke?"

They respond by saying, "I'm going to be an electrical engineer." Or, "I'm going into medicine."

But then we note that the average American goes through *seven* job changes in a lifetime. Someone from the engineering school told me the other day that they did a study of their graduates and only thirty percent of them were in engineering just twenty years after graduation!

See my point? These students had better be preparing for a more challenging life than merely figuring out what you want to do for the rest of your life, getting that, expecting to do that for the rest of your life.

Is that why increasing numbers of educators are coming to speak of intelligence not in terms of IQ, a fixed intellectual quotient in you since birth, but rather intelligence defined as *the ability to adapt*? Life is this long series of adaptations, moves, changes, beginnings and endings.

As a pastor, I've watched a good number of people move into retirement. I'm moving ever closer there myself. And though, from what I've observed, there are a number of challenges of the allegedly "Golden Years," one stands out above all the rest:

Retirement is a whole new life.

I'm here paraphrasing from a great book by my friend, Reynolds Price, *A Whole New Life* (New York: Atheneum, 1994). It's Reynolds's moving account of his struggle through cancer surgery, recovery, and beyond. Some of you may have read it. What Reynolds has to say there is far too rich to be condensed, but I think it fair to say that one of the most important insights of the book, and the insight which lends its title is that he experienced his illness as an invitation to a whole new life.

Reynolds tells how he denied his cancer, how he was filled with anger and resentment when he realized that he was very sick, how he struggled in the painful months after his debilitating, but life-saving surgery. Here was a once robust, active man, at the prime of his life, the peak of his career, reduced to life in a wheelchair.

But Reynolds depicts his path back as a dawning realization that, in his words, "The old Reynolds has died" (Ibid., 183). His old self, so many of the aspects of his former existence that he loved, were over. He could not get them back. Now, he could spend the rest of his life in grief for what he had lost, pitifully attempting to salvage some bits and pieces, or he could begin "a whole new life."

Reynolds chose the latter. He began again. He started over. It was not the life he might have chosen, if he were doing the choosing, but it was a good life, a life worth living. He now enjoys the greatest period of artistic productivity of his life, turning out more novels, plays, and poems, than ever.

"Find your way to be somebody else," he advises, "the next viable you—a stripped-down whole other clear-eyed person, realistic as a sawed-off shotgun and thankful for air, not to speak of the human kindness you'll meet if you get normal luck" (Ibid.).

Now, retirement is rarely as traumatic as spinal cancer. Yet I do think there are analogies to be made. From what I've observed, the people who fail miserably at the challenges of the later years are those who fail to see retirement as a definite transition from one plane of existence to another. They attempt to salvage too much of their former life.

I'm haunted by what a woman told me of her mother. Her mother had worked at minimum wage in a garment factory for over forty years. When she retired, her children thought she would be thrilled. She was miserable. She cried. She hung around at the gate of the factory many mornings, vainly hoping that they would call her back to work. She even took an assumed name and tried to get hired, representing herself as another person.

That won't work. Your old life goes on without you. They somehow get by down at the office without your services. The school doesn't fall in after your last day in the classroom.

You can't get the old life back. You need to lay hold of a whole new life. I think those of us who are moving toward retirement (and isn't that just about everyone here?) could do much more to prepare ourselves better to make that transition to a whole new life. If our only life is our work, we are in big trouble unless we can find some new life after work. Churches could do a better job of helping our members to prepare themselves and to support one another during the transition into retirement.

We need some good rituals for retirement. In Japan, for instance, there is a tradition in which, when a woman reaches retirement age, she takes all of her pots and pans and presents them to her daughter or daughter-in-law. From then on she is expected not to enter the kitchen. That part of her life is over. A new life has begun.

Many Japanese men begin retirement by dressing in a red kimono and doing something adventuresome that they have not done before, like climbing Mount Fuji. People need to be encouraged to do something visible and physical which will symbolize their important transition.

Thomas Naylor and I wrote a book arising out of our first-year student seminar called *The Search for Meaning.* To our surprise and delight, a number of churches have reported using the book in congregational preretirement seminars. We're delighted that the book we wrote with college freshmen in mind has proved to be helpful for those in their sixties. We are reminded that one of the most important skills one can have is the ability to take a deep breath, to look out over your life, and start over with a whole new life.

As Christians, we do not believe that history is a meaningless cycle going nowhere, one thing after another. We believe that God is Alpha and Omega, the Beginning and the End. God not only gets us going at the beginning but also meets us at the end. More to the point of the challenges of retirement, God gives fresh beginnings, new days, new lives. The Bible opens with the Genesis declaration, "Let there be light!" as a new world comes into being and, as today's Scripture has reminded us, closes with the Revelation, "Behold, I make all things new!"

Between here and there, we are asked to make many transitions, each with their attendant pain, uncertainty, and their promise. One of the most important of our life transitions is retirement.

My father-in-law spent his entire life as a pastor in a variety of United Methodist churches in South Carolina. Mr. Parker had thus spent his whole life in black suits and white shirts as moral exemplar of the community, doing his duty in the week-in-week-out care of his churches.

When he retired, he bought a large camping trailer and he and Mrs. Parker pulled the trailer toward New England for a long-awaited retirement celebration trip. Somehow, on the way from South Carolina to New England, he took a wrong turn and found himself driving down the middle of Manhattan, pulling that trailer, lost, not knowing which way to turn.

A car blew its horn at him, pulled up beside him, and the driver shouted, "Old man, I wish you would figure out where you're going or get out of the way!"

Mr. Parker said that he thought to himself, "I'm up here in New York, a long way from South Carolina. Nobody here knows that I was a Methodist preacher. I'm retired."

So he rolled down his window, looked over at the man in the car beside him and said, "And I wish you would go to hell!"

Retirement. It's a whole new life.

36

Unspectacular Faithfulness

September 28, 1997

ESTHER 7:1–6, 9–10; 9:20–22

This sermon, early in the school year, was motivated by an article by a feminist inter-preter where I read, "Esther, precisely because she was a woman and therefore basi-cally powerless within Persian society, was the paradigm of the diaspora Jew, who was also powerless in Persian society. Because she was successful in attaining power within the structure of society, she served as a role model for diaspora Jews" ("Esther," by Sidnie Ann White, in Carol Newsom and Sharon Ringe, eds., The Women's Bible Commentary *[Louisville, KY: Westminster/John Knox Press, 1992], 126).*

To be a young Christian in a modern, selective, first-rate university is also to be powerless and in diaspora. In this thoroughly narrative sermon I sought to link the powerlessness of sophomore Christians with that of this heroic woman. Most of the sermon is consumed with a simple retelling of a biblical story that I assumed came as new information to most of my collegiate congregation.

He told me how much he was enjoying his Bible study group here at Duke.

"Were you in a Bible study group in high school?" I asked.

"Are you kidding?" he asked, "I told you I was an Episcopalian."

I persisted. "Well, why do you think that Bible study has become so impor-tant to you here?"

Exasperated he replied, "Dean Willimon, have you ever tried to be a Chris-tian and a sophomore at the same time?"

Weird that increasing numbers of Christians are beginning to feel like strangers in the very culture we thought we had created.

Let me tell you a story. Once upon a time there was a king who ruled over the world from India to Ethiopia; his name was Ahasuerus. He decided he needed a queen, so he ordered that the most lovely women from his 127 provinces be brought before him that he might choose the loveliest as his queen. He chose Esther.

Though the king did not know it, Esther was an orphan, a Jew in the care of her uncle, Mordecai. Mordecai advised Esther to marry the king, even though he was not of her faith or her people. Besides, Esther was a poor nobody, a woman, and Ahasuerus was a king and in the socioeconomic, gender-based, class-dependent politics of the day, what could she do?

Now, in the king's employ was a wicked toady named Haman, who wasn't only a bureaucrat—similar to those who work today here in the registrar's office or the department of motor vehicles—but he was a bad bureaucrat, if you will accept the tautology. Haman plotted to kill all the Jews in all the king's lands, seeing these foreigners as troublesome aliens who would never be loyal subjects.

He set a date for the mass executions. Then, in good little toady, bureaucratic kiss-up fashion, Haman slithers up to the king and says, "Dear king, it has come to our attention that there is a certain ethnic group in your kingdom who consider themselves above your laws. Although multiculturalism and ethnic diversity is an otherwise good thing, a rule is a rule. Allow me to help my king by destroying them."

This sounded good to the king, Ahasuerus agreed, and ordered that on the thirteenth of Adar all Jews would be slain.

The Jews were distressed by this horrible news. Mordecai sent news of the plan to Esther in the palace, begging her to help. "Who knows?" asked Mordecai, "maybe you have been put in the palace for a moment such as this."

Now a word about palace etiquette. In those days, it was hard to get to see the king—even if your were a Taiwanese businessperson with a fat donation to make, you couldn't get in. Even the queen had to ask permission. If she showed up unsummoned by the king, even the queen could be killed.

Esther reminds Mordecai of the rules. You bother the king when he doesn't want to be messed with, honey, you could be a dead queen. Mordecai reminds Esther that she is the only hope her people have.

Esther is in great fear. She lies awake in torment for three days. Finally, she decides that she will go, saying, "If I die, I shall die."

Esther entered the throne room. She was terrified. Yet the king bid her to speak.

"Dear king," she said, "would you grant to me just one little favor?"

"Just name it," said the king, "even half my kingdom, whatever." (She had obviously caught him in a great mood.)

"Would you and your trusted lackey, er, uh, I mean advisor Haman do me the honor of attending a great dinner with me?"

Haman, when he learned of the invitation, was even more full of himself, so proud that he was being invited up to the big house for a great party. He was obviously in tight with the king and the queen. Passing old Mordecai on the way to dinner, he told him to get ready to swing from a rope by morning.

Esther spent the whole next day wondering how in the world she was going to talk to the king about Haman's plot against the Jews. The banquet was a great affair, but Esther couldn't bring herself to speak to the king about her people.

At the end of the evening, Esther said that the food and the wine had been so great, the dinner table conversation so scintillating, that she was going to give another dinner tomorrow. Would the king and his toady . . . advisor be good enough to come?

They agreed. Next night, maybe it was the wine, or maybe it was the beef bourguignon, but King Ahasuerus blurted out, "Esther, you are such a great queen, tell me what would make you happy."

Esther finally had the courage to say, "Dear king, there is an evil man in this palace who wants to kill me and those whom I love. Let me and my people live; that's all I ask."

"What?" asked the king. "Tell me who this scoundrel is."

"He's over there," she said, "the fat one just finishing his chocolate mousse."

Was Haman shocked. He didn't even know Esther was Jewish! He was even more shocked when the king ordered him taken out and hanged on the very gallows Haman had been preparing for old Mordecai.

And that's how the people of Israel were preserved, even to this day. A savvy woman, laying aside her own safety, speaking up in behalf of her people, saved them in a foreign land.

I expect that this is the first time most of you have heard this story of Esther. I think this is the first sermon I have preached on it. Esther has never been one of the top ten books of the Bible. For one thing, Esther is a woman, and most of history seems most interested in the actions of men. For another thing, some Christians have been a little perplexed by Esther's morality, becoming the mistress, then the queen of a pagan.

For yet another thing, God is never mentioned in the entire book of Esther. God doesn't speak, or intervene, nothing.

So why should I tell you this story, and on a Sunday, and in church? If you are young, then a major job is looking for appropriate adult role models. If you are young and a woman, your task is especially tough, because there aren't many. If you are young, a woman, and a Christian, then your choices of adult role models are few indeed.

There are heroes out there, grand names like Teresa of Calcutta, or Madame Curie, or Eleanor Roosevelt. But sometimes these great, grand heroes are no role models at all. Their attainments are too great, their accomplishments so spectacular that how can an average, everyday person like you possibly hope to match your life with theirs?

Esther was a hero, but a reluctant one. She did a great deed for her people, but she took small, hesitant steps on the way there. She assimilated herself into the dominant culture, so much so that most of her people probably thought that she had given away the store, had allowed herself to be so thoroughly enmeshed in pagan culture that she was no longer a Jew.

As a woman, she was powerless, even though she was queen. Yet Esther used what power she had, maneuvered skillfully within the limits imposed upon her by the culture, and did a great thing.

What she did was not particularly spectacular but that's good because most of us are not very spectacular ourselves. Fortunately, most of the good that God needs doing is not too spectacular. Someday, someone here may be required to die for the faith that you profess, but not likely. More likely you will be given the opportunity, or the dilemma, of summoning up the courage to speak out at some elegant dinner party, to put in a word to the boss in behalf of someone who can't speak for himself. Not large. Not grand. But still good.

Today's story is about that. As Christians and Jews we live in a world that, on the whole, neither worships nor obeys our God. The motto of our age is not, "What doth the Lord require?" but rather, "What do I have to do to get along?" In such a climate we are tempted to let ourselves off the hook too easily, to say, "I'm no martyr, I'm just one little guy, what can I do?"

This story is for us. In little, ordinary, unspectacular ways, the kingdom of God is being defeated or advanced through us, the battle is being lost or won on the basis of our little words, gestures, and acts.

Esther is a story about that.

37

Washed in the Blood

Maundy Thursday 1999

This is my blood, poured out for you . . . for the remission of sin.

An article on cockfighting (Burkhard Bilger, "Enter the Chicken: On the Bayou, Cock-fighting Remains Undefeated," Harper's Magazine, March 1999, 48–57) got me to thinking about Maundy Thursday. Looking back more than a decade, it's hard to remember why I was motivated to preach this odd sermon on one of the highest, holiest nights of the year. Blame it on a Savior who could say, without flinching, "Unless you eat my flesh and drink my blood you are unworthy of me." Blame it on a church that invites a congregation of urbane university-related folk to huddle in a darkened church in order to hold up before them a cup of wine and say, "Here, this blood's for you."

My usual Sunday assumption, in dealing with you in sermons, is that you are all sinful, fallen, and utterly depraved.

However, if you will come out to worship on a Thursday night, well then you must not be all bad! Thursday evening piety ought to count for something, you're thinking. That you are feeling rather righteous, by being here tonight at table with Jesus, is proof-positive of your *unrighteousness*.

Cockfighting is legal in Louisiana, and in four other states, though it is estimated that there are at least half a million cockfighting enthusiasts in this country. Cockfighting involves taking two roosters specially, expensively bred to fight (all chickens are natural born killers), strapping surgical steel blades (gaffs) to their legs, putting them in a ring, and watching as they slash one another to shreds. Pent up for two days prior in total darkness, injected with testosterone (all you feminists take note), as well as vitamin K to make wounds clot quickly, it's pure blood sport. It often takes only a few minutes for one cock to kick and claw another to death, but sometimes the blood and feathers fly for half an hour. Not many cocks leave the ring alive, even the winners. Cockfighting is a big part of the culture in the Philippines, in Bali, and Puerto Rico. George Washington and (of course) Andrew Jackson dearly loved the sport. Abe Lincoln was a cockfighting referee and when asked if cockfighting ought to be banned replied, "As long as God permits intelligent man created in his own image to fight in public and kill each other while the world looks on, it's not for me to deprive the chickens of the same 'freedom.'"

It has been estimated that there are more cockfights today than at any time in our nation's history. I know more on this subject than any Methodist preacher alive, having seen Western North Carolina's Professor Fredrick Hawley's dissertation on the subject. And we can be glad, you and I, that cockfighting is relegated to the realm of illegal, redneck recreation. It really is quite horrible what these ignorant people will watch.

Tyson Foods slaughters 1.3 million birds a week. We consume seven billion chickens a year. It now takes only about six weeks for an egg to roll down a conveyer belt, be incubated, hatched, and be a four-pound victim whose feet have never hit dirt, to be hung up by the feet on a conveyer belt to be decapitated by a buzz saw. Of course, all this is kept from the sight of a people who so want to believe that we have risen above a taste for blood. Who are the chicken killers now?

Augustine (in *De Ordine*) tells of noticing a couple of barnyard cocks in bitter battle just outside his front door. "We chose to watch," he said. And Augustine noted his choice to watch as visible evidence of his depravity.

Interesting that we would have no such moral qualms. "At least our birds live a pampered life and get to die heroically," said a cockfighter, "which is more than you can say for the ones *you* eat."

Ernest Becker (*The Denial of Death*) mocked modern humanity who lifted up its head, smacked its lips over a mountain of animal carcasses and proudly declared, "Life is good."

And so, in a classroom discussion about corporate greed, about the badness of multinational business tycoons, an honest student pointed to the Nikes he was wearing and said, "I'm guilty."

If only we could pin the sin on other people, some gaggle of grinning redneck fools clustered about a bloody cock pit. No, I had dinner tonight. I'm guilty. We are washed in the blood.

"The dragging death of a black man in Texas at least ended in a vindication of our belief in the American justice system with the conviction of that white supremacist monster," he said.

"That you think a white supremacist monster is rare in this country is a vindication of my belief that you need to travel more widely in America," I said.

So when an alleged "theologian" at Union Seminary, New York, declares, "We don't need some man bleeding on a cross to save us," I say, "Well, *I* sure do."

Any God too good to get his hands a little bloody, any savior unwilling to stoop, to suffer, can't do me much good, so deep is my sinful self-deceit. We're all natural-born killers, and I'm not just referring to the murder rate in New York City. To get to us, to do something decisive about us, blood must be shed, for we are a very bloody lot. Our sin is a life-and-death matter. If we could contain our carnage to a few billion chickens, maybe we could be improved. But, God help us, we can't.

God help us.

A cup is lifted over a table filled with sinners, over the burned body of the sacrificial paschal lamb. Jesus, the host, turns to his disciples (who are also his betrayers) and gives us the good news, *"This is my blood, poured out for you . . . for the remission of sin."* Amen.

38

Easter as an Earthquake

Easter 1999

MATTHEW 28:1–10

Suddenly there was a great earthquake; for an angel of the Lord, descending from heaven, came and rolled back the stone and sat on it.

Matthew 28:2

My Maundy Thursday sermon on cockfighting is followed by an Easter sermon on an earthquake. Who can account for the machinations in the mind of a preacher? The Gospels' marvelously metaphorical presentation of the truth of Jesus Christ generates peculiar proclamation.

John says that they got to the tomb on Easter morning, and it's empty. Then, they go back home.

Go back home? Reminds you of the two disciples in Luke on the way to Emmaus. "Some women told us that Jesus had been raised from the dead, but we had already planned to have supper over in Emmaus, so we couldn't change our reservations." A man is raised from the dead and you can't cancel lunch? How dumb are these disciples?

So my friend Stanley Hauerwas, in dialogue with dear Marcus Borg of the errant Jesus Seminar says, "Marcus thinks the disciples had an experience. They said, 'Wasn't it great being with Jesus before they killed him? You remember those great stories he told? The lectures, er, *sermons?* Just thinking about it makes him seem almost still here. Yep, by God, he *is* still here. Let's all close our eyes and believe real hard that he's still here. Okay?'"

Hey, Jesus Seminar, the disciples weren't that creative! These were not imaginative minds we're dealing with here. They were the sort of people who could see an empty tomb and not let it spoil lunch. You don't get an idea like the bodily resurrection of Jesus out of people with brains like Simon Peter's.

In short, *the disciples were people like us.*

People like us are the sort of folk who like to believe that you can have resurrection and still have the world as it was last Thursday. We want to have Easter and still have our world unrocked by resurrection. We are amazingly well-adjusted to the same old world.

I think that's why Matthew says that when there was Easter, the whole earth shook. Luke does Easter as a meal on Sunday evening with the risen Christ. John has resurrected Jesus encounter Mary Magdalene in the garden. But Matthew? Easter is an earthquake with doors shaken off tombs and dead people walking the streets, the stone rolled away by the ruckus and an impudent angel sitting on it.

I've been in an earthquake, even though I'm not from L.A. I was preaching in Alaska and during my sermon the earth heaved a moment that seemed forever. The little church shook. The Alaskan Methodists sat there like it was another day at the office. Their only response was the woman who said, "How about that, the light fixtures didn't fall this time." I ended my sermon immediately. I was shaken by the earthquake, but also a bit shaken by those nonchalant Alaskans. Afterwards (at lunch!) I asked the pastor, "What the heck would it take to get this congregation's attention? I'd hate to have to preach to them every Sunday."

Matthew says Easter is an earthquake that shook the whole world.

We modern types try to "explain" the resurrection. One says that Jesus was in a deep, drugged coma and woke up. Another said that the disciples got all worked up in their grief and just fantasized the whole thing.

But you can't "explain" a resurrection. *Resurrection explains us.* The truth of Jesus tells on the faces of the befuddled disciples who witnessed it. Not one of them expected, wanted Easter. Death, defeat, while regrettable, are utterly explainable.

"It was a good campaign while it lasted. But we didn't get him elected Messiah. Death has the last word. We had hoped . . . but you've got to face facts. You want some lunch?"

The world is in the tight death grip of the "facts." All that lives, dies. The good get it in the end. Face facts. It may be a rather somber world, but it is *our* world where things stay tied down and what dies stays that way. And there are few surprises. This is us.

But Easter is about God. It is not about the resuscitation of a dead body. That's resuscitation, not resurrection. It's not about the "immortality of the soul," some divine spark that endures after the end. That's Plato, not Jesus. It's about God, not God as an empathetic but ineffective good friend, or some inner experience. It's about God who makes a way when there was no way, a God who makes war on evil until evil is undone, a God who raises dead Jesus just to show us who's in charge here.

I don't know this for sure, but I think Matthew's Easter earthquake angel perched on the rock rolled from the tomb was the same angel who, earlier in Matthew 1 (vv. 8–25) shook Joseph awake one night with the news that his fiancée was pregnant. (Talk about an earthquake!)

See my point? God did on Easter in invading the tomb what God did on Christmas in a virgin's womb: Made a way when there was no way. Took charge. The same angel who was sent to tell Joseph, "Name the baby Emmanuel, God with us," was the angel who told the women, "Don't be afraid. He isn't here. He's been raised."

Little God with Us grew up, got crucified, made the earth shake, and is on the move to take back the world.

On the cross, the world did all it could to Jesus. At Easter, God did all God could to the world. And the earth shook.

You don't explain that. You witness it. That's why the risen Christ appeared first to his own disciples. They had heard him teach, seen him heal, watched as he loved the poor and attacked the rich, watched him be arrested by the soldiers, tried by the judge, and crucified. Why would Jesus come back first to his disciples? Because they were the ones able to recognize that this risen Lord was none other than the crucified Jesus. Crucifixion wasn't just an unfortunate mistake in the Roman legal system, the first-century Judean equivalent of the O. J. Simpson fiasco. Crucifixion was the inevitable, predictable result of saying the things Jesus said, and doing the things Jesus did, and being the Savior Jesus was. This is what the world always does to people who threaten the world. Face facts.

But . . . on Easter God inserted a new fact. God took the cruel cross and made it the means of triumph. God (the same Creator who made light from darkness, a world from void, a baby in a virgin's womb), God took the worst we do—all our death-dealing doings—and led them out toward life. And the earth shook.

A new world was thereby offered. Jesus came back to forgive the very disciples who had forsaken him. The world is about forgiveness, as it turns out, not vengeance. And the earth shook.

Jesus picked up a piece of bread and ate it and you could see the nailprints in his hands. The world is about life, as it turns out, not death. And the earth shook.

In the fifties, in China, there was a devastating earthquake. But as a result of the quake, a huge boulder was dislodged from a mountain thus exposing a great cache of wonderful artifacts from a thousand years ago. A new world suddenly came to light.

When the stone was rolled away, and the earth shook we got our first glimpse of a new world, a world where death doesn't have the last word, a world where injustice is made right, and innocent suffering is vindicated by the intrusion of a powerful God.

The women came out to the cemetery to write one more chapter in the long sad story of death's ascendancy, one more episode of how the good always get it in the end. This is the way the world ends, not with a bang but a whimper of resignation at death's dark victory.

And then ... the earth heaved, an angel appeared, the stone was rolled away, Caesar's soldiers shook. The angel plopped himself down on the stone in one final act of impudent defiance of death, and the soldiers, and all that, and said to the women, *"Don't be afraid.* You're looking for Jesus? He isn't here."

Then that angel turned to the soldiers and said, *"Be* afraid. Everything which your world is built on is being shaken."

We will never go back home by the same path we came. Alleluia.

39

The Extravagance of Trinitarian Faith

May 30, 1999

MATTHEW 28:16–20

To those who expected a mercifully short sermon for a warm May Sunday I said, "Settle down. It's Trinity Sunday. This will take some time."

I know this is a prejudiced preacher comment, but I have never had much empathy with those dear modern souls who whine that we know too little for sure about Jesus, that we are not told enough about God in the Bible, that we lack enough evidence to decide anything for sure about Christianity. The God who supplies my sermons is extravagantly revealing. This God has shown us more than we'll ever be able to assimilate in a century of sermons. Thus my sermon on the Trinity.

"Good teachers are big talkers," he said to me. I found this an interesting observation coming from a man who had spent his entire life preparing teachers to teach in elementary schools.

"I haven't worked this out in any exact way, but from my observations, good teachers are big talkers. They are people who are effusive, ubiquitous in their interaction with others. They are everywhere, all the time, talking, interacting with the children."

And I thought about some of the great teachers I have known, particularly teachers of young children. It seemed to me that he was right. Good teachers are good talkers. I am thinking now of a woman who taught one of my children. When you visited her classroom, you saw a person who somehow managed to be everywhere, all the time, moving, interacting with the children, talking to them, full of opinions about their work, full of encouraging words and constant conversation. Their constant reaching toward their

199

students evokes the best from their students. There does seem to be a sort of effusiveness and loquaciousness about good teachers.

Scripture says that our God is a big talker—effusive, loquacious. Think of the Bible as a long story of God's attempted conversation with humanity. We keep rejecting the words of God, turning in another direction, worshiping false Gods, attempting to hide, evade, or end the conversation. But God keeps coming back to us. God comes to us in the lives of the patriarchs, in the words of the prophets, in the gift of God's law. Then, stooping at nothing, God comes to us as the Son, coming to us as Jesus. Then, even when we killed his only Son, hung him on a cruel cross, thinking that that had probably ended relations between us and God, in three days, God came back to us as the risen Christ, came back and resumed the conversation with the same disciples who had forsaken him. God keeps coming back, again, and even again.

We are now, on this Sunday, ending the church's celebration of the Great Fifty Days of Easter—God's supreme coming back to talk to us as the resurrected Christ. But we end Easter in the confidence that we do not thereby end God's continuing conversation with us. What we thought, with the cross, was the end, was, with the resurrection, the beginning because it is of the nature of this God to be loquacious, effusive.

Our appointed Scripture comes from the very end of Matthew's Gospel when the risen Christ tells his followers to "Bed down here, get some real estate, build a church for me with accessible parking, and hold on tight to the experience that we have shared together." No! Christ resurrected and victorious tells his people to "Go!" "Get out of here and go into the whole world and make disciples. Tell them, baptize them, teach them in the name of the Father, the Son, and the Holy Spirit."

The same God, who had come to them, now tells them to go to others. The same resourceful, creative, talkative God who had spoken to them, in life and in death, now commands them to speak to others about him. To say that they are to do this in the name of the "Father, Son, and Holy Spirit," is not just a pious tag added on to Christ's mission mandate. It is the source of that mandate. It is the nature of this God whom we call Father, Son, and Holy Spirit—the Trinity—always to reach, always to go, to address, to summon, and to speak and those who would be in the world (us) in his name must also be on the go, always talking as we go. Wasn't that what we heard the angel say to the women at the tomb, "Go! Tell!" Act toward the world the same way that God as Father, Son, and Holy Spirit has acted toward you!

Martin Luther, in speaking of the real presence of Christ in the Lord's Supper, spoke of God's "ubiquity." Our God is ubiquitous, everywhere and at all times present, though peculiarly, particularly, and especially present in the

Eucharist, the Lord's Supper. Our God is not only loving, caring, and acting, our God is ubiquitous.

There is a kind of effusiveness about God, an effervescent, overflowing quality.

Augustine spoke of this in a passage in his great book, *The City of God.* Augustine spoke of the "plentitude" of God. As evidence of this, Augustine mentioned the effusiveness whereby God created all of the flowers in the world. We might have stopped creating flowers after one or two beautiful specimens. But God didn't stop. God kept creating multitudes of flowers, all in different shapes and colors and kinds. Not only are they beautiful, Augustine notes, but see the glory in how they will turn their heads toward the sun, bending toward the light. We might have been content, as humans, with just a few flowers and their splendor. God didn't stop with a few, because God is effusive, overflowing with love and creativity. God is ubiquitous, plenitudinous . . .

I feel sorry for fundamentalist Christians who earnestly attempt to reduce this effusive, overflowing God to five or six "fundamentals." It is tough to get this God down to a list of five or six of anything because our God is effusive.

I sorrow for the self-described "progressive Christian" scholar who recently dumbed things down to "the essence of Christianity"—five or six vague platitudes that allegedly sum up Jesus. This isn't progress but regress to a "god" who is considerably more flat and dull than the Trinity.

So, as Christians, we don't have one Gospel, we have four. Four Gospels! One might have thought that we could have stopped with one, saying to ourselves, "Matthew fairly well got it right, let's all go with Matthew. Why confuse the children with all these Gospels? Let's go just with Matthew." But no, an effusive, ubiquitous, plenitudinous, and overflowing God requires at least four Gospels to talk about God and Christ.

And one way the church has historically attempted to talk about God's plenitudinousness and effusiveness, God's ubiquitousness and loquaciousness is through the Trinity. Don't think of the Trinity as some incomprehensible doctrine of the church, though God's plenitudinous is beyond our comprehension. Think of the Trinity as our earnest, though groping attempt, somehow to put into words what has been revealed to us of the overflowing love of God.

Sometimes you hear people say, "Well, you are a Christian, and I am not, but the important thing is that we all try to believe and serve God. Right?"

Wrong.

Christians are not those who believe in some amorphous, vague concept of "god."

Christians are those who believe that God is best addressed as Trinity. God is not simply a monad, "God." God is the Father, God is the Son, and God is the Holy Spirit. And these three are One.

We might have been able to say, at some early point, "Well we all believe in the same God." However, we believe that God came to us as Jesus. We believe that Jesus is God in the flesh, the fullness of God. The one from Nazareth was as much of God as we ever hope to see. This crucified Jew was raised from the dead, which was God's way of saying, "You wonder what I'm like. Here's what I'm like—crucified, suffering, forgiving love."

And after experiencing that, all of our notions of God had to go back to the drawing table. If Jesus Christ is God, then we have a challenge in talking about God. After Easter, it just wouldn't do to talk about God as anything less than Trinity. As masterful interpreter of the Trinity, David Cunningham, puts it, in the Trinity Christians attempt to account for the complex biblical testimony that "(1) God remained all-powerful and transcendent, and yet (2) Jesus, who died and was raised by God, was somehow also God; moreover, (3) the Spirit, poured out on the Church, is also God, and yet (4) there is only one God" (*These Three Are One: The Practice of Trinitarian Theology* [Oxford: Blackwell Publishers, 1998], 23).

When God came to us as the Son, Incarnate in Jesus, God did not say, "Call me by my proper name, Trinity." God didn't have to. *We* did. That is, on the basis of our experience of God as complex, ubiquitous, and overflowing with love as the Father, the Son, and the Holy Spirit, we just naturally started speaking of God as Trinity. We experienced one God in these three ways. Though it was the same God whom we had experienced as the great Creator of the world, the Father of Israel, now we also experienced that God in the flesh as the Son, as well as the power flowing from God, the Holy Spirit.

Augustine, one of the greatest minds of the Western world, put his head to thinking about the Trinity. Augustine, a master of words, took fifteen books to talk about the Trinity, fifteen books that took him over a decade to write. Augustine's *On the Trinity* continues to be helpful in thinking through that which is difficult to think about, namely, the nature of God who comes to us as Father, Son, and Holy Spirit.

Early on in his massive treatise, Augustine had seven statements about God: The Father is God. The Son is God. The Holy Spirit is God. The Son is not the Father. The Father is not the Holy Spirit. The Holy Spirit is not the Son. And then, after these six statements, Augustine adds one more. There is only one God.

This is the thinking that is tough to get into our brains. We have experienced three rather distinctive modes of the one God's presence. God is the Father, the Creator of us and the world. God is the Son, the One who comes to us as Jesus, living, suffering, dying, and rising among us. We experience God as Holy Spirit, that power which has intruded into our world as the near presence and power of God.

And yet, we are not tritheists, we don't believe in three gods. We know, with Israel, that there is only one God. These names—Father, Son, and Holy Spirit—are not three names for the same thing. They are the three names that describe the nature of one God.

In book 7 of *On the Trinity*, Augustine tried to think of an analogy of God and he looked within himself. In looking within himself, Augustine noted how the human soul itself is triadic, trinitarian. There is a kind of triune way in which we experience ourselves, as if the Trinity is built right into the structure of our reality.

We say, for instance, "I love myself." According to Jesus, it is all right to love ourselves, for we are to love our neighbors as we love ourselves. So we can say, "I love myself." When we do so, we are speaking in a triune way. When I say "I love myself," there is a lover that is doing the loving, namely, me loving myself. There is also the beloved, the object of my love, which is also me, then, there is the loving, the act and energy of the lover upon the beloved. So even with the one there is the lover, the beloved, and the loving.

Thus, within our own hearts, in our own experience, Augustine said that there is the *vestigia trinitatis*, vestiges of the Trinity. Reality is trinitarian—complex, revealing, and communicative.

One of the church fathers said that "when we talk about the Trinity, we must forget how to count." He was simply recognizing that, at first glance, the Trinity is a mathematical impossibility. After all, how can one equal three?

We must throw away our math, not because the Trinity is a logical muddle, but because we need a different kind of logic. It took Augustine fifteen books to try to think about it, because God is God and we are not. Because God comes to us with a complexity and effusiveness, a ubiquity and a plenitude that boggles our modest minds, no wonder we have trouble thinking about God. No wonder the Trinity boggles our imaginations. And that is probably the right way to put it. The problem with the Trinity is not that this is a bunch of nonsense, but that God is God, in God's particularly glorious, effusive way, and we are creatures, the recipients of a love so deep we cannot find words to describe it. When we think about the Trinity, we must forget how to count.

Watch a newborn infant coo and smile, reach toward you and interact with you and you may rightly conclude that we ourselves are trinitarian in being—we have been created to reach out, to speak, to be in relationship and we are restless until we make contact.

There is a modern word for talking about this dynamic structure—synergy. Within the Trinity, there is constant movement, interaction, as the

Father gives to the Son, and the Son is constantly returning praise and glory to the Father, and the Father and the Son give to the Holy Spirit and the Holy Spirit constantly draws everything back to the Father and the Son. There is the Beloved, the Lover, and the Love.

So in today's Scripture the last thing that the risen Christ commands us to do is to go out of here and live in the world as he—Father, Son, and Holy Spirit—is in the world. A church that doesn't reach out, that is not going and telling, is not the church formed by the effusive Trinity. A Christian who doesn't want, in love, to go out and tell somebody is not one who is formed by the relentlessly reaching out and drawing in that is the Trinity.

Thank God that our relationship with God is not dependent upon our talking to, listening to, reaching toward, and loving God. The Trinity refuses to leave it all up to us. In Jesus Christ, through the promptings of the Holy Spirit, in the wonder of a good creation, the Trinity keeps reaching toward us, keeps leaving hints for us, indications that we live every moment of our lives upheld by a living, resourceful, loquacious God.

As one of you put it to me, when you were in the midst of a terrible, life-threatening illness and I asked you if you were afraid of death, you said to me, "Not really. When I think of all the trouble that God has gone to for me, all the tricks that God has used to grab me, all the traps that God has laid to catch me, I can't believe God will let a little thing like death stump him."

That struck me as a very Trinitarian sort of observation, the fruit of a life lived in the light of the God who is Father, Son, and Holy Spirit.

40

Who Do You Say That I Am?

August 22, 1999

MATTHEW 16:13–20

That which makes Christians, Christian is Christ. That which makes a sermon interesting and relevant, disturbing and faithful, is Christ. So often we preachers are tempted to present the Christian faith as something that makes sense, or something that will be helpful in getting whatever it is that you think you must have to give you a reason to get out of bed in the morning. This Sunday I attempted to come clean with the congregation and say that the gospel is not about any such drivel; it's all about Jesus. I thank Karl Barth for doing all he could to keep my theology christological in a time when preachers appear to want to talk about just about anything other than whom it's all about.

One of the things I love about students is when they don't know any better than to ask a wonderfully basic, absolutely essential question. Maybe it's a question that some of us have long ago asked and thought we answered. Maybe it's a question that we haven't asked in a long time because we've given up on an answer. Students sometimes don't know any better than to just ask it.

A student came to me and asked me to explain to her the difference between Christianity and Judaism. She is in love with a student who is Jewish. They are both law students, thinking about marriage. How will they deal with the difficult differences?

I told her that I had known people who marry lawyers and go on to have happy marriages, despite the difficulties!

Just kidding. The differences that trouble her are between two related but disparate faiths. Well, we discussed rituals, festivals, beliefs. Then she asked a fundamental question.

"When it comes down to it, what is the one thing that makes Christians, Christian?"

The answer is not potluck dinners, WWJD bracelets, or pushy preachers. The thing that makes us who we are is who Jesus is. Jesus Christ is Christianity.

Other faiths have love, have beliefs about the good and the true. Only Christianity has Jesus. If God had kept aloof from us, if God had only given us a book, then we would have the Bible, but we wouldn't be Christians. We would be another noble philosophy of life, or a system of ethical virtues.

But what God did, we believe, is to come to us in the flesh, as a Jew from Nazareth named Jesus, or more Hebraically named, Joshua, meaning God saves. We believe that the peculiar way God saves, that God gets to us and gets us, is Jesus. It is our astounding claim that we look at the Jewish carpenter's son—who was born, lived briefly, died violently in his thirties, and rose from the dead unexpectedly—and we see as much of Almighty God as we hope to see.

Now, we can sympathize with those folk who look at Jesus and see only a noble teacher, or only a great moral example, or even a wild-eyed revolutionary. After all, from the very beginning, who Jesus was, what he was about, was far from self-evident. There were people who stood face-to-face with Jesus and said, "This is God incarnate." There appear to be many more who said, "This man is nuts."

So, from the first, that God came to us *as Jesus* meant lots of people didn't get it. Jesus frustrated people's expectations about how a Messiah ought to act. Jesus didn't directly say who he was. He didn't walk around with a sign on his back saying, "Son of God." Messiahs were supposed to have power, were supposed to take charge, set things right, fix all of our problems.

Jesus refused to stiff-arm anybody into following him. He refused to dominate or to take up arms. Looking at his life work, many people would say that Jesus was one of history's most noble failures.

Sometimes when alumni ask, "How many students do you get in Duke Chapel on a Sunday?" I say, "Probably more than Jesus got for his sermons."

So it wasn't just that God came as Jesus, it was that God came *as Jesus*. He just didn't seem like we thought God ought to be God. Eventually, Jesus was executed for doing the things he did and saying the things he said. He wasn't killed for walking around bragging, "By the way, I'm God."

Jesus was killed for saying, "This is God's way: the poor are precious, the rich are in big trouble, Caesar isn't God despite what his spin doctors claim, not everybody who cries 'Lord, Lord' is going into God's kingdom. In fact, whores and tax collectors get in before you."

You just don't say things like that to people and get tenure. And Christianity, being a Christian, is about following Jesus, doing what Jesus did, speaking as he spoke. Certainly we don't all succeed at that. After all, Jesus warned that his way was "narrow."

Time and again Jesus said things we wish he had not. I don't know what he was getting at when he said, "Hate your mother," or "Go sell everything you have and give it to the poor."

Well, to be honest, I knew what he meant when he said some of those things, but I don't like it! For most of us, it isn't that we've listened to Jesus and found him incomprehensible. It's that we've listened to him and found him darn difficult.

So someone came out of the chapel one Sunday after service saying, "I know that you would never want to hurt anyone in your sermons, but I was hurt by your comment in your sermon that . . ."

And I thought to myself, "Where on earth did you get the notion that we wouldn't want to hurt you? This is Jesus! It's going to get rough from time to time!"

Being Christian is about the challenging, lifelong struggle to be friends with Jesus and to allow him to be friends with you.

It's about a relationship. I think it was Richard Niebuhr who said that conversion happens when the God whom you thought was your enemy to be feared is really your friend to be loved.

We love God because, we believe, God first loved us in Jesus. So Christianity is not first adherence to a set of great ideals (ethics), nor is it the comprehension of a set of great ideas (philosophy), it is a way of life, a way of walking with Jesus, a relationship.

We really believe, not only that Jesus spoke to us but that he came to us, he speaks to us, comes to us. If Easter had not happened, who would still think about Jesus? Most of his teaching was unoriginal, his inheritance from the faith of Israel. He was not particularly effective in getting his program across to his followers.

But when he came back to us, even from the dead, we then say that Jesus—who he was, what he taught, what he did—had been vindicated by God. That's what those early Christians meant when they exploded out into the world shouting, "God has raised Jesus from the dead!" Easter was like God saying to us, "In case you have ever wondered whether or not Jesus was truly, truthfully revealing my will for the world—with all his talk of forgiving enemies, and loving the unlovable, and finding the lost—then be assured, this is exactly the way to see it. When he speaks, I'm speaking. When you look at Jesus, you're looking at me, the one who hung the stars and flung the planets into their courses."

I know this seems an astounding assertion to those who have not experienced it, but Christians believe that Jesus is present with us, walks with us, is closer to us than we are even to ourselves.

I've been rereading Augustine's *Confessions*. Someone wrote a book not long ago titled *Augustine and the Invention of the Modern Self*. Augustine, with his searching, relentless gazing upon his soul, invented the modern sense of the self. How do you find out what's what in the world? Look in yourself. "Discover yourself." "I'm trying to find myself," we moderns say. We owe that, says this scholar, to old Augustine who in the fourth century picked through his own soul for a couple of hundred pages.

But that's not quite right. Augustine begins by saying, "I'm going to tell you the story of my life." But after a few pages of this, you become aware that he's not saying much of "I" and is more frequently saying "You," "Thou." He thought that his desires and longing arose from within himself; he finds that it was really God desiring and longing for him. "I was searching everywhere for you, O God, only to find that you had been searching everywhere for me."

That's the presence I'm talking about that Christians learn to name as the risen Christ. Say a prayer, tear open a loaf of bread, have a sip of wine, we believe Jesus is with us. When just two or three of us show up on Sunday, Jesus has promised, "I'll be there."

So that's what makes Christians who we are—Jesus. We're here, not because we were searching for more meaning in our lives and found Jesus. Rather, most of us were minding our own business and from out of nowhere Jesus found us. Or we were just biding our time trying to make it through a Sunday service without dozing off and he grabbed us. We stood to sing a hymn only to sit down after the last note saying, "I believe."

It's about Jesus.

41

Our Advocate

Day of Pentecost 2000

JOHN 15:26–27; 16:4B–15

After lots of Pentecosts with Acts 2, I decided to celebrate Pentecost with John 15—the promise of the Paraclete. As I recall, my sermon was well received, particularly by the lawyers and lawyers-to-be in the congregation.

Not long ago I had the opportunity to meet with a group of students of law, people preparing to be attorneys. They wanted me to speak on the subject, "On Being a Lawyer and a Christian at the Same Time." Some of you are snickering. Some of you are thinking, Isn't that the definition of oxymoron? A "Christian lawyer"?

Now I've been guilty of laughing at those lawyer jokes. I have liked them as a welcomed respite from preacher jokes!

But I confess to being quite touched by these young attorneys as they spoke of their fears at going into the practice of law. They wondered what would happen to their character. They said that they were troubled by the public perception of lawyers. Perhaps their fears are testimonial to what the legal profession has become. Or perhaps it is testimonial to our society's ambivalent feelings about law.

However, I am sure that there are people here today who could testify that, if you are in trouble, and find yourself in a situation where it's your word against that of the police, or see your name across the docket from "The People of the United States" in some legal action, suddenly lawyers look good.

It is a frightening thing to stand before the bar of justice as the accused and be forced to defend yourself. What do you say? Which legal precedent should you invoke?

My wife spent a week on jury duty and came home saying, "I learned one thing. If you are ever called before the court, you better get a good lawyer. I saw people who lost their cases, not on the lack of merit of their case, but purely because they had a lousy attorney. I saw people get more than they deserved because they had a skillful attorney who wisely argued their case."

We believe that the art of rhetoric, the art of using language skillfully and persuasively, arose in ancient Greece during a time when there were lots of disputes over property rights and therefore lots of cases brought to court. People hired skilled speakers to argue their case in court. Philosophers began studying language and how language works and thus was born the science of rhetoric.

The profession of law was born in a time when people needed others to stand before the court and skillfully argue their case using the best possible arguments, the right words, the right appeal to the good judgments of the court.

"And why did you decide to go to law school?" I asked. He had left his job in sales, gone back to school, earned enough credits to get his undergraduate degree, then he applied and was accepted at law school.

"I read John Grisham's book *The Street Lawyer*," he answered. "A young lawyer on his way up in a prestigious firm is jolted off course by a strange encounter with a homeless person. The homeless man threatens the young lawyer with death, but the whole experience causes the young man to rearrange his priorities. He exchanges the prospects of wealth to become a street lawyer, a lawyer whose only practice is to help homeless people."

The portrayal of an attorney out for the good of others reminds one of Atticus Finch in *To Kill a Mockingbird*. We all thrill to stories of those lawyers who speak for the voiceless.

In today's Pentecost Gospel, Jesus is preparing to leave his disciples. He says that he is leaving them so that he might send them an even better, more effective presence. He promises to send them an "Advocate." He promises to send them an attorney, for who is a lawyer but an "advocate"?

We speak of Christ as king, teacher, savior, Lord. Today, at Pentecost, at our festival of the Holy Spirit, the Gospel of John encourages us to speak of the Holy Spirit as Advocate.

Scripture says, "If anyone sins [and who doesn't?] we have an advocate with the Father, Jesus Christ the righteous" (1 John 2:1, my trans.).

Imagine yourself standing one day before the throne of God, holding your life in your hands, all that you have said and done over the years, the battles you've fought and won, as well as the battles you have lost. What would you say to God in defense of yourself?

A few years ago, when the president of the United States was being investigated for his improprieties and misdeeds, more than one person asked, "How would you like for fifty million dollars to be spent investigating your life?"

Who could stand up under such investigation? And once your secret misdeeds and mismanaged acts were uncovered, by what argument would you defend yourself? If God knows everything you have done, every word spoken in anger, every deed done in the darkness, remembers every sin that we so quickly forget, then what hope have any of us standing before the throne of God? Who could defend us or make our case?

Are you good with words? Is public speaking your strength? Do you know what it's like to be charged and have to stand and defend yourself? It's tough.

Jesus says he is going to send us an Advocate. He departs, but he sends One to us who becomes our argument, our defense, our defender, our spokesperson before God.

You need, when you stand before God, when your life is held up for divine scrutiny, you need an advocate, someone to argue your case.

In my last church we had a clothes closet and a food pantry for the needy. People in need came by the church two mornings a week looking for help.

There was a businessperson in our church, a man who had spent his life in an upper level management position in a large corporation. Without warning, things at the company changed and he was fired. The company called it "early retirement" but he called it "put out early to pasture." He became depressed, sullen. We were worried about him.

Out of concern for him, I asked him to help out a couple of mornings a week at the church clothes closet. He was reluctant at first. Maybe he thought this quite a comedown for one who had previously been in a high position of power. But he consented.

While working there, he met a woman, mother of three, trying to make ends meet in her little family on her meager wages as a domestic worker. She happened to tell him about her problems with the electric company. She had paid her bill late, but the company still turned off her electricity and now they wanted the unbelievably huge sum of fifty dollars to restore the power. What was she to do?

She had called the electric company half a dozen times, she said, but no one could help her. A rule was a rule, etc.

The retired executive said he would call for her. When he inquired into her bill, he was shocked at the way he was treated. He demanded to talk to the manager, an old friend of many years. He agreed to help the woman with her problems.

This led to another poor person asking him to call a loan company about a problem she had with her loan. He did so and he got action.

A new area of ministry opened up for this man. In giving he received. He learned what a gift it is to be able to talk on the phone, to cut through the red tape, to speak up.

"I never knew what it is like to be unable to figure out all the levels of red tape and organizational smoke screen," he said. "Having spent my life in business, I knew how to cut through the garbage, go to the top, and get these people the help they needed."

He had become an advocate for the poor, someone to plead their case before the powerful.

Jesus says that he is going to leave us. He will not be present to his disciples as he has been before. But he will not leave us desolate. He will send us the Holy Spirit, the near presence of God to stand beside us, to speak up for us, to plead our case, to take our cause.

Because the Holy Spirit shares in the life of Jesus, the Spirit knows our need, finds words that articulate our groaning. You are not alone. You don't have to speak up for yourself before the throne of God or argue your case in the courts of the Almighty. You have an Advocate. The Holy Spirit intercedes in your behalf. Thanks be to God.

42

To Bethlehem

December 24, 2001

Christmas Eve is huge in Duke Chapel, with crowds swarming in to see the place at its best. It's risky to confront such a throng with a relatively obscure story—Ruth and Naomi, not to mention Leviticus and homosexuality. Yet I thought I might give it a try in 2001 on the eve of the Feast of the Incarnation. With a standing-room-only congregation every year, we could use some culling of the Christmas crowd!

I've got a charming story for you this Christmas Eve. The story of Ruth and Naomi. Poor Ruth. She had married one of Naomi's sons. But he soon died, before they had any children. So, in accordance with the custom of the day, she married Naomi's other son. He also died, leaving her without children. Surely you understand what that meant, in that day, in that part of the world. Ruth was utterly without hope. No husband, no children to care for her in her old age. A woman who was husbandless and childless was called "barren." And those were her prospects for the future. Barren. Now alone, completely vulnerable, her ex-mother-in-law Naomi says to her, "I have no more sons to offer you. You had better go back and live with your own people."

You see, Ruth had come down to Judea from Moab. She was a Moabite—a person of another race, another religion. Naomi advises Ruth to go on back to her own people. Maybe she will receive the care and protection she needs there.

But then Ruth says something to Naomi, maybe the only thing you have ever heard of out of the book of Ruth. Ruth says to Naomi, the younger woman speaking to the other, "Entreat me not to leave you. Where you go, I will go. Your people shall be my people" (Ruth 1:16, paraphr.). It's a thought that is put into music and often sung at weddings. Though in context it is an older woman speaking to a younger woman, it is often used to express the beauty of marriage in which a person, in marriage, takes on the family and the name of another person.

For Ruth to say this to Naomi was rather amazing. For here we see someone of another race, another religion and nationality, another generation saying, "I will stick with you, I will be with you, where you go, I will go. Your people will be my people."

Thus the book of Ruth is also a story of tough women, two resilient people who, after life has dealt them a couple of bad breaks, cling together, and with clinch-fisted determination, attempt to make it in the world.

And survive they do. One day Naomi stops an old, fairly well-to-do man, Boaz, at his threshing floor. Naomi rushes to tell Ruth to put on her best dress and meet Boaz at the threshing floor.

"Though he is old, sometimes old men can be effective too."

Ruth meets Boaz, marries Boaz, and the rest is history. They have children, and those children go on to have other children, and they thus become part of the glad story of the perseverance, even the triumph of God's chosen people. Ruth and Boaz meet, marry, and begin life together in a little town named Bethlehem.

Which explains, in case you are wondering, why I am telling you this story on this night of nights. The story of Ruth is a story that takes place in Bethlehem. It is a story about two resilient women, who, against all odds, make a good life for themselves, make a future where there has been none, and triumph. Ruth, at Bethlehem, was the great-great-great-grandmother of Jesus.

The story of Ruth and Naomi is inspiring, and charming. It is an everyday story. It is a story without any miracles, or visions. There is not much vision of God in this story. It is so mundane and everyday and ordinary. And yet that is part of its glory. In a mundane, ordinary, everyday place, named Bethlehem, two ordinary women become part of the purposes of God. Their stories are woven into the story of what God wants to do for the whole world.

This is often the Bible's way with the divine. The extraordinary arises within the ordinary. The heavenly breaks out amid the earthly. What we tend to call earthly and ordinary, the Bible wants to depict as the realm of God's amazing work among us. If you want to meet God, then the Bible implies that you don't have to go off on some mountaintop. You don't have to rummage around in the recesses of your ego, or move to some high spiritual summit. You just have to be in a place like Bethlehem, trying to make your way in the world, attempting to make ends meet, getting along as best you can with what you've got.

This is a counterview of "spirituality" than that which is abroad today. Many people have noted, in the last few years, a dramatic outbreak in "spirituality" in

America. Increasing numbers of Americans are becoming interested in spiritual matters. Most of this tends to be rather fluffy stuff, vague, ethereal, an attempt to inflate one's spirit and rise above the messy mundane quality of life. Spirituality is when we float above the grubbiness of the stuff of everyday life.

But when it comes to Bethlehem, don't believe it.

Archbishop William Temple once said, "Christianity is the most materialistic of all the world's religions." Or as C. S. Lewis said in *Mere Christianity*, "[God] likes matter. He invented it." Or, as one of my friends puts it, "Any God who won't tell you what to do with your pots, your pans, and your genitals is not worth worshiping."

Christmas is a time for great music, and great poetry, but it also ought to be a time for great prose. Here is a prosaic, mundane vision of how God deals with us. If we want to meet God, we need not go up to some mountaintop, some aloof, heavenly situated place. We need to be living in a place like Bethlehem, an ordinary and everyday place, where women have to get by by their wits, and do the best they can in a bad situation, where the cards that life deals us are not always easy to deal with.

Do you want to get close to God? Then the story of Ruth, as well as the story of the babe at Bethlehem, suggests that we will meet God in our times of grief, when people leave us in untimely ways, people on whom we are dependent. In times of vulnerability. When we have issues with our in-laws, when we are worried about what is going to become of us tomorrow.

My wife conducts a weekly Bible study for graduates here at the university. They work through the entire Bible in a year.

When they got to the book of Leviticus, one of the members of the Bible study opened up their discussion by saying, "I have been dreading this night. I have been dreading when we got to the book of Leviticus. Because I had heard that the book of Leviticus is down on people like me. I had heard that Leviticus has some nasty things to say about people of my sexual orientation. Well, what I learned this week, is Leviticus is down on lots of things! Leviticus has negative opinions about how we eat, how we make dinner, how we treat livestock, and how we make love. It isn't that Leviticus is opinionated about homosexuality, it's opinionated about just about everything! Maybe the deal with Leviticus is that you should only read Leviticus if you read the whole book!"

Then another member of the Bible study group asked, "Why does God care about all of that stuff? I can't believe that God would have enough time to form an opinion about how we behave in the kitchen, how we behave in bedrooms, in living rooms. Why on earth does God care?" Yet another member of the group responded, "But that is kind of great, when you think about it. God cares. God cares even about the stuff that happens in the kitchen. The pots and the pans and everything are not religious."

Take that as a good definition of incarnation. Now that God has come into the world, through a couple like Mary and Joseph, in a place like Bethlehem, now even the pots and the pans are religious.

What a God we've got. Or, more to the point of incarnation, what a God has got us. Now, after what happened in Bethlehem, with Ruth and Naomi, and with Mary and Joseph, if we are going to meet God, we need not climb up to the top of some mountain, or rummage about in our psyche, we can meet God right here. Or better, God meets us here. In mundane ways, God meets us, in something as common and everyday as a bit of bread or a sip of wine, in common things like people, like Ruth and Naomi are people like us.

Now, the word has been made flesh and dwells among us. Made flesh. Our flesh.

43

Christmas in the Empire

December 24, 2002

LUKE 2:1–20

Things got decidedly "political" in this Christmas Eve sermon of 2002. A few of the worshipers that evening, on their way out to Adeste Fideles, let me know this was not their idea of a Christmas sermon.

You will notice, when it comes to thinking about Christmas, suddenly the camera goes out of focus and everything gets a bit blurred. Inside, fruitcake is cooking on the stove and outside snow is beginning to blanket the earth. At the mention of the magic word "Christmas" everything becomes nostalgic, comforting, and sweet.

Christmas in the Bible, as opposed to Christmas at the mall, is not like that at all. Christmas here drowns in nostalgia, carols, candles, happy children in the warm firelight. There's nothing like an old-fashioned Christmas.

Christmas in the Bible might agree with that. There's nothing quite like an old-fashioned Christmas, first-century style. This world is not a winter wonderland, covered in a blanket of snow. This old world is a shockingly bad world, where kings rage and wickedness flourishes, babies are murdered, and countries who think of themselves as the most civilized people in the world make and sell the weapons to the countries they regard as uncivilized, in order that the uncivilized can blow each other up.

Christmas, real Christmas, is light—light coming into the darkness, our darkness.

Odd, in our hands, Christmas becomes a dream, an escape. In the Bible, Christmas is reality. Today's newspaper headlines—it's all there in Matthew

217

and Luke and their stories of Christmas, for they are the only two of the four Gospels that tell us much about the first Christmas. There is a massacre of innocent children, political intrigue, lies, deceit, fear, and the Holy Family just barely escaping with their lives as political refugees in an unwelcoming world.

Somehow this really came home to me last Christmas. Last Christmas we launched our "War on Terrorism." The war really didn't get into full swing until about Christmastime. That's how long it took us to get our troops into Afghanistan, in order to liberate that suffering country. It took about four thousand civilian casualties in order for us to liberate them. Even this Christmas, the war goes on.

And on Christmas Eve we read from the Christmas story—the story about how a poor couple named Mary and Joseph were forced by imperial political decrees to pack up, to journey across the countryside (even though Mary was expecting a baby), to hole up in a cow stable, all as the result of Caesar's enrollment. The Romans had the most power, and the biggest army of any Western country ever to conquer the Middle East. How are you going to keep these Jews in their place if you don't enroll them? So Caesar Augustus decreed, and cruel King Herod enforced, the order that everybody had to go to the city of his or her ancestors and get registered. That's how Mary and Joseph got to Bethlehem. Mary and Joseph were Jews, under the heel of the vast Roman Empire, the greatest empire the world has ever known, with the largest army—that is, until us.

In reading the Christmas story last Christmas it suddenly occurred to me—*we are the empire*. We are the Romans. We're in the East, doing all sorts of important things for which we have worthy justification. But in spite of the justifications for our being there, it is a bit unnerving to have to admit that Imperial Rome has become Durham, North Carolina. We are the empire.

That means that, when we are reading the Christmas story, it is unfair for me to read myself into the places of Mary and Joseph, the shepherds, or even the wise men. This was their home. They are under the heel of the empire, their lives jerked around by imperial decrees.

If I have a place in this story, thanks to the aftermath of 9/11, my place is in Rome with Caesar Augustus, or maybe in Jerusalem up at the palace with that quisling King Herod, lackey for the Roman overlords.

I'd rather see myself as one of the relatives of Mary and Joseph, or at least among their friends, if they had any, together around the manger that night in Bethlehem. I wouldn't even mind being one of the shepherds, out working the night shift, surprised when the heavens filled with angels. I'd like to be numbered even among those poor shepherds who were among the first to get the good news.

I wouldn't even mind being one of the magi—strange Persian visitors who have come to the Christ child bearing gifts.

But alas, that is not my place in the story. My place in the story is as a member of the empire. I am well-fixed. I don't live up in the palace, but I live in a home that—with its modern conveniences and security—the majority of the world's people would call a palace. I am not a king, but I certainly have more control over my life, and more control over a number of people, than most of the kings who have walked the earth in the past. I am not a civilized and cultivated Roman (I hated the four years that I was forced to take Latin), but I am a member of the academic establishment. I have been the beneficiary of a great classical education, and I am a citizen of a country that has dominated other countries, often without even trying to dominate other countries. We are the empire.

I don't like my particular place in the story of the first Christmas.

I wish the star that was seen by the wise men had shown for me. But I am no stargazer. I don't dabble in gold, frankincense, and myrrh. I dabble in stocks and bonds. I get my news from CNN, not from the heavens. So that star does not shine for me.

I would have loved to hear the songs of the angels who sang so wondrously before the shepherds. But my job runs from 9 to 5. I sit behind a desk, not out in the fields with sheep. I am not one of those people who has to work the night shift, or whose job is smelly, dirty, and difficult like those shepherds. By nightfall, I'm safely tucked away in my suburban home, climate controlled, secure, and well protected. Therefore, the angels have not sung their songs to me.

So when you think about it, in our context, it is odd in a way that so many of us should flock to church on a Christmas Eve. It is a bit strange that we should think that, in Christmas, we hear such unadulteratedly good news, that we should feel such warm and happy feelings, and think that we are closer to God now than at any other time of the year.

I guess we ought to be of the same frame of mind as our cousin, King Herod. When he heard the word about the first Christmas, the Gospels say that he was filled with fear, agitation and contempt. He immediately started lying, tried to get the magi to show him where the baby was so he could come "worship him," when what he really meant was, "so that I can exterminate him." Failing to find the baby, he just killed all the boy babies around Jerusalem.

You have to at least give Herod credit. He knew bad news when he heard it. He knew that the songs that the angels sang meant an attack upon his world, God taking sides with those on the margins, the people in the night out in the fields, the oppressed and the lowly.

But for the people up at the palace, the well-fixed, the people on top, the masters of the empire, Christmas was bad news. And many of them were perceptive enough to know it.

So maybe that is why we cover up Christmas with cheap sentimentality, turn it into a saccharine celebration, nostalgia, a lost world that was, or probably never was. Maybe, in our heart of hearts, we know that Christmas means that God may not be with the empire, but rather the empire may be on a shaky foundation, and that, if we told the story straight, as the Bible tells it, we might have reason, like Herod (when he heard about the first Christmas) to fear.

O great imperial power, O ones who feel so well-fixed that we don't need a God to help us, much less save us, did we not hear the words that the angels sang? Did we miss the full scope of their singing?

"Do not be afraid; for see—I am bringing you good news of great joy for all the people: to you is born this day in the city of David a Savior, who is the Messiah, the Lord" (Luke 2:10–11).

The angel did not say good news for some people. The angel was bold to say good news for *all the people*. All. Though the angel was singing to the shepherds, I suppose the angel meant the song for everybody, all. Herod no doubt had difficulty hearing the song, safely fortified as he was with his troops and his thick-walled palace. Augustus, behind his facade of classical learning, Augustus, that smooth dictator, was in the wrong place to hear. Herod, the old fox, missed it.

But you haven't missed it. Even though you are a card-carrying member as am I, of the greatest empire that has ever ruled, you are in the right place to hear the news.

Good news this day. There is born for you a savior. For you. All people. Your flags, your government, your armies, cannot save. Only that baby saves. One who is born among the lowly and the poor, only that one can save.

And the good news is *he is born for you*. He comes not only for the oppressed, not only for Israel, but for the oppressor, that is, for all. O that we in the empire could hear that song, O that we could turn back to the Lord, change our ways, bow down before the manger, rather than before our power, acknowledge our need, and pledge allegiance to the Prince of Peace.

Because he is our prince too. He comes to form an empire, not the way this world builds its empires, called the kingdom of God. And he shall reign forever and ever, and of his reign there shall be no end.

Good news. For this day in the city of David is born a Savior, Christ the Lord. Good news *for all*. Amen.

44

Super Woman

September 21, 2003

PROVERBS 31:10–31

A preacher ought never, ever take a biblical text and be so presumptuous as to preach against that text. Except sometimes. I took such liberty during a September sermon series on memorable women in the Bible. A distinguished Old Testament professor at the divinity school pled with me to change my angle on Proverbs 31, to no effect, as you can see in my unorthodox (and probably unjustified) exposition of Proverbs 31.

For the past few Sundays we have introduced you to a number of wonderful women. Most of these women are termed "wonderful" because God utilized their lives in some wonderful ways. Few of them had spectacularly good qualities. Most of them simply stumbled through their bit parts, saying, "yes" when God had something important for them to do. In that way they are a model for us. Because let's face it, most of us are not spectacularly good people. The best that can usually be said of our discipleship is that we simply stumble along and do the best that we can when God calls.

But today I want to introduce you to a wildly wonderful woman, a spectacularly superior woman, the best of all good women in the Bible. We don't know her name, but she is the one who brings the biblical book of Proverbs to its grand finale. Some of you may have met her. She has been known to make an appearance in churches on Mother's Day, testimonial in part to the paucity of good Scripture that deals with mothers. And she is a spectacularly good mother.

Or sometimes she appears at the funerals. When someone dies who has been a wonderful mother, they think of this woman, the mother of all good mothers. A good woman is hard to find, and a woman this good is almost impossible to find and, by the time you have found her, I think you'll agree with me that she is—impossible. Here is a good woman in the very worst sense of the word.

First, note that this woman meets us at the very end of the book of Proverbs. The book of Proverbs is not one of my favorite books in the Bible. There is virtually no God in Proverbs. What you have in Proverbs are lists of dos and don'ts. Don't drink too much. Get up early in the morning. Go to bed early in the evening. Don't talk too much in groups. A fool and his money are soon parted. That kind of thing. There is not much God in the book of Proverbs because, well, if you can do all of these good things that the book of Proverbs urges, why would you need God to do anything for you? The book of Proverbs is that book of the Bible for people who find it easy to be good, people who are high achievers, spiritually speaking. That kid in the fourth grade whom the teacher left in charge of the class, to take names of malfactors while the teacher went down to the principal's office. That kid loves the book of Proverbs. That is probably the reason that I can't stand this book any better than I could stand that kid in the fourth grade.

And here at the grand finale we meet a woman who manages to embody most of the proverbial virtues. She is introduced in a sort of hymn, a hymn to the "capable wife." She is "far more precious than jewels" (31:10). No need for false modesty, "capable" is an understatement.

Proverbs 31 is a paean to the superwife. Each line begins with a successive letter of the Hebrew alphabet. Maybe somebody thought this was poetry, but in our Bible it's a ridiculous shopping list of desirable traits for the allegedly "capable wife."

The poem begins with a rhetorical, "Where can one find a capable wife?" A good woman is hard to find. If you find such a woman, she is more valuable even than rare jewels (31:10). She is an amazingly productive woman, getting the job done, therefore, "Her husband trusts her." Then begins an almost laughable list of all the tasks at which this productive woman excels: She works in both wool and flax, harvesting these fibers, processing them, and making them into garments. She hauls in massive amounts of food "from far away." Rising when it is still dark, when all of the men in the house are still asleep, she gets to work. But this woman's expertise is not limited to domestic activities. As it turns out, she is a real-estate tycoon, she's a master at grape cultivation, the management of vineyards, and wine production. She has strong arms and her lamp never lacks oil. This woman makes Martha Stewart look like a slouch, a shirker. Looking at what this woman achieves in a given day, we wonder what Martha Stewart is doing with all of her spare time. Spinning, giving generously to the poor, clothing members of her own household in crimson—she does everything, and does it well. Though the Bible doesn't say so, we expect that all the other women in the neighborhood must hate her guts. That's the effect of these Martha Stewart types on others.

After clothing members of her household in crimson, she dresses herself in "fine linen and purple." Sometimes she sells this clothing at a profit. Thus we find that she is not only in production, but also marketing and distribution. When you heard this woman was "far more precious than jewels" (31:10), you thought this was merely metaphor. Think again; she's worth a fortune to her admiring husband.

Even amid all of her household tasks and mercantile activity this domestic dynamo still has time to be a wise teacher (31:26). In short, in the patriarchical culture of the Bible, this woman is every man's dream, every man who believes that the chief virtue of a woman is in service of a man.

And yet, praise her though you might, I still can't stand her. Far from being a woman to be praised, I really worry about this woman and her spiritual health. For one thing, the writer praises this woman almost exclusively in terms of her value for others, particularly her value for her husband. She's not introduced to us as a good person, she's a "capable wife." Furthermore, when measure is taken of her life, the standards of measurement are ridiculously high. "A husband of such a wife may have no lack of gain" (31:11). I ask you, is it really a virtue to praise someone as a valuable commodity for her mate?

As I said, one sometimes meets this woman at a funeral of a woman. I think that context seems odd, unless the deceased woman literally worked herself to death. If I were a woman, I certainly wouldn't want this woman at my funeral. Because no matter how industrious and productive the deceased may have been, there is no way that she could measure up to this super woman who excels at so wide a range of endeavor.

Another thing, most of the praise for this woman is for domestic activities and her management of the private space of the home. She runs her home so well, she rules over her children so wisely, that her husband is free for important public work like "taking a seat among the elders of the land" (31:23). This capable wife stays home, from morning till night, getting up before dawn, working like a slave, so that the husband may take pride in his valuable wife, sit around with the boys up at city hall, someday write some poem about her, and keep to more important work "near the city gates."

Where, anywhere else in the Bible, are we told that a woman is to serve her husband as if he were a god? Christ calls us to service to others, not to mere servility. Where are this woman's children when she is rising up before dawn to work for her family? Is there no household chore that the children could do to help? And where is her husband? Probably out on some political junket with the other "elders of the land." Has he no responsibility for his marriage and his family other than periodic praise to his relentlessly over-achieving wife? Is this woman doing her family a favor by bearing all the burdens, working from before dawn until well past dusk, while they merely rise up occasionally and praise her for being such a good woman? Ought we to join our voices in praising this premodern Martha Stewart who out Martha Stewart's Martha Stewart?

I say no. What we ought to do is question how this woman's self-sacrificial life may be warping the lives of the children and her husband, relieving them of their God-given responsibility to serve and to create and be responsible, warping them into selfish and irresponsible people. How this woman, in the days before electric dishwashers and trash compactors, still manages to be a real-estate tycoon (31:16) is a wonder.

But please don't make the mistake of thinking, just because you are a liberated, modern, feminist-type person that you feel superior to this pre-modern Jewish woman for her fevered servility. This is Duke. The office of undergraduate admissions exists to weed through the thousands of applica-tions that are received by the university, and try to get women—and men too, that look just like this woman. Slouches, people who spend their teen-age years lounging by the pool, or lying in the grass and staring up at the trees, people like that don't get in places like here. The people who get in here are the people who are captain of their football team, first-chair violin in the school symphony, won the Latin prize, built houses with Habitat for Humanity on weekends, as well as fixed automatic transmissions for the poor on Sundays. People like that. And though we honor these people and praise them, though we admit them to Duke, there is a price to be paid for such capability. A downside.

Eating disorders may be the number one health risk among Duke women. Counselors at Duke Counseling and Psychological Services (CAPS) are over-burdened with people who, during what ought to be the wonderful years of their lives, find this place oppressive. As one of the campus ministers said, when we were discussing problems of alcohol abuse by students, "Alcohol gives Duke students a temporary vacation from the misery of having to be a success all the time."

They have to be best of everything, to cram everything into a day, be so good in so many areas. This costs something. Take too much responsibility on your back for making your family work, relieve others of their God-given responsibility, though this be praised as remarkable activity, there is a dear price to be paid.

It is a fairly predictable Duke experience, during your first year, after a quiz, it dawns on you that you are not Number One. So many of us here have been so accustomed to being Number One, this can be traumatic, to find that we are number two, or worse. And what then? If our lives are built upon having to be Number One, we are in crisis.

If our entire sense of self-worth and value is built upon our productivity, others' impressions of us, we are building our lives on shaky ground.

The Christian faith has always claimed that we are saved, not by our good works, but by the good love of God. The key to our eternal significance is not what we do, but what God has done for us in Jesus Christ.

About this time of the year, a few years ago, I got a call from a parent, a mother who had ordered flowers to be sent to her daughter's dorm room for her daughter's birthday. She wondered if I would be good enough to check to be sure that the florist had come through with the delivery. Obviously, she was a spectacularly attentive, wonderfully successful mom, this mother who managed to send her daughter fresh flowers on her birthday, even in Jarvis. And yet, when I met the daughter, I felt sorry for her. Do you understand what a burden it can be to have a mother this good? I bet you do. Pity the poor child of "capable wife" who is left no room to blossom and flourish.

Even the Lord Almighty took a day off a week to rest. Not this woman. That's why there is no mention of God in today's Scripture, no room left for God to reach in, to help out, to lift up. She doesn't need a God to save her, so she gets none. She is perfect, she is busy, capable, productive. She is headed for disaster and warps everyone around her. She is not real. She is an atheist.

I've never met a woman I didn't like, until I met her.

45

Lucky to Be Here

August 29, 2004

ACTS 20:7–12

A young man named Eutychus, who was sitting in the window, began to sink off into a deep sleep while Paul talked still longer. Overcome by sleep, he fell to the ground three floors below and was picked up dead.

Acts 20:9

Here is my last sermon in Duke Chapel, a sermon about a student delivered with gratitude before a new group of Duke students on Orientation Sunday, students on their way in as I was on my way out.

I asked the class to write an essay, "My Life." Just to introduce themselves. One essay, I shall never forget, began, "Last year I awoke from an eighteen-year coma that was my life."

He went on to tell of the influence of an incredibly wonderful art teacher who had, in his words, "awakened me from the mediocrity to which I had become accustomed."

When I read that line, I knew that he had come to the right place. That's what we do well at this university, when we're doing our job. We snap people awake out of their coma. We call it "enlightenment," or "the acquisition of knowledge," but we could as well call it "awakening."

I teach for the privilege of seeing the eyes light up, the lids spring open, the neck crane forward.

I fear the somnambulant, etherized, anesthetized morbidity of a class at three in the afternoon. My brilliant lecture killed by zombielike night-of-the-living-dead drooping eyelids.

I have found that if I continue to talk in a low monotone, quietly, serenely and then, carefully, ever so carefully, slam a large book down on the desk while screaming, "WAKE UP!" it will do the trick.

Last year we were told that a study of students showed that sleep deprivation was the major health problem on campus. We needed to study to know that? Just visit my afternoon class about three-thirty, you could have learned that for free!

Church is a favorite quiescent location for sleeping. I can see some of you bedding down out there! A few years ago, we broadcast our services on the local cable channel. I was excited about this extension of our ministry. I rushed home, flipped on the television to see how we looked on TV. There I was horrified to see one of our sopranos bedded down, head thrown back, soprano mouth gaping open throughout my sermon!

I complained to Dr. Wynkoop. He excused her sleeping with, "Look, she's a student. Sometimes it's hard for me to stay awake too." I said, "She was dead to the world, brought a pillow in with her, a stuffed teddy bear and duvet! It was an outrage!"

She is no longer in our choir.

Last Sunday of last term, April, we had two services, the early service for the alumni who were with us that weekend. I concocted a different sort of sermon on Christian music and its effects. I was helped by the choir. I spoke, then the choir sang a favorite anthem, then I spoke again—the sermon was my commentary with the choir's anthems interspersed throughout.

A couple of days before this sermon I asked Craig if he would like to take some of the speaking parts of the sermon. He was eager to do so.

Well, after the first service and our first time with this dialogical sermon, Robert Parkins, university organist, who spends the service up there, encased within the Flentrop Organ where he can hear but can't see what we are doing, came up to me and said, "I didn't know that Craig was helping you out with the sermon so, after you spoke, and the choir sang, when I heard Craig speak I assumed that you had collapsed and died and that Craig had to take over the sermon."

"You idiot," I replied. "You mean that you thought I had died and that Craig just stepped over my body and continued the sermon?"

"Right."

Church has become, for many, a place of slumber, a place of death. Sad. It ought to be a place of resurrection, awakening.

Back in the summer when we thought we would do a "young heroes of the Bible" sermon series, it seemed like a good idea to me. Trouble is, there aren't that many young people in the Bible, heroes or otherwise. So I have to go with who we've got, so today we look at a young man named

Eutychus. Maybe he's no hero, but he was young. He reminds me of some of you.

Paul arrives with Luke in Troas. On the "first day of the week," that is, Sunday, they join other Christians for worship. "First day of the week" is surely meant as an echo of that phrase as it appears in Luke's first book, the Gospel of Luke. First day of the week was when Jesus rose from the dead. So there's a good chance that we'll hear something about Easter. The congregation meets to "break bread" and to "hold a discussion" (v. 7). This is the very first, the very oldest description of a Christian Sunday in all the New Testament. Why do Christians meet on Sunday, the "first day of the week," rather than on the Jewish Sabbath, Saturday? It's because it's the day when Jesus was raised from the dead. Every Sunday is supposed to be Easter all over again.

Paul was preaching, and he's on a roll. Paul's come a long way to be at First Church Troas and so he gives them everything he's got, the whole ball of wax. The sermon begins about 11:20 a.m. and continues "until midnight" (v. 7). (And you have the nerve to criticize the length of my sermons!)

Well, Paul is going on at some length about the doctrine of the Trinity, or explicating the mystical connections in the book of Numbers or whatever; "a young man named Eutychus" is mentioned. This is where you come in. If you are a sophomore. His name "Eutychus" means in the Greek, "Lucky." Young Lucky is precariously seated on a sill at an open window where, as Paul drones on about the awfully interesting last chapters of Leviticus, Lucky falls asleep just before midnight, topples out the open window, falling to his death three stories below, where Luke says that a couple of ushers "picked Lucky up dead" (v. 9). (I guess his Mama goofed when she called him "Lucky.")

Well, Paul stops just long enough to go downstairs, resuscitate Lucky and announce to the others, "Do not be alarmed, his life is in him. Now, as I was saying . . ." (v. 10).

That's it? Paul's not going to let a little thing like the violent death of the president of the Methodist Youth Fellowship and his subsequent resuscitation from the dead stop him. Paul's on a roll, it's only one o'clock in the morning, and so he continues with the sermon.

As one commentator says, Paul's resurrection of this dead boy "appears as a mere hiccup" during the middle of his lecture!

Lucky is brushed off, his breathing resumes, and church continues. Next day Paul is off to Melitus and Lucky is back at school with a bad headache but raised from the dead and no worse for wear.

In a mere two verses we are told that Paul has paused just long enough in his sermon to raise a young man from the dead and then church goes on as if nothing happened and young Eutychus, Lucky, was named patron saint of all those of you who have trouble staying alive during church.

Maybe Luke is saying, in this curious story about young Lucky, that *this is the way church is supposed to be, not just then, but now*. Somebody seated in the third pew from the back left, once was dead, now alive? Somebody near the left transept door awakened from a coma, big deal! Now, can I continue with my sermon? It's another day at the office for the church, just your average, predictable, raising of the dead.

"How was church last night?"

"Fine. Preacher had some good points to make about Leviticus, but he went on too long. Lucky died during the service, but Paul raised him from the dead and we continued."

The resurrection of Jesus means not only that Jesus is loose, on the move among us but it also means that we can get loose. Something about this God that just loves to wake people up, shake people up, raise people up. Something about this God's preachers like Paul just loves to raise the dead without missing a beat in the sermon.

"Do you really think he can get over his addiction to heroin?" she asked. "I'm told that most people don't. I'm told it's terminal."

"I think it's possible," said I. "But what do I know? I'm just a preacher who's accustomed to seeing people raised from the dead all the time on Sunday."

Some of you are quite new here in this church. This church probably impresses you as old, heavy, ponderous, and stable. It's meant to. But don't be deceived by first appearances. I could line up before you a whole gang of people named Lucky who, on some Sunday, some first day of the week, stumbled into this place, sleepy-eyed and somnambulant only to be jolted, rocked, shocked awake. We were just reading Scripture, just singing a hymn, just finishing a sermon, and they fell out of line, sat straight up in bed, eyes opened—like they were raised from the dead.

And I love to tell stories about the dead raised. I preached not long ago at a clergy conference, and after four of my sermons, a fellow clergyman asked, "What would you do without all those great stories of students who scorned their parents and thumbed their noses at the establishment?" God only knows what I'll do, in my new life as a bishop, for sermon material when I don't have clueless sophomores raised from the dead.

I've seen young people here, fall out the window, land on their heads, die, get born again, be raised from the dead, get a life they wouldn't have had had they not come in here on the first day of the week. One of the great joys of preaching here is to get a front-row seat on resurrection. I was lucky to be here.

Episcopal Sermons

46

Guess Where You're Going

November 14, 2004

My world rather remarkably, quite unexpectedly, changed in the summer of 2004 when I was elected a bishop. I was determined to do my best always to preach a biblical sermon whenever I preached as a bishop—always to take a biblical text and try to preach from that text, rather than to pump up denominational programs. As a Methodist bishop one of my chief duties was to administer the itinerancy system in my conference, to appoint over six hundred clergy to more than eight hundred churches. Thus my sermon of Installation*—an attempt to talk myself, and those six hundred clergy, into the wisdom of my episcopacy and the joys of ministerial itinerancy.

By the time balloting was completed and the last bishop was elected, it was very late on Friday evening at Jurisdictional Conference, Lake Junaluska. The new bishops were hurriedly assembled behind the stage at the auditorium and the chair of the Episcopacy Committee said, "Give me your cell phone numbers, go home and try to get some sleep. We will call you sometime before 2 a.m. and tell you where you are being sent."

I said, "So when we are bishops and we are appointing pastors we're to say, 'Give me your cell phone number and I'll call you in the middle of the night and tell you where you are being sent'?"

He said, "No, don't ever treat your pastors the way we're treating you."

Well, we go back to the room. At 3:40 that morning the phone rings. The voice on the other end says, "Good morning, Will. Guess where you're going."

---

*Service of Installation as Bishop of the North Alabama Conference of the United Methodist Church.

233

Of course, I don't have a clue.

"Birmingham," says the voice.

When I sang that beloved new hymn, "Here I am Lord, I have heard you calling in the night," little did I know it meant 3:40 a.m.!

Thus began the journey that brought us here.

Now I know that most of you here this afternoon got here differently from the way that we got here and yet all of us are Christians, disciples of Jesus, so in a sense we all got here the same way.

Moses hiding out in Midian (Exodus 3). He killed a man back in Egypt and he's hiding out, working for his father-in-law, a "priest of Midian" who does a little sheep farming on the side to augment his ministerial income. Suddenly, a bush bursts into flame. A voice. "I am the LORD your God, the God of Abraham, Isaac, and Jacob. I have heard the cry of my people. I have seen their suffering. I have come down to deliver them. . . . Now guess where you're going."

Even though Moses had no theological or oratorical gifts or training, even though he was scared to death of the mighty Pharaoh, he went, reluctantly. Who would call a tongue-tied murderer to do a prophet's work?

Little boy Samuel, asleep in the middle of the night (1 Samuel 3). At 3:40 a.m., the child hears his name called. Called three times before the child gets the point. Who would call a child to do a grown-up's work? "The house of Eli will be cast down and the voice of God will be spoken to a new generation," says the voice. "Now guess where you're going."

Young adult Isaiah (Isaiah 6). Didn't want to go to church that Sunday but his mother made him. Didn't get anything out of the sermon, couldn't stand the music. (Bach was not his bag.) Then, without warning, the heavens open, there is a vision, a voice, "Whom shall I send? Who will go for us?"

Young Isaiah says, "Not me! I've got baggage from my freshman year of college. Done things, said things I shouldn't have said."

The voice says, "Perfect. Just the sort of truth-teller my people deserve. Guess where you are going."

See? Many of you think that you are here because you chose to be here, or your preacher made you feel guilty so you drove over to Birmingham. No. No. You are here because God put you here, in this faith, walking this way, in this ministry. You are here because God said to you, in some way or another, "Guess where you're going. . . ." And you simply said, "Yes."

It is no mere coincidence that all of the Gospels depict Jesus as always on a journey, always on the move. It's rare that Jesus ever sits down and alights somewhere. Get the point?

Jesus walked along a road. Saw some men bending over their nets in the boat. "Follow me!" he called, "Guess where you're going. . . ." And they did!

He took them places they would have never gone by themselves. Know anything about that? I think you do.

Back where I used to work, occasionally some student would wander in and ask me, "How did you get here?" I always found it a threatening question. I wondered if she had been sent to ask that question by the president of the university, "How on earth did *you* get here?"

I tell them. I was a junior in college, thinking about a lot of things, none of which included the ministry. A friend talked me into going with him to a conference, "Exploring Ministry." I drifted through most of the weekend until late Saturday night, a group of South Carolina pastors sat in a hotel room, talking about their lives. These were the days of the civil rights movement. One had been a victim of the Klan. Had a cross burned in his yard. Another had a concrete block thrown through the back windshield of his car after a church meeting. The wife and the children of another had been snubbed, persecuted, in a small Southern town.

I, in my low undergraduate imagination thought, "This sounds great! I didn't know that being a Methodist preacher was this much fun!"

Didn't know it at the time, because I didn't know much about Jesus or the church, but that was my, "Guess where you are going."

Sometimes, in popular, American, evangelical Christianity, we get this wrong. We say, "Since I took Jesus into my heart . . . ," or "Since I gave my life to Jesus . . . ," or "Since I decided to follow Christ . . ." That's not the story! The story—Moses, Samuel, Mary, Paul, Peter, you and me—is that you don't take Jesus anywhere—he takes you places. You can't "give your life to Christ." He takes it! It's not all that important that you "decided to follow Christ"; the Bible says that in Jesus Christ God has decided for you!

Everyone is here, because you got put here. For some of you, it was dramatic and life-changing, for others it was a lifetime of quiet leading and coaxing. For every last one of you, God reached in, grabbed you. You got called, summoned.

I got put here as an infant. I can't remember a time when I was not a Methodist Christian. My mother told me I was about three months old when I got baptized. Without my asking, they poured water over my head. I screamed and said, "Boy, I'm glad that's over!"

And in response the church stood and said in unison: "Guess where you're going."

The last Bush war in Iraq, visiting with a woman, secretary at the university. She asked me, "Got any yard work that needs to be done? Any chores around the house?" She then told me about how she had befriended an Iraqi student in graduate school at the university. Then the war started and he was cut off, totally without funds. Couldn't go home. Couldn't continue as a student. She and her husband had taken this young man into their home and she was trying to find him odd jobs so that he could get a little money.

What does he think about the war? I asked. "Oh he thinks we're terrible and Saddam is just wonderful," she replied.

"Well, I find it interesting that you took this Iraqi into your home, wanted to care for him."

With some indignation she replied, "*I* decided? *I* wanted?"

"Well, why did you do it?" I asked.

She slammed her fist down on her desk and said, "Because I'm a Christian, darn it! You think it's easy?"

Some of you are here tonight as the ordained. Clergy. But whether you be clergy or lay, we are all here as those under orders. We are here because we've been put here. We are on a mission. The word *mission* means "to be sent." We are not here because we were searching for deeper meaning in life and stumbled on Jesus. Not here because we did a study of all the world's great religions and decided that Methodism made the most sense. We are here because we got a call and the voice at the other end said, "Guess where you're going."

Preachers should never talk about their children in a sermon. But, take my daughter. The week after Harriet finished the school of social work, she was in a wedding. A Baptist wedding. During the rehearsal party, a fellow brides-maid said to her, "You're going to be sorry that you wasted all that time and money becoming a social worker. I got my MSW degree. Worst mistake I ever made. Made only twenty-two. I got out and got a good job."

I said, "Harriet, I can't believe that she said that to you, and the first week after you had become a social worker. That's terrible!"

Harriet said, "I told her that I would be stupid to go into social work for the money. I'm a social worker because I'm called by God to do this. It's my vocation."

And I said, "The girl has had good preaching!"

Patsy and I are excited about being here and thank the Lord that in the church's wisdom we have been sent to work in a place as good as this with people as good as you. But above all we're excited because we get to work with people who have been called to do good work by a good Lord.

It isn't easy work. We are prone sometimes to fail. I'm sure that I won't get everything accomplished that I set out to do with you. You will, before we're done here, see me at my worst, and so will I see you. Thank God we're not called to be successful, or nice, or even friendly. Just faithful. We preachers didn't volunteer to get a raise in salary with each appointment, or to live in a good parsonage, we just pledged to go where we are sent. The Good News is that Jesus is going places and we are the ones who get to go with him.

Reporter interviewed me the week after I was elected a bishop. Reporter asked, "I've been following your career a long time," she said. "I was a bit surprised by all this."

"You and me both," I said.

"I never knew that this was part of your plans, that you *wanted* to be a bishop."

And I thought, "You poor, ignorant thing. What *I* wanted? *My* plans? That's just not how Methodist preachers think."

Jesus is once again on the move. *Guess where we're going*!

47

Untimely Easter

July 2005

MARK 5:2 1–43

When Jesus had crossed again in the boat to the other side, a great crowd gathered around him; and he was by the sea. Then one of the leaders of the synagogue named Jairus came and, when he saw him, fell at his feet and begged him repeatedly, "My little daughter is at the point of death. Come and lay your hands on her, so that she may be made well, and live." So he went with him.

And a large crowd followed him and pressed in on him. Now there was a woman who had been suffering from hemorrhages for twelve years. She had endured much under many physicians, and had spent all that she had; and she was no better, but rather grew worse. She had heard about Jesus, and came up behind him in the crowd and touched his cloak, for she said, "If I but touch his clothes, I will be made well." Immediately her hemorrhage stopped; and she felt in her body that she was healed of her disease. Immediately aware that power had gone forth from him, Jesus turned about in the crowd and said, "Who touched my clothes?" And his disciples said to him, "You see the crowd pressing in on you; how can you say, 'Who touched me?'" He looked all around to see who had done it. But the woman, knowing what had happened to her, came in fear and trembling, fell down before him, and told him the whole truth. He said to her, "Daughter, your faith has made you well; go in peace, and be healed of your disease."

While he was still speaking, some people came from the leader's house to say, "Your daughter is dead. Why trouble the teacher any further?" But overhearing what they said, Jesus said to the leader of the synagogue, "Do not fear, only believe." He allowed no one to follow him except Peter, James, and John, the brother of James. When they came to the house of the leader of the synagogue, he saw a commotion, people weeping and wailing loudly. When he had entered, he said to them, "Why do you make a commotion and weep? The child is not dead but sleeping." And they laughed at him. Then he put them all outside, and took the child's father and mother and those who were with him, and went in where the child was. He took her by the hand and said to her, "Talitha cum," which means, "Little girl, get up!" And immediately the girl got up and began to walk about (she was twelve years of age). At this they were overcome with amazement. He strictly ordered them that no one should know this, and told them to give her something to eat.

On a hot, summer Sunday at Lake Junaluska, North Carolina—beloved Methodist watering hole—I preached this sermon to the gathering of mostly senior citizens. (Like I said, it was a mostly Methodist gathering.) When I read the assigned Gospel for this Sunday, it seemed the wrong text for the time of year. Then it occurred to me that talk of resurrection, anytime, is always out of sync. I was on my way to an Easter sermon three months after Easter.

I know, I know. Easter is over. Here we are deep in dead summer. Yet still the church never quite gets over the inopportunity of Easter. We still keep being surprised that, whenever resurrected Jesus shows up, even in midsummer, the dead don't stay that way.

And I know there's no Easter in the Gospel of Mark. Mark ends abruptly with no resurrection appearances. There is a promise that hints of resurrection, but no resurrected Jesus in Mark. The last sentence of Mark, the response of the church to the good news that Jesus is raised from the dead? *Fear.* The women who came to the tomb in mourning left the empty tomb in fear.

Now, why would they be scared of Easter?

This absence of Easter in Mark has led some biblical scholars to say that Mark's Gospel, the earliest of the Gospels, is one long passion story, one long account of Jesus—faced with constant misunderstanding and opposition—walking grimly toward his cross. There's no resurrection in Mark, or so it seems.

Well, this Sunday we're barely in the middle of Mark's Gospel. Jesus has been working outside our boundaries, on the wrong side of the tracks, out over in Gentile territory. But now Jesus crosses back home, back to the faithful, the Bible believers, back to us. Jesus is home among his own, home where he began his work, just a few months ago.

Home, as it turns out, is a place of death and dying. There is a poor woman who has been suffering sickness for twelve years. A synagogue official has a dying daughter who is twelve years old. (Israel, I remind you, had twelve tribes. Jesus gathers twelve disciples. Is Mark about to tell us a story that challenges the inner circle, the insiders, us? That's opportune because anyone who would get out of bed, get dressed, and come to church—and in the dead of summer, mind you—has got to be a quintessential insider! All you insiders, listen up.)

Jesus is accosted by a church official who pleads, "My daughter's dying." Jesus and the official, Jairus, go home together. On the way the woman, who has been hemorrhaging for twelve years, who has used up her life savings on medical bills and ineffective therapies, pushes through the crowd and touches Jesus. We don't know her name. She is introduced as a woman who is sick and has suffered much at the hands of doctors. Her sickness has named her, dominated her, consumed her, which is what dying tends to do.

"If I could just touch him, I'd be healed," she says. She would have an identity other than her sickness.

And she is healed. This woman, enslaved by sickness for over a decade, as good as dead, named by her dying, is healed, brought back from the dead. We don't know what theology she adhered to, or if she was active in the synagogue. All we know is that she reached out, touched Jesus, and received resurrection, just by touching him.

Now this healing on the way is wonderful but by the time Jesus gets to Jairus's house, it's all over. His beloved little girl is dead. The weeping and wailing tell the sad news. Unfortunately, Jesus has come too late to help the little girl.

"Why are you making such a fuss?" Jesus asks. "Mr. Lord of Life is here!" And the crowd turns from tears and mourning to mocking laughter. "Sure, like she's only asleep!" Nice timing, Jesus. You're late.

And Jesus touches her, announces, "It's time to get up!" And the derisive laughter becomes shocked wonder. Jesus' disciples, the ones gathered in this house of death, were "astounded." And even though it's not Easter, even though it's the dead of summer, whenever Jesus shows up, it's Easter. They were astounded.

We still are.[1]

---

1. Scripture makes Jesus' encounter with hometown sickness and death an even greater challenge: the little girl is dead. Levitical law says that the dead are not to be touched, for the dead defile (Lev. 21). As for the good-as-dead anonymous woman with the discharge of blood, Scripture suggests that she is in this fix because she must have failed to be righteous. She wouldn't be sick if she had not done something wrong so she is probably an outcast from the faith community, that is, *us* (Lev. 15:25–30).

Here is the church, the insiders, us, all adjusted to death. Stoic resignation is about the best our theology can deliver. Mainline, Protestant Christians, in our membership malaise, console ourselves with "Everybody's losing members." Amen. Decline is prevalent. Amen. Death is normal, we say with a knowing smirk. Declining birthrates among liberal, mainline Protestants lead to declining congregations. Simple as that. Church growth? It's a gimmick, a simplistic quick fix best suited for less progressive and well-educated congregations, we say with a progressive sneer.

"Do you think my son will ever get over his drug addiction?" she asked me. And I, as her enlightened pastor replied, in love, "Recovery from heroin? What are the chances of that? Get serious. Get real." Mocking laughter is the way a sophisticated, stoic disposition refers to talk of Easter.

That expression, "Get real," translated into today's Scripture means "adjust to death." So when this desperate father presses in upon Jesus, when this poor, harried woman reaches toward Jesus, the homefolks react with a sardonic smile. Jesus responds by offering some sufferers new life, hope, a future. Jesus doesn't say some magical incantation, doesn't offer some esoteric technique. Jesus just shows up. He allows the woman just to touch him. He speaks to the dead girl. And there is resurrection.

Jesus commands, "Little girl, get up!" Arise! Be resurrected! Jesus apparently resuscitated only three throughout his ministry: Jairus's daughter, the widow's son at Nain (Luke 7:11–17), and Lazarus (John 11:1–44). Why didn't he raise all the dead whom he encountered in his journeys?

Of course, the reasons are known only to Jesus, but perhaps we are not to see Jesus as a spectacularly, though sporadically successful doctor (unlike the "diverse physicians" who have plagued the poor bleeding woman). Rather Jesus is a revolutionary, a challenger of the status quo, a teacher who teaches us how to overturn the world, a subversive who has invaded deadly enemy territory (which happens to be his own homeland) in order to wrench it from the grip of death, conquer it and hold it for his own.

Sometimes biblical scholars point out that what we have here, in this raising from the dead, is more precisely "resuscitation" rather than "resurrection" since, though Jesus raised these people from the dead, they eventually died. The resurrection, they note, is participation in God's eternal life, not a temporary respite from death.

Yet I think it's fair to read this as Mark's rendition of the meaning of resurrection. Jesus is the one who is raised from the dead. That would be wonder enough. But wonder of wonders, Jesus is the one who raises others from the dead. Whenever Jesus shows up, even in the fifth chapter, long before the time for Easter, the dead are raised. Mark just can't wait until the end to tell these miraculous stories because, with Jesus, the time is always right for resurrection. By telling these stories here, resurrection gets political—a political challenge to the mocking bystanders and to the stupefied disciples. Who gets to name what's real, what's really going on in the world and when? Jesus refuses deferentially to wait until a more auspicious time to go on the attack. Whenever Jesus walks into town, even when he is on the way, even in the dead of summer, the time is right for resurrection. Whenever Jesus commands, "Get up!" or allows somebody just to reach out and touch him, then, even if it's July, hot, and dry, it's Easter.

In conversation with Marcus Borg of the Jesus Seminar, Marcus asked me, "Why do you need a supernaturally resurrected body of Jesus to make your faith work?"

And I responded, in love, "Marcus, I don't need a resurrected Jesus. Come to think of it, I'm not sure I *want* a resurrected Jesus. In fact, if I got one, it would be a real nuisance for me, personally. I've got a good life, I've figured out how to work the world, on the whole, to the advantage of me and my friends and family. My health is good, everybody close to me is doing fine. I have the illusion that I'm in control, that I am making a so significant contribution to help Jesus that I may be eternal on my own. No, I don't need a bodily resurrected Jesus. In fact, if I ever got one, my life would only become much more difficult."

When the possibility of resurrection really comes through to you, when the rumor that something's afoot becomes a reality for you, well, you can see why the women were scared that first Easter.

At the Monday morning clergy coffee hour, one of the young pastors excitedly reported some rather spectacular growth in the past year at a megachurch in another town.

"It's really a miracle," he said.

One of the older, wiser pastors at the table responded with a chuckle, "It's no miracle. That guy has gathered a little group of admirers around himself. He's not made a church; he's made a personality cult to himself."

Another laughed, "He's such a showman! Have you ever seen him perform on Sunday morning? He's just got a good act that attracts a crowd."

Mocking, cynical laughter is the way that death keeps control and attempts to keep Mr. Life at bay.

When I heard the size of the projected budget for the coming year (I was away on vacation when the finance committee voted) I laughed. "Let me get this straight. A church which is this year ten percent behind in collections for the budget is going to have an increase of ten percent for next year's budget? Get real!"

Still, the lay leadership persisted. (Laity are often unrealistic in their expectations.) My contribution to the fall stewardship campaign was frequently to smirk, "You'll never make that budget."

Three Sundays into the campaign, the stewardship chair made his Sunday report. "We've had something of a miracle here, folks," he said. "Just three weeks into the campaign we have met our goal."

Spontaneous applause.

He continued, "Which is all the more amazing because next year's budget is ten percent more than this year's."

Widespread applause.

"Now as I recall, there was someone who said, when we started this venture, 'You will never make that budget.' Who was it who said that? Help me. I can't rightly remember. Who said, 'You will never make that budget'?"

"Sit down and shut up," I said, in love.

I don't know, this summer day, where there is a shadow in your life. I don't know what dead end you are dealing. I don't know what you may have lost or where you might be hemorrhaging. I do know that Jesus is the Lord of Life, that he is master, even over death, anyplace, anytime.

I'm a United Methodist bishop so a big part of my job is to send pastors to churches. Some of the churches are so difficult, or so dead and deadly, that sometimes a pastor doesn't want to be sent there. The pastors are afraid that they might catch what the church has got. One of my district superintendents was telling me that a pastor was resisting his appointment, protesting, "That church is hopeless! There is no way to turn around the downward slide there. It's dead! I'll just die if I'm sent there!"

The district superintendent defended our appointment by saying, "Well, I'll tell the bishop what you said. But I need to warn you, this bishop truly believes that the resurrection is a fact. He actually believes that Jesus bodily, really, truthfully rose from the dead on Easter. He even thinks that Jesus still does. So you need to know that when you say something like, 'That church is dead,' it really doesn't mean a thing to the bishop because he thinks Easter is true."

It was a great compliment, probably undeserved. Still, I couldn't help thinking to myself, "Imagine that? After sixty years of trying, this church has almost made me a Christian."

48

Disrespect

Baccalaureate Sermon at Birmingham-Southern
May 27, 2006

My office is on the campus of Birmingham-Southern College, a fine Methodist school where I'm also a trustee as well as teach a course a year on Jesus. Asked to give the baccalaureate, I stood before the class in a long robe, and played the biblical scribe egged on by Jesus encouraging contumeliousness among the graduates.

Dear Class of 2006. Shortly before he was tortured to death, Jesus issued this short sermon to the youth of his day:

> Beware of the scribes, who like to walk around in long robes, and to be greeted with respect in the marketplaces, and to have the best seats . . . and places of honor at banquets! They devour widows' houses and for the sake of appearance say long prayers. They will receive the greater condemnation! (Mark 12:38–40)

If you ever wondered why a wonderful person like Jesus was murdered, it was because of his baccalaureate sermons! Just for a moment I want you to overlook that when Jesus condemned "scribes" he was talking about people like me, religious authorities, people in power who sit at head tables. You will note that—despite Jesus' condemnation of such attire—I stand before you in a "long robe." Though Jesus loved the poor, he despised religious authorities, people who have the "best seats" and wear long robes and offer long prayers.

Yet despite all that I beg you to overlook Jesus' condemnation of long-robed, long-winded people like me and allow me just a few moments to condemn people like you.

I come before you today, on the eve of your graduation from the Hilltop, to say a word of praise for the virtue that Jesus so well and so often embodied—contumeliousness.

244

I know, your mother told you that contumeliousness is a vice, not a virtue, no matter what Jesus said. I know that "human dignity," "respect" have been themes of your senior year at Birmingham-Southern. We have had panels and symposia where you were told that respect and dignity were what you most owed us and what we most wanted out of you. As Jesus says, this is what people who wear long robes always want from the young—respect for us and the world we are handing you.

But now, on your way out, this long-robed, long-winded preacher, taking Jesus as my model, would like to put in a good word for disrespect, even insolence. I taught a class here last fall and in that class I was confirmed in one of my earliest impressions of your generation. You are noted by people of my generation for your unfailing politeness. Back when I was a student, in the sixties, we were mad at our parents and we told them so. Our parents had deceived us about Vietnam and civil rights and we didn't like it and we were determined to push them out of the way, take charge and to do better than they.

You, on the other hand, are generally respectful and deferential to us old people. I know what you are thinking: "One reason why we appear to be so civil and kind to you faculty in class is not only that many of us are polite Southerners but also because you, as faculty, have power over our lives, our future's in your hands. We had to act like we liked you in order to get out of organic chemistry!"

True. But now that you are graduating and, because you have a degree from a first-rate college, we are handing the world over into your hands. I beg you to overcome your inbred graciousness toward us, the aging infirm and the often inept, and let youthful disrespect blossom.

True, the Bible says that we should "honor our father and mother" and we in Alabama are very big on the Ten Commandments, even if we don't always know or follow them! Still, I want to say a word on behalf of disrespect of your parents.

The world we're giving to you is not what we intended it to be. We are handing you not only a bright future but a future with huge problems—global warming, national debt, energy shortages, terrorism, governmental ineptitude, poverty. We, your elders and your superiors, have shown you time and again that we have little inclination, courage, or creativity to address these problems. (President Bush is my age, as is ex-President Clinton.) We need you therefore to show less deference and politeness toward us and more determination to run the world better than we. That's one of the things that I have difficulty respecting about your generation—you have too much respect for my generation. An excess of politeness, a surfeit of civility can be just another sort of slavery, a totalitarian attempt to keep you pacified and unthreatening to the status quo. Is that why a national survey of college students, taken your

freshmen year, indicated that yours was the most politically apathetic generation since the peak of political engagement in the 1960s?

In his day, Thoreau (in *On the Duty of Civil Disobedience*) said a truly great
education ought to cultivate among the young less respect for the law and
more respect for the right. Claiming that respect for the law tends to go hand
in hand with injustice, Thoreau said that a good education is one that teaches
us to respect the good that is always higher than conventional, received
standards of what is good. Perhaps that's what a higher education should be
about—the glorification of the good that is higher than present arrangements
coupled with a *dis*glorification of where we happen to be right now.

Take, therefore, as your motto as you go forth, that which the hip-hop
subculture rendered into a verb, the word "disrespect." Or as it is often abbre-
viated "to dis." The New Oxford Dictionary says that "dissing" specifically
means "failing to show sufficient terror in the face of intimidation." That's
what I'm pleading. Don't be intimidated by the achievements of my generation, nor by our unaddressed and even unacknowledged global problems.

Idealism, vision, hope, these are all noble virtues. But maybe for your generation, at this time and place, the engine that will drive you into a better
future is *dis*respect, *mal*contentment, *dis*-ease with the inherited world.

When asked to comment on the genius of the artist, Joan Miró, the French
poet Tristan Tzara said that Miró brushed off "the history of art with a dis-
respectful wave" (1948). The basis of Miró's genius was in his determined,
creative disrespect, his unwillingness to be bound by the art he inherited. And
when the great southern Catholic novelist, Walker Percy, went into a funk, he
blamed his writer's block on his now being, "Fresh out of malice . . . the love
of God, hatred of things as they are." In short, the things that are essential for
any artist to make great art.

I'll admit that for many of you, merely by accidents of birth, the world we're
giving you looks fairly good. A recent survey of your age group (according to
Natalie Davis who knows so very much about these things) shows 65 percent
of you said you think, "Alabama is basically headed in the right direction."

When I read that, I'm thinking that maybe the blessings that you have
inherited have become a kind of curse, lulling you into a false contentment
with things present when you ought to be just dying to get out there and do
better than we have.

I say this with some nervousness, recalling that even someone who spoke
as well as Socrates was executed on the charge of "corrupting youth," which
by that the long-robed Athenian establishment meant making the kids discontent with Athens.

One of you was telling me about a summer internship that you had in the
office of some legislator. You were thrilled to get the internship because you

respected him so much. Well, by the end of the summer when I asked you how it went, you replied, "He's in over his head. He doesn't know what he is doing." I predict that experience may give birth to a new breed of politician. What passes for "reality," or the "way things are" may be considerably more pliable and responsive to your touch than you think.

When asked how he became a humorist, Stephen Colbert said that the night his father and two of his brothers died in the crash of an Eastern airlines jet, he turned to humor out of disrespect for those who thought they were in charge of the world.

The great Christian apologist, Narnia's C. S. Lewis, said that our greatest sin is not that we do great wrong but rather that "we are far too easily pleased," too satisfied with things as they are, too adjusted and accommodated. Jesus blessed those who hunger and thirst for righteousness and couldn't stand the way things are now.

As an aging long-robed person, I yearn for your respect, admiration, and deferential obeisance. However, in my better moments I know: What we most need from you today is to dream dreams that we forgot how to dream, to think of things that we haven't thought of, to come up with ideas, in a society that has a shortage, not only of light sweet crude, but also of dreams and ideas. It's healthy for there to be a gap between what we've done, and what you hope to do. That gap is a free, liberating space within which you can work your wonders.

I respect you because I believe God has given you all we need to address the problems that lie before us. Cultivate in yourself a holy discontent with present arrangements, and practices.

The great anarchist, Emma Goldmann, when she was not trying to overthrow the government or organizing labor, worked as a midwife. It was said that when Emma Goldmann assisted at a birth, if the baby was a female infant, as the babe was being born, Emma would whisper in the child's ear, "Rebel! Rebel!" I apologize for taking almost twenty minutes to tell you what Goldmann said in less than one.

So tomorrow, at commencement, if we should bump into each other as we parade about in our long robes, I shall not take offense if you greet me not with your typical deference and respect but rather with, "Old man, get out of my way. It's my turn now to clean up your mess. God has sent me to take over!"

49

To Galilee

Easter 2007

And very early on the first day of the week, when the sun had risen, they went to the tomb. . . . As they entered the tomb, they saw a young man, dressed in a white robe, . . . he said to them, "Do not be alarmed; you are looking for Jesus of Nazareth, who was crucified. He has been raised; . . . he is going ahead of you to Galilee; there you will see him, just as he told you."

Mark 16:2–7

For I handed on to you as of first importance what I in turn had received: that Christ died for our sins . . . that he was raised on the third day . . . that he appeared to Cephas, then to the twelve. Then he appeared to more than five hundred brothers and sisters at one time. . . . Then he appeared to James, then to all the apostles. Last of all, . . . he appeared also to me.

1 Corinthians 15:3–8

On Good Friday one of my pastors called. His troubled adolescent son had committed suicide. As I attempted to comfort the distraught father, I asked if there was anything I could do for him. He asked me to preach at his church on Easter.

Amid the tragedy and the gloom, the thing that impressed me that year about the Easter story was not just that Jesus came back from the dead but that he came back to a set of sad losers like us. Therein is our hope in life, in death, in life beyond death—Christ came back to Galilee.

Mark says that on that first Easter, women went to the tomb to pay their last respects to poor, dead Jesus. To their alarm, the body of Jesus was not there. A "young man, dressed in a white robe" told them, "You are looking for Jesus of Nazareth, who was crucified? Well, he isn't here. He is raised. He is going ahead of you to Galilee."

Here's my Easter question for you: *Why Galilee?*

Galilee? Galilee is a forlorn, out-of-the-way sort of place. It's where Jesus came from (which in itself was a shock—"Can anything good come out of Galilee?"). Jesus is Galilee's only claim to fame. Jesus spent most of his ministry out in Galilee, the bucolic outback of Judea. He expended most of his teaching trying to prepare his forlorn disciples for their trip up to Jerusalem where the real action was. All of Jesus' disciples seem to have hailed from out in Galilee. Jesus' ultimate goal seems not to focus on Galilee but rather on the capital city, Jerusalem. In Jerusalem he was crucified and in Jerusalem he rose. Pious believers in Jesus' day expected a restoration of Jerusalem in which Messiah would again make the Holy City the power center that it deserved to be, the capital city of the world. Which makes all the more odd that the moment he rose from the dead, says today's Gospel, Jesus left the big city and headed back to Galilee. Why?

One might have thought that the first day of his resurrected life, the risen Christ might have made straight for the palace, the seat of Roman power, appear there and say,

"Pilate, you made a big mistake. Now, it's payback time!"

One might have thought that Jesus would do something effective. If you want to have maximum results, don't waste your time talking to the first person whom you meet on the street, figure out a way to get to the movers and the shakers, the influential and the newsmakers, those who have some power and prestige. If you really want to promote change, go to the top.

I recall an official of the National Council of Churches who, when asked why the Council had fallen on hard times and appeared to have so little influence, replied, "The Bush Administration has refused to welcome us to the White House." How on earth can we get anything done if the most powerful person on earth won't receive us at the White House?

But Jesus? He didn't go up to the palace, the White House, the Kremlin, or Downing Street. He went outback to Galilee.

Why Galilee? Nobody special lived in Galilee, nobody except the *followers of Jesus.* Us.

The resurrected Christ comes back to, appears before the very same ragtag group of failures who so disappointed him, misunderstood him, forsook him, and fled into the darkness. He returns to his betrayers. He returns to us.

It would have been news enough that Christ had died, but the good news was that he died *for us.* As Paul said elsewhere (Romans 5), one of us might be willing to die for a really good person but Christ shows that he is not one of us by his willingness to die for sinners like us. His response to our sinful antics was not to punish or judge us. Rather, he came back to us, flooding our flat world not with the wrath that we deserved but with his vivid presence that we did not deserve.

It would have been news enough that Christ rose from the dead, but the good news was that he rose *for us.*

That first Easter, nobody actually saw Jesus rise from the dead. They saw him afterward. They didn't appear to him; he appeared to them. Us. In the Bible, the "proof" of the resurrection is not the absence of Jesus' body from the tomb; it's the presence of Jesus to his followers. The gospel message of the resurrection is not first, "Though we die, we shall one day return to life," it is, "Though we were dead, Jesus returned to us." If it was difficult to believe that Jesus was raised from the dead, it must have been almost impossible to believe that he was raised and returned *to us.* The result of Easter, the product of the resurrection of Christ is the church—a community of people with nothing more to convene us than that the risen Christ came back to us. That's our only claim, our only hope. He came back to Galilee. He came back to us.

I visit churches where they have a "seeker service" on Sunday mornings. Sometimes they have a "seeker service" on Saturday night. What's a "seeker service"? It's worship trimmed to the limitations of those who don't know much about church, where the music is all singable, and all the ideas are understandable, and the preachers are adorable. It's designed for people who are "seeking" something better in their lives.

Of course the church should reach out to people, including those who seek something better in their lives. Trouble is that's not the way the Bible depicts us. Scripture is not a story about how we kept seeking God. As we demonstrated on Good Friday and Holy Saturday, we can adjust to death. We can get along just fine without Jesus. So back to work, back to what we were doing before Jesus called us, back to Galilee. Nobody expected, even less wanted a resurrection.

But on Easter we were encountered by a Christ who was unwilling to let the story of us and God end in death. Easter is the story about how God keeps—despite us—seeking us.

On Easter, and in the days afterward, the risen Christ showed up among us while we were back at work out in Galilee—when he "appeared to Cephas, then to the twelve. Then he appeared to more than five hundred brothers and sisters at one time, then to James, then to all the apostles. Last of all, . . .

he appeared also" to the great persecutor and murderer of the church named Paul. The risen Christ was only doing what the crucified Jesus always did: *he came back to us.*

"Show us God!" we demanded of Jesus. God? God is the shepherd who doesn't just sit back and wait for the lost sheep to wander back home, God goes out, seeks, risks everything, beats the bushes night and day, and finds that lost sheep!

God is the father who does not simply fold his hands and sit back and wait for the wayward son to come home; God is the heavenly Father who leaves heaven and reaches down in the mire and pulls out the prodigal son that he may be at home with the Father forever.

We thought, what with the blood and the betrayal of Friday, this was the end. We thought it was over between us and God. At last, we had gone too far away, had stooped to torturing to death God's own Son.

Then on Easter, he came back. He came back to the very ones who had forsaken, betrayed, and crucified him. He came back to *us*.

Christians are the people who don't simply know something the world does not yet know, or believe something that non-Christians don't yet believe. We are the people who have had something happen to us that the world appears not yet to have experienced. The risen Christ has come back to us. In one way or another, you are here because the risen Christ sought you, met you, caught you, and commandeered you for God's purposes. We live not alone.

Implications? When we walk through the valley of the shadow of death, time and again we look up and realize that we're not walking by ourselves. When we come to some dead end in life, we look over the brink, into the dark abyss and, to our surprise and delight there He is, awaiting us, a light in the darkness. We pick up the morning newspaper and delude ourselves that if we can just get some really good political leadership, some really effective defensive weapons, all our problems will be solved. Then comes the risen Christ who confronts and overpowers those politicos who thought they were in charge. We give up, give in, despair only to be surprised to find Him near to us.

A student, asked to summarize the gospel in a few words, responded: "In the Bible, it gets dark, then it gets very, very dark, then Jesus shows up." I'd add to this affirmation, Jesus doesn't just show up; he shows up *for us.*

As the psalmist declared:

> Where can I go from your spirit?
>   Or where can I flee from your presence?
> If I ascend to heaven, you are there;
>   if I make my bed in Sheol, you are there.
>   (Ps. 139:7–8)

I was visiting a man as he lay dying, his death only a couple of days away. I asked him there at the end what he was feeling. Was he fearful?

"Fear? No," he responded, "I'm not fearful because of my faith in Jesus."

"We all have hope that our future is in God's hands," I said, somewhat piously.

"Well, I'm not hopeful because of what I believe about the future," he corrected me, "I'm hopeful because of what I've experienced in the past."

I asked him to say more.

"I look back over my life, all the mistakes I've made, all the times I've turned away from Jesus, gone my own way, strayed, and got lost. And time and again, he found a way to get to me, showed up and got me, looked for me when I wasn't looking for him. I don't think he'll let something like my dying defeat his love for me."

There's a man who understands Easter.

To the poor, struggling Corinthians, failing at being the church, backsliding, wandering, split apart, faithless, scandalously immoral, Paul preaches Easter. He reminds them that they are here, *ekklesia*, gathered and summoned by the return of the risen Christ. Earlier God declared, "I will be their God and they will be my people." That's the story that, by the sheer grace of God, continues. That's what this risen Savior does. He comes back—again and again—to the very ones (I'm talking about us!) who so betray and disappoint him. He appears to us, seeks us, finds, grabs us, embraces, holds on to us, commissions us to do his work. In returning to his disciples, the risen Christ makes each of us agents of Easter. "As the Father has sent me," Jesus says, "so I send you" (John 20:21).

What the young man in white tells the women is in effect, "Jesus is raised! You had better get yourselves back to Galilee, there you will see him." This was a wonderful, frightening thing to hear: the risen Christ is at work, on the loose, and will appear where you live. By the way, Christians, from the first, seem to have worshiped on Sunday. Sunday for Jews was not a holy day of rest; it was the first day of the Jewish work week. Isn't it curious that Jesus wasn't raised on a Saturday, a holy day, but was raised on the day when everybody went back to work? In so doing I think God demonstrated that faithfulness is the willingness to be confronted by Christ even at the office. Jesus is raised into our time and our place. Now every day is sanctified and the whole creation, even Alabama, is the Holy Land. From this perspective, tomorrow, Easter Monday, may be more to the point than today, Easter.

In life, in death, in any life beyond death, this is our great hope and our great commission. Hallelujah! Go! Tell! The risen Christ came back to Birmingham, uh I mean *Galilee*.

50

Last Easter

March 30, 2008

ACTS 12:1–19, 24

About that time King Herod laid violent hands upon some who belonged to the church. He had James, the brother of John, killed with the sword. After he saw that it pleased the Jews, he proceeded to arrest Peter also. (This was during the festival of Unleavened Bread.) When he had seized him, he put him in prison and handed him over to four squads of soldiers to guard him, intending to bring him out to the people after the Passover. While Peter was kept in prison, the church prayed fervently to God for him.

The very night before Herod was going to bring him out, Peter, bound with two chains, was sleeping between two soldiers, while guards in front of the door were keeping watch over the prison. Suddenly an angel of the Lord appeared and a light shone in the cell. He tapped Peter on the side and woke him, saying, "Get up quickly." And the chains fell off his wrists. The angel said to him, "Fasten your belt and put on your sandals." He did so. Then he said to him, "Wrap your cloak around you and follow me." Peter went out and followed him; he did not realize that what was happening with the angel's help was real; he thought he was seeing a vision. After they had passed the first and the second guard, they came before the iron gate leading into the city. It opened for them of its own accord, and they went outside and walked along a lane, when suddenly the angel left him. Then Peter came to himself and said, "Now I am sure that the Lord has sent his angel and rescued me from the hands of Herod and from all that the Jewish people were expecting."

As soon as he realized this, he went to the house of Mary, the mother of John whose other name was Mark, where many had gathered and were praying. When he knocked at the outer gate, a maid named Rhoda came to answer. On recognizing Peter's voice, she was so overjoyed that, instead of opening the gate, she ran in and announced that Peter was standing at the gate. They said to her, "You are out of your mind!" But she insisted that it was so. They said, "It is his angel." Meanwhile, Peter continued knocking; and when they opened the gate, they saw him and were amazed. He motioned to them with his hand to be silent, and described for them how the Lord had brought him out of the prison. And he added, "Tell this to James and to the believers." Then he left and went to another place.

When morning came, there was no small commotion among the soldiers over what had become of Peter. When Herod had searched for him and could not find him, he examined the guards and ordered them to be put to death. Then he went down from Judea to Caesarea and stayed there. . . .

But the word of God continued to advance and gain adherents.

Acts 12:1–19, 24[1]

I was struck by how, among many Alabama Christians, the grand message of Jesus' resurrection had been reduced to, "Christ has risen. I will now be able to be resurrected and see my loved ones again in heaven." The political claim of Easter was lost in such a diminished theology of resurrection. Preaching in a small congregation, I decided to take a text from Acts 12. Easter continues. The first sermon, "He is risen!" carries political consequences.

We had a great Easter, didn't we? Rented trumpets, a bank of lilies, TV. Crowd so large that we had to bring out extra chairs. Two of you graciously phoned to tell me how much you liked my sermon—and I'm sure many, many more of you intended to call. What an Easter!

But it didn't last. On Monday I learned that U.S. deaths in Iraq topped 4,400. Suicide bombings doubled from last year. While we were celebrating with Easter lilies and trumpeted "hallelujahs," Caesar reminded us who is really in charge. The real news was from Iraq, not Jerusalem, where a presumptively democratic Caesar dukes it out with a gaggle of allegedly terrorist Caesars. An Iraqi man whose son was shot dead by Blackwater mercenaries cries out for revenge; an entire wedding party is wiped out by a Taliban mine

---

1. Why was this fecund story omitted from the Revised Common Lectionary? I can only surmise that the reason for exclusion was political—the lectionary committee was mostly Republican.

in Afghanistan. It's the little, ordinary, powerless people on both sides who suffer for Caesar and who kill and who die for Caesar's empire. Caesar has outdone us. Enough of Easter.

Easter never seems to last because the powers-that-be are determined to let death be the last word.

Easter once lasted fifty days, "the Great Fifty Days of Joy" the church called it. But that was then; this is now, and Easter seems shorter every year. We have these great spiritual highs, predictably followed by these dismal, mediocre ecclesiastical lows. Bright Resurrection is overtaken by Grim Reality. Easter joy wilts even sooner than the florist's Easter lilies.

Jack Canfield is America's success guru, telling you how you can uplift yourself, by yourself. Yet even Canfield wrote a book titled *After the Ecstasy the Laundry*. I don't care how high you jump, there is always the morning after, the week, the fifty-days-afterward letdown.

But I'm not talking about that. I'm talking about the way Jesus' great Easter success gets wrestled from his people by Caesar so shortly after our victory celebration. It is as if a powerful policing makes sure that Easter is short-lived.

Up to this point in the Acts of the Apostles we've had quite a ride. The Holy Spirit wildly descended upon the church at Pentecost, shaking up everything, the word of God leaping over all boundaries, overcoming all obstacles, spreading like wildfire over the whole world. All kinds of enemies, including Church Enemy Number One—Saul—have been brought to the faith. Is anything more powerful than the word of God? Is there anything that's too much for the Holy Spirit?

Apparently, there is—the empire. "About that time (that is, time just after Easter, that is, our time right now) Herod (lackey for the Caesar) laid hands on the church"—a polite Bible way of saying that Herod's soldiers went on a murderous rampage. He killed James and, when he saw that his public opinion polls took an upward turn, he decided to kill Peter, the rock of the church, too. That's what kings do best—put powerless people to the sword. We didn't ask Iraq if they wanted to be liberated for democracy by us. When you have got the largest army in the world, you don't have to ask.

Well, Herod has the largest army in the Near East (at least before Operation Iraqi Freedom) backing him up, so he doesn't ask, he tells. Peter, premier disciple, the first spokesman for the church, is in jail. Herod is going to shut up these uppity, talkative Galileans once and for all. Herod has imprisoned Peter during Passover, Israel's Fourth of July Independence Day celebration, just to show who's really in charge. But this is no minimum security executive prison. Peter is really, really in prison.

Peter is not only in chains, he is guarded by no less than four squads of soldiers. He's not only got guards outside his jail cell; he's forced to sleep between guards in the cell. He's really in jail. Peter is as good as dead.

And there's Peter pacing back and forth in his cell, terrified? No, this is Peter, the same one who fell asleep while Jesus was in anguish in Gethsemane. He's sleeping like a baby, dead to the world. As good as dead.

From out of nowhere an angel shows up, enters the cell, slaps Peter in the side, commands, "Wake up! Get dressed!" Peter staggers about in a stupor. The angel leads him out of the cell as first one door, then another swings open before them. Peter, rubbing his eyes, now standing out in the street before the jail, says, "Hmm. I thought it was just a vision. This is for real!"

(A curious comment, that one. You would think that Peter, as the "rock" of the church, would be a specialist in visions. But no, this is Peter, never noted for a surfeit of imagination.)

Peter scurries through darkened streets to Mary's house where earnest prayer is being offered up to God for Peter by the church. Peter bangs on the door.

(What kind of organization is this that meets in unmarried women's homes, and at night?)

While Peter bangs at the door, the little prayer group prays, "Lord, do something about Herod. And please consider helping poor Peter. O Lord, please help, if it be thy will. And if it is not thy will, help us to accept reality and to adjust to our circumstances without complaint. Amen."

A maid, Rhoda, answers the knock, opens the door, sees Peter, and "in her joy" slams the door and runs to tell the prayer group, "Hey, he's loose! He's alive! He's here!"

And the church, in unison responds, "You're nuts, Rhoda. You get back in the kitchen where you maids belong."

At last Peter stands undeniably before them, risen, free and then he disappears elsewhere. And the church in unison dumbfoundedly mutters, "Hmm, Rhoda was right."

Remind you of another story that we read here last Easter? Luke 23–24? Jesus wasn't just dead; he was crucified. Caesar at last shut him up by torturing him to death on a cross. And he wasn't just entombed. He was sealed shut with a big stone, with a squad of Caesar's finest to guard the tomb. (Soldiers making sure that a dead man doesn't go anywhere? Talk about waste in the military budget!)

And women were there too. Unarmed women came out in the darkness and, to their surprise and joy, discovered that God had defeated death and Caesar. The women ran back to the boys in Jerusalem shouting, "He's loose! He's free! God won!"

And the church with one voice responded, "You're nuts."

The first Easter preachers were joy-filled women. And the last people to believe in resurrection, when we get one, is the church—until Jesus himself knocked on our locked doors (John 20) and spoke to us, leading us to mutter, "So, the women were right?"

And we thought that was the last of Easter. But here in the Acts of the Apostles what we've got is Easter remade, *Deus redivivus*, resurrection repeated. You thought Easter was a once-and-for-all thing with Jesus. Well, think again. Easter lasts.

See? You thought Easter was over. You thought we heard the last of a powerful, victorious God last Easter. Well, think again. Easter keeps happening. All over town, jail cell doors are swinging open, the military is put in disarray, and uppity women like Rhoda are spreading seditious news.

Easter lasts. Easter isn't over until God says it's over.

Back when Peter preached to the street mob on Pentecost (Acts 2), Peter cited the prophet Joel. In the old days, God's Holy Spirit was outpoured upon just a few men named "prophets" who, with lively words, preached the mighty works of God, spoke truth to power, and made kings nervous. But there will come a day, said Joel, when God's Spirit will be poured out on old people, your sons and daughters, janitors and maids (that is, people who are usually silenced by the powerful). There will be a day when the once powerless will get to stand up and speak truth to power. That promised day is fulfilled as maid Rhoda preaches Luke's second Easter sermon titled "Hey! He's Loose!"

The resurrection is more even than the promise of eternal life for you and me after we die. Easter is the promise of the universal, cosmic triumph of God over all the forces of death and sin. Easter is whenever in the dark—out at the cemetery or at a prayer meeting at Mary's house—God dramatically demonstrates who's in charge. Easter is God's justice accomplished, God's kingdom come, God's will being done at last on earth as it is in heaven.

Luke ends this wild, wonderful Easter story by saying that there was quite a commotion at the Roman garrison in Jerusalem. "What in the world became of Peter?" they asked. And after an official court-martial, King Herod put the soldiers to death. As we said, that's what kings do. The only way Caesar knows to accomplish any good in the world is through violence. We are in Iraq only for good, noble reasons. It's crazy to die for a god but patriotic to die for a government. More people died in the twentieth century at the hands of their own government even than those who died in war. All governments kill. That's how they do good. That's how they stay in charge.

But then, just when we thought that Death had the last word, God moves, kicks open the iron gate, slaps us in the side, gives us a vision, leads us into the darkness and through it, knocks on the door, turns the key in the lock, servant women begin to preach the good news, the church laughs at itself, and the word of God continues "to advance and gain adherents."[2] And despite our attenuated political imagination, it's Easter all over again.

Death-dealers, doom-doers, beware. You tried to shut Jesus up, once and for all. But you can't. God is at last on the loose. The smart-mouthed talk continues. Prison doors swinging open, ordinary, powerless people speaking up like prophets, maids getting uppity, death defeated, and God is getting back what belongs to God—and not just last Easter. Who's that knocking at our door? Easter continues. Easter lasts!

Epilogue: All you good church people, you now weeded-out, post-Easter elite, truly committed and naturally religious ones take note: The people most reluctant to believe in resurrection—when we get one—is us.

---

2. I love the way the old Revised Standard Version rendered this Greek phrase as "The Word grew and multiplied"—like rabbits, God's word proliferated.

51

The Self Saved with C. S. Lewis

August 8, 2008

ACTS 9:1–8

ISAIAH 6:1–8

Summers are for conferences of various sorts. Here is the sermon I preached for C. S. Lewis aficionados in Cambridge, noting the peculiar Christian notions of "self" and "salvation." My sermon was meant to be a critique of the conference theme, "The Search for a Meaningful Self."*

In Harold Ramis's endlessly rewatchable movie *Groundhog Day*, Bill Murray plays the most superficial of men engaged in the most inane of jobs (reporting the weather). One drab morning in a dumb Pennsylvania town he awakens to the radio blaring Sonny and Cher's whining rendition of their most pointless song "I've Got You Babe." He then plods through his day, encountering a group of wearisome people along the way.

The next morning the radio awakes him at the same time, with the same song—Sonny and Cher all over again—and the same weather report, which he thinks a bit odd. But things become even stranger as he stumbles through exactly the same day with the same boring people as yesterday. And then the next day and the next. After the twentieth repetition of the same meaningless day Murray realizes he is in hell. In a number of vain attempts to end it all he tries to commit suicide, leaping from a building, falling in front of a speeding truck. But after each attempt, he awakes the next day to the same song, same day, Sonny and Cher again. He becomes desperate to find some sense of meaning amid the boredom. He engages in a life of crime, doing all those things that he was reluctant to do before his days became gruesome

---

*Closing Worship, the C. S. Lewis Society, King's College, Cambridge.

repetition. After even the worst of crimes, he awakens the next morning to "I've Got You Babe" and begins his day all over again.

Realizing that he has no way of escaping the humdrum of the same day hellishly repeated, he launches into a program of self-improvement. He takes up piano. He memorizes poetry. He makes love like a Frenchman. He transforms himself into an interesting person and, in the process, the people around him, for whom he once had such contempt, become meaningful to him. Only then is he freed from the wheel of the eternal return.

Murray attempts to free himself from hellish repetition through heroic self-improvement. This is the story that the modern world (and Joel Osteen's sermons) thinks it is now living—take charge of your life and transform yourself into someone worth loving and use your time to make a life worth living. You can have meaning if you choose to have meaning.

Christians believe that story to be a lie. Christians believe another story than that of *Groundhog Day*.

Our theme is "search for meaning." Scripture suggests that "meaning" is not to be pursued. Meaning ensues. Meaning is not what we put together for us but what God puts together in us. Scripture knows nothing of our search for God; rather more typical of the Bible is to assert God's search for us, as illustrated so well in both of tonight's lessons.

My most ready illustration for these assertions is, of course, C. S. Lewis. He wasn't really searching for meaning. He was being searched for until that time when, as he put it, "God closed in on me," and he exclaimed with surprise, "So, it was you all along." Lewis didn't find meaning; meaning found him.

Well, enough about Bill Murray or C. S. Lewis, let's get this sermon focused back upon me. How did I get here? How did I come to possess the self that now possesses me? Note how I am trained to narrate myself: "It all began in a small town in South Carolina. I was born to two loving, but often inept parents, raised in a middle-class environment plagued by racial segregation but even at an early age I began to question . . ."

See? Modernity teaches us to describe ourselves as mostly self-contrived. Our lives are the result of historical, psychological, genetic development that occurs within the self. Everything unfolds, developmentally, from some historical beginning. This is the story we have been taught to tell about ourselves.

Now if you study C. S. Lewis's self as it developed from not much of a believer, to a believer in some vague "theism," to robustly orthodox "Christian" you will be disappointed. Lewis's biography is singularly unrevealing.

Lewis grew up negative about Christian faith in his grandfather's church in Dundela where he said, "we were offered dry husks of Christianity." The main point of Protestantism in Northern Ireland was to demonstrate that whatever they believed in, it was not what Roman Catholics believed. College, army, the war were all, for Lewis, negative experiences of Christian faith.

He read G. K. Chesterton and concluded that "Christianity was very sensible—apart from its being Christianity." As a bright young scholar he knew that the Gospels were ahistorical nonsense. Yet in rereading the Gospels he felt that they were so appallingly unimaginative and artless that they must be historical fact! They certainly weren't great literature.

Then, as if out of nowhere in 1931, Lewis wrote Arthur Greeves, "I have just passed on from believing in God to definitely believing in Christ." He received Communion at the church in Heddington for the first time since boyhood in 1931.

Where did this come from? In the most famous passage of *Surprised by Joy* ([New York: Harcourt, Brace & Co., 1955], 228), he writes:

> Picture me alone in that room in Magdalen, night after night, feeling, whenever my mind lifted even for a second from my work, the steady, unrelenting approach of Him Whom I so earnestly desired not to meet. That which I greatly feared came upon me. . . . I gave in, and admitted that God was God, and knelt and prayed: perhaps, that night, the most dejected and reluctant convert in all England . . . a prodigal who is brought in kicking, struggling, resentful, and darting his eyes in every direction for a chance of escape? The words *compelle intrare*, compel them to come in, have been so abused by wicked men; . . . but, properly understood, they plumb the depth of the Divine mercy. The hardness of God is kinder than the softness of men, and His compulsion is our liberation.

Surprised by Joy describes a mostly intellectual journey. One is left wondering how Lewis got from the vague Hegelian absolute spirit to the Jew from Nazareth who is God Incarnate?

From whence came this new self? Lewis is clear that his belief was not his intellectual achievement, not that which ends a good argument; it was pure gift, grace, the result of the surprise, "so, it was you, all along."

I think this is why Lewis deliberately made *Surprised by Joy* nonautobiographical. From the first, this disappointed some critics. (His doctor and friend, Dr. Humphrey Havard said the book should have been called, *Suppressed by Jack*.) From out of nowhere comes this dramatic turn around toward faith. Yet we search in vain for something in the earlier life of Lewis that leads to this and we find nothing in his biography that accounts for his conversion.

It is as if Lewis wants to make clear that his "self" in Christ was not the result of earlier influences, not the end of some earnest intellectual search (and not the result of attending a conference on having a more meaningful self); it was divine gift. It came from outside the self, reforming the self, transforming the self in ways the self did not previously intend.

Lewis's great moment of spiritual insight came as he rode in a sidecar to Whipsnade Zoo on a sunny morning in September of 1931. This has always struck me as the most ridiculous of situations for a religious conversion—stodgy C. S. Lewis, bobbing along in a motorcycle sidecar on his way to a second-rate zoo. At least St. Paul was on a road going somewhere to do important business. Yet of that moment Lewis wrote, "When we set out I did not believe that Jesus Christ is the Son of God, and when we reached the zoo I did." That's it? This is rather uneventful spiritual stuff, even for the English.

In modernity the self becomes an exclusively human construct, something we fabricate through our astute decisions and adventurous choices. "I choose, therefore I am." Lewis illustrates a very different conception of the self; *the self as surprising gift of a creative God.*

Christians believe that there is no "self" there until God makes a move, until the embrace, the intrusion, the surprise. Of course, we are modern women and men who have had years of education designed to insulate ourselves from even considering the possibility that something's afoot other than that of our own devising. We do not expect to be addressed by voices other than those that are self-derived.

So the story of C. S. Lewis—who wasn't worrying about the meaninglessness of his life, who wasn't searching for anything, whom God surprised by joy—is a jolt to our sense of self. What if the life I'm living is not my own? What if I am not only the sum of my choices and decisions, but also the result of "the steady, unrelenting approach of Him Whom I so earnestly desired not to meet"? Lewis's conversion is akin to tonight's Scripture: Saul who had a wonderfully fulfilling life as a "Pharisee of Pharisees" and therefore wasn't looking for more meaning but rather for more Christians to persecute, Saul whom God blinded by light while on Damascus Road. Young Isaiah in the temple, out of habit, just trying to stay awake during the service and suddenly, the heavens open and he sees, hears God Almighty. In these stories there is no development, no history, no precedent, nothing but a God who shows up and, in showing up in a life, transforms the self into that which the self could have never been on its own.

We're all here this week because we're interested in C. S. Lewis. But I believe that Lewis would back me up when I declare that C. S. Lewis is not as interesting as the God who took an interest in C. S. Lewis.

The god of American, popular Christianity is the utilitarian, instrumental god who is moderately helpful and never disrupted, the god who is sometimes useful in getting whatever it is we happen to want in life other than God. Flaccid, therapeutic deism reigns. We are told that God loves and cares—mainly about me, my family and my felt needs—but this urbane, deistic, therapist of a god never actually gets around to doing anything. Not the sort of God to show up and strike someone blind. Lewis called it "surprised by joy." Theologian Robert Jenson says that's how you can tell the difference between a true, living God and a dead, false god. A fake, noninterventionist god will never surprise you.

Only God knows the self I'm meant to be. Only God knows the self I shall, by God, become. Only God can give me a self worth having. And God does, in those surprising moments, when we're proceeding down our accustomed ruts, just busy looking after ourselves, and there is, as if out of nowhere, light, a voice, a summons, and we know we have been cornered, and we mutter with C. S. Lewis in astonishment, "So, it was you, all along."

52

Be Young

Service of Ordination 2009

LUKE 22:24–27

Our 2009 Annual Conference theme was "A New Generation of United Methodist Christians" with particular focus upon a new generation of pastors. Thus my ordination sermon.

Leadership is all the rage these days. Courses on leadership proliferate on campuses. I'm a bit uneasy about an eighteen-year-old who shows up at college saying, "Point me to the leadership courses. I enjoy giving orders to others. I'm a leader." Still, we certainly have enough quandaries to need good leaders. What are the qualities of a good leader? Fortunately, Jesus defined leadership:

> A dispute arose among them as to which one of them was considered to be greatest. Jesus said to them, "The kings of the Gentiles lord it over them. . . . But you are not to be like that. Instead, the greatest among you should be like the youngest, and the one who rules like the one who serves. . . . I am among you as one who serves" (Luke 22:24–27, paraphr.).

I have never had a course on leadership (as many of you can testify from watching me at work these past five years, it shows!). But I doubt that Jesus' words on leadership make it into anybody's course on leaders.

Tonight's Scripture takes place on the way to the cross. At his last supper with them, just hours before his horrendous crucifixion, Jesus' disciples—his inner circle, his closest friends, us—get into an argument over who is the greatest. "When we get him elected Messiah and the kingdom is come, who will sit on the cabinet?" Oh the sad irony.

Jesus is on his way to the most humiliating, belittling event—the cross. And we argue over who among us is the greatest. Jesus must have despaired. Here are those who were with Jesus every day, heard all his teaching, saw his work and here, at the end, his own disciples show that they don't have the foggiest notion of what he's been talking about. "You're talking like a bunch of pagans," Jesus says. "If you would be great, as I define greatness, revert, turn and become as a child, be young." In Jesus' topsy-turvy world, the master is the one who serves and the most mature is the youngest.

Most of you ordinands think that you have spent years in school in order to grow up. The Board of Ordained Ministry thinks that it has overseen you through a laborious process of examination and credentialing that proves that you are sufficiently mature for ministry. The main factor in the clergy appointive process is seniority; anybody can see the correlation between our largest congregations and their pastors' years of service. And, it's a wonderful system, if I do say so—particularly if you're like me, sixty-three years old with forty years of experience!

But here comes Jesus—if you lead in my kingdom, you've got to be young. The person who spoke those words was a young adult about whom we know next to nothing save between the ages of thirty and thirty-three. Is that why Jesus says so few words to help me toward retirement? As I read the Gospels—with Jesus lurching from this place to that place, always on the move, talking fast, dropping one bomb after another without giving us sufficient time to reflect and ponder what he's talking about—I think to myself, "Christianity may be a faith best suited for people under thirty-three! And yet my beloved church has an average age of fifty-nine. We have one of the most generous clergy pension plans in the world. The new clergy whom I will ordain tonight have borrowed over half a million dollars to get the education we require."

Before you tonight are those called by Jesus and the church to be leaders of the church. Like those first disciples, these before you tonight have all answered Jesus' "Follow me!" with "Here I am, send me!" Note that Jesus had no screening process for the twelve. He required no education, training, or experience. The only thing they had to commend them was Jesus' "Come!" Leave your marriages, families, revert to your youthful wanderlust and itinerate!

Few early Methodist circuit riders worked past their mid-thirties. Didn't need a clergy pension fund back then; Methodist itineracy was a young person's vocation.

It's difficult for many of you ordinands to be that young because we've taken so many years of your lives to get prepared to be preachers. I had breakfast with John Mullaney the week after the Board of Ordained Ministry approved him for ordination. John said, "I began this process when I was sixteen years old! I reached puberty, married, and had a child all under the watchful eye of the Board of Ordained Ministry!" Is something wrong with this picture?

This Annual Conference focuses upon one of our conference priorities—empowering a new generation of United Methodist Christians. Our two-hundred-year-old Annual Conference needs the questions, criticisms, ideas, and innovations of people under thirty-five. When we content ourselves with a church that limits its ministries mostly to the needs of one generation (those of us over thirty-five) we deny ourselves the energy, insights, and good that youth has to offer. A pastor in the Northwest District (who's more ancient even than I) told me that he simply convened the few young adults in his congregation and asked, "What ought we to be doing truly to make this congregation *your* church?" Within five minutes he was writing madly on his notepad, overwhelmed with stunning ideas that God would have never given him had not he dared to ask and to listen.

New United Methodist pastors, we can't wait for you to expend twenty years in ministry "paying your dues," before you step up and lead by following Jesus into the future. We need you to take over now and do what novice, youthful, uninformed, inexperienced people do so well. As Jesus says, you are a leader who imitates the servant leadership of Jesus. And at this time in the history of our movement what we need most is not wisdom, continuity, and deference to the past but rather Holy Spirit-induced originality, innovation, risk, and transformation.

And yet, I take a closer look at tonight's text. Jesus didn't say, "I want all of my followers to be under thirty-five." Rather, he said that he wanted his disciples to lead *as if* they were all under thirty-five. We are not to be like the aging, Social Security gobbling, AARP entitlement-loving pagans. To quote Jesus, "*Instead, the greatest among you should be like the youngest, and the one who rules like the one who serves.*"

It's easy to ask questions, seek help, crave mentoring, read, learn new skills when you are under thirty-five, just starting out, unsteady, green, and goofy. But that's hard for those of us over fifty. We have been in this ministry so long we think we actually know just how to do ministry. We would rather tell you how to do ministry, just like we did it, than to say, "Our church really has some great needs. We've tried some things, some of which God blessed and some which God didn't. Kid, has God given you any bright ideas? Tell me!"

What would it mean for me as bishop, in my fourth decade of ministry, to "be like the youngest"? I bet it would mean to ask more questions, to be more honest about the limits of my way of doing things, to look for help from whomever God gave it, and above all to remember that, in the words of Jesus, "God is of the living and not the dead." Jesus is always in motion and, if we are going to follow Jesus, we've got to be willing to itinerate, to relocate! In short, to "be like the youngest."

We are moving dramatically toward longer pastorates. Research says that churches thrive under longer pastorates. But many of you can testify to the good of short pastorates. Indeed, Francis Asbury believed that Methodist preachers ought to travel, not simply to keep them on the move with the westward frontier, but because, when a Methodist preacher stays in one place too long, that pastor sometimes suffers the worst of all possible fates—"location." Every Annual Conference began with a roll call with each preacher asked, "Brother Smith, are you traveling this year?"

As Dale Cohen says, one of the goals of our new "First Ninety Days" program is to keep clergy supple and adaptive, never to show up at a new church saying, "Here's what I did in my last appointment, so here's what I'm doing again."

Patsy and I have noted that since coming to this ministry in Alabama, we feel oddly younger, as if we're in the first days of our marriage, as if we're at our very first church. I don't think we feel that way because of the climate. I think it may be because the church has called me to a ministry for which I have no experience, few qualifications, and little knowledge! I meet with the young and new clergy, seeking to give them advice, and Jack Hinnen says to me after the meeting, "You don't know what you're doing either!" I'm having to ask for help, read boring business books on management, get a coach, like I was twenty something. And it's . . . wonderful to be young.

When Rome was sacked by the pagans, a whole world died. St. Augustine asked his congregation at Hippo, after the sack of Rome, "You are surprised that the world is losing its grip? You are sad that . . . the world grows old. . . . Don't hold on to the old world; do not refuse to regain your youth in Christ. The world is passing away, the world is losing its grip, the world is old, short of breath. Do not fear, thy youth shall be renewed as an eagle."

There is something about our God that loves to raise the dead, to bring new worlds out of nothing, life out of death, a future where we thought all was past. Because of Easter, we have more tomorrows with this God than yesterdays. We cannot worship a living God without continually turning and becoming, "as a little child." Discipleship is a young person's vocation.

You newest pastors are fortunate to be vowing to submit to a clergy deployment system—the itineracy that, when it works, keeps pushing you to keep learning, keep adapting your ministry. And we older pastors are fortunate that tonight God is continuing to look out for us, to send us fresh new vitality. And all of us are fortunate to be saved by a living, itinerate God who keeps rebirthing us, keeps refreshing us in our life's journeys, promises even at the end of our journey to say to us, "Surprise! Your life has not ended, it's begun. Arise! Be young."

53

Reunion Sunday

April 18, 2010

REVELATION 5:11–14
JOHN 21:1–19

It is fitting that the last sermon in this collection is the sermon I preached upon being invited back to preach at Duke Chapel. My six years away had dimmed neither my affection for the place nor my desire to mix it up with university people. It was the seventy-fifth anniversary of Duke Chapel, University Reunion Weekend, the Third Sunday of Easter, and my first time back in the chapel pulpit. How to do justice to all that in less than twenty minutes? In a way, that outrageously full assignment is every preacher's, every Sunday, everywhere. We'll never say enough about the gospel to say it all. Thank God for next Sunday.

Well, you may imagine what a privilege it was for mere Methodist, self-effacing South Carolinian me to preach here for two decades. I've missed it greatly.

I've also missed shagging (state dance of South Carolina!) under the great tent on Reunion Weekend. When Sam graciously invited me to preach, I excitedly inquired, "Isn't that Reunion Weekend?" Sam didn't know. "You don't know? What has become of Duke values since me? In my day Reunion Weekend was the best part of being faculty."

"I know that it's the Third Sunday of Eastertide," Sam responded, in an accent other than mine.

"Who cares? Is that the Sunday of Reunion?" I implored.

A professor advised me when I was in college, "You may get an education while here but you won't get wisdom until you return for your tenth college reunion. You can learn more that weekend about life, human nature, women than we can teach you in four years."

Reunions are times when dispersed classes reunite. There are memories: "Aren't you the random I met in Duke Gardens, three a.m., last weekend in June, '89, third magnolia from the gate?" Reckonings: "Wow! Is that your hair?" Presence: "Is that you? Really?" Confrontations: "Remember me? Kryshevskyville? 1999, third magnolia?"

One thing I love about this chapel: *God has utilized Duke Chapel for seventy-five years as a place of reunion.*

Karl Barth, theologian of more notoriety even than Stanley Hauerwas, once sneered, "Christians go to church to make their last stand against God."

Guilty. Sometimes the dignity, order, beauty, and spiritual fuzz of church are perverse defense against a death-defying God. Duke Chapel, like any church, can be abused.

Still, I've seen people flee inside this seemingly safe sanctuary only to get smacked upside the head, jumped by God who refuses to stay put.

I recall the student who muttered on his way out one Sunday, "So? It really is true, after all?" I took him as a victim of the divine dragnet of grace. Perhaps he thought he had come away for a polite academic discussion of God, only to get whopped by a real God who loves to surprise.

Or the visitor who exited, not with the usual, annoying, "Isn't Dr. Wynkoop wonderful?" but rather with, "I just met the God I've spent most of my life avoiding." Gotcha.

Israel had a tabernacle—portable tent housing the ark with the tablets of Moses. "Tabernacle" means "tent of meeting." Some of you grads got up this morning, even after you overdid it last night, because in your student days this great towering church was for you a tent of meeting.

"In the beginning was the Word, . . . and the Word . . . dwelt among us," says John's Gospel (John 1:1, 14). It's literally, "the Word tabernacled among us."

And like any reunion, divine-human reunion can be a bittersweet experience, which may be why we are so well defended against it.

One Sunday, after service, a then resident *grand dame* was filleting me at the door of the chapel, charging my sermon as "insensitive, disconcerting, and utterly inappropriate." Of course, a crowd gathered—students relish attacks upon the clergy.

After she had given me her best shot, storming off under full sail in a histrionic huff, a student remarked, "Well, I guess somebody didn't want to be as close to Jesus as she first thought."

Why didn't I think of that retort?

In today's Gospel the disciples are getting back to what they did before Jesus called them and so disrupted their lives—they're fishing. The response of Jesus' disciples to his cross and resurrection? Disbelief, doubt, and a relentless determination to get back their world before Jesus.

"It was a good campaign while it lasted but we didn't get him elected Messiah. The road trips were fun, but I didn't find the preaching, healing, and exorcisms that fulfilling anyway," said one. "Let's go fishing."

"We ought to get together sometime and remember the good old days back on the road," one chirped.

"Yeah, like a reunion weekend for veterans of the Jesus campaign," said another.

Ah, back to the reassuring, anesthetizing calm of the normal and the everyday! (Sometimes our yearning for Monday is a means of escaping the weirdness of Sunday.)

A stranger calls out to them from the beach, "Kids, caught any fish?"

"No."

Those who weren't much good at discipling are not much better at fishing. The stranger gives fishing advice, then kindles a fire for breakfast. Peter is the first to figure out that the stranger is none other than Jesus. He's back. Jesus, true to form, has returned to the same group of losers who so disappointed him in the first place. He is back, doing what he did for them before; feeding them, inviting them to table, taking, breaking, giving the bread. Having seen this action before, they see, "So? He's back!" they say in unison.

The risen Christ doesn't just come back to them but as usual enlists, summons, commands them—love me; feed my lambs. Three times he tells them, love me by loving others. Repeating it three times. (He's worked with these idiots before.)

There on the beach, on Monday morning, there is reunion, meeting. Reunion unsought, unexpected, maybe even unwanted.

That's Jesus for you. Like I say, I've seen it here. Some random student staggers into my dark, Gothic chapel office ("Who let you in here?" I ask, in love.). Tells me some bizarre story of a voice, a light, a summons offered to the wrong person at the wrong time and—having read John 21:1–19—I mutter, "How typical. I can't get into the dorm without permission from Dean Wasiolek and Jesus just shows up anytime he pleases."

It wasn't just that Jesus was raised from the dead; it was that he immediately engaged in reunion. He came back to those who had failed him and, once again, ordains them to be about his work. "Love, as I loved you. Do the same things I've done to you," he commands.

The Bible may be read as a book of reunion—Abraham and Sarah met by God on a starry night, Jacob wrestled to the ground by the River Jabbok, Mary hailed by an angel, the disciples found on the beach by the Jesus they thought they had lost.

Do you know what Jesus' name, "Emmanuel," means in the Aramaic? Look it up.

Sometimes we want reunion and sometimes we don't. Reunions can be sad or glad. But one point of this Easter story is that it's not up to us anyway. Tabernacle, meeting, reunion is something that Jesus does.

A student tells me that he has taken a philosophy course and has decided that God is bunk. He's now an atheist, so he says. I, as his spiritual advisor respond (in love), "You sophomore! You're an Armenian for God's sake. Do you know what the Turks tried to do to your great-grandparents? With a name like Klonic Gregarian there's no way you'll ever get rid of Jesus!"

Met him a few years ago. He's teaching at Harvard, volunteer organist at his church. "You were right, I'm back," he said glumly. Ah the reach of a God determined to have reunion!

After floundering about in my first years here—giving unsolicited advice to students, exploring whether they think they were or were not a Christian, how little they can believe about Jesus and still make it under the bar, how good they have to be and still be considered a member of the flock, what feelings they ought and ought not to have to qualify as a real Christian—I finally came to a simple definition of Christianity (academics hate simple definitions): *A Christian is anybody who has been met by Jesus. A recipient of reunion.*

Richard Niebuhr defined "conversion" to Christianity as that moment when you wake up to the reality that the God whom you feared as your enemy is in truth your long-lost friend. Reunion.

Which is good news for some: Relax, Christianity is not what you think or feel about Jesus—it's what Jesus does to you. Not a technique for how you can use him but rather his plans for using you.

For others reunion is bad news: Cease your attempts to escape. If Jesus means to show up to you in church or at the beach or in the classroom, you might as well say yes. Come to the reunion.

A preacher hears some great stories: people minding their own business, full of a host of personal reservations and doctrinal questions, only to get encountered, summoned, dragged into a reunion for which they had not registered.

I remember a conversation in which I lamented the relatively small number of students we attracted to the chapel. A student responded, "Go easy on yourself. I've heard you preach. It's amazing that you get anybody. Look. Duke is a selective university. These people are smart enough to know that if Jesus showed up in their lives it would make their lives more difficult than they already are. No wonder they sleep in."

There are perfectly understandable reasons for not registering for reunion.

Today's first lesson is from the last book of the Bible. It's a metaphorically charged vision. In the end, God will at last get what God wants. All God's

separated, far-flung family shall be summoned to reunion. God will tabernacle with humanity. Heaven will at last alight on earth. Jesus, the one whom we
tried to push out of our world on a cross, shall reign. And he shall gather every
living creature to himself, around the throne, singing to high heaven, the living reunited with the dead, the lost, found, everybody, in the end . . . home.

And then we shall know; we are not fated for separation, loneliness, exile,
and autonomy, isolation in the cold, dark, demystified and uncaring cosmos.
We were made for meeting. Creation moves toward communion. We shall
be raised for reunion.

Scripture Index